Reconstruction and Redemption in the South

Reconstruction
AND Redemption
IN THE SOUTH

Edited by
OTTO H. OLSEN

LOUISIANA STATE UNIVERSITY PRESS
BATON ROUGE AND LONDON

Designer: Robert L. Nance
Typeface: Caledonia
Typesetter: LSU Press

The editor gratefully acknowledges permission to use material from the *Alabama Review* and *The Scalawag in Alabama Politics, 1865–1881* (1977), © The University of Alabama Press, in "Democratic Bulldozing and Republican Folly" by Sarah Woolfolk Wiggins.

Louisiana Paperback Edition, 1982

Library of Congress Cataloging in Publication Data

Main entry under title:

Reconstruction and redemption in the South.

   Includes bibliographies and index.
   1. Reconstruction—Addresses, essays, lectures.   I. Olsen, Otto H.
E668.R38   973.8   79–10342
ISBN 0-8071-0496-5 (cloth)
ISBN 0-8071-1033-7 (paper)

328517

Contents

Introduction

I

THE so-called radical Reconstruction of the Confederate South was the final bewildering act in the great drama of the American Civil War. It involved the startling elevation of a recently enslaved and still despised race, an attempt at the most radical redistribution of political power in the history of the nation, and an overwhelming and dreadful reaction well symbolized by the terrorism of the Ku Klux Klan. Included were all the requirements for classic tragedy—heroes by the score, monumental evils to be opposed, and seemingly inevitable defeat. Altogether it constituted an episode of remarkable change, aspiration, and trial, and it has remained a topic of lasting fascination and debate.

The political history of the Reconstruction experience in the South is obviously central to the history of that age. Whatever its limitations in the way of wisdom, implementation, or sincerity, the enfranchisement of the freed slaves was the prescribed solution to a variety of problems created by emancipation and the Civil War. The ten-year history of southern Reconstruction was the testing ground of that proposed solution. Just what really did happen during those years? What were the aspirations of freed blacks, and what was their record as voters? Who were the white Republicans, and what were their desires and goals? Who were their opponents, and what did they seek? Why was the opposition to this experiment in democracy so intense, and why did it soon collapse? These are but some of the many questions about that tragic era that continue to perplex us all.

The six original essays collected in this volume are intended to provide an up-to-date assessment of the politics of this obscure era by reviewing the rise and fall of Reconstruction Republicanism in six selected states. It is hoped that these essays will serve as both a sophisticated introduction to the topic and a suggestive guide to historiographical issues and further research. Individual state studies appeared an advantageous means of approaching this topic because southern Reconstruction was, in fact, a state-by-state process. There was no central southern government to serve as a focus, and variations in the history of each state have always served to hinder an effective general synthesis. In addition, this approach has been able to directly exploit the appearance over the past decade of a number of important studies that have superseded long-outmoded and racially biased interpretations of Reconstruction in individual states. The essays presented here were written by six historians who have published such new studies, and their work invites the kind of comparative consideration that will contribute to a solid understanding of Reconstruction in the South.[1]

The states that are discussed have been selected with the intent of providing not only an expert author but also as diverse a picture as possible of the varieties of the Reconstruction experience. The periods of Republican rule that are involved range

1. William C. Harris, *Presidential Reconstruction in Mississippi* (Baton Rouge, 1967); Jack P. Maddex, Jr., *The Virginia Conservatives, 1867–1879: A Study in Reconstruction Politics* (Chapel Hill, 1970); Otto H. Olsen, *Carpetbagger's Crusade: The Life of Albion Winegar Tourgee* (Baltimore, 1965); Jerrell H. Shofner, *Nor Is It Over Yet: Florida in the Era of Reconstruction, 1863–1877* (Gainesville, 1974); Joe Gray Taylor, *Louisiana Reconstruction, 1863–1877* (Baton Rouge, 1975); Sarah Woolfolk Wiggins, *The Scalawag in Alabama Politics, 1865–1881* (University, Ala., 1977).

from the complete lack of a radical regime in Virginia, through the relatively short-lived Republican government of North Carolina, to the last stands of Reconstruction Republicanism in Mississippi, Louisiana, and Florida. A consideration of the brief resurgence of Virginia Republicanism in the 1880s provides a suggestive added dimension. Geographically the states cover every tier of the Confederate South, and they include a wide variety of racial ratios, differing constitutional and political heritages, and both the urban and rural centers of the South. Although all of the authors reflect modern interpretive trends, they differ significantly in their approach and conclusions.

II

Following the decisive military defeat of the Confederacy in the spring of 1865, the North soon found itself thoroughly befuddled by the task of satisfactorily defining the lasting meaning of emancipation and the Civil War. As unconditional victors in a brutal and costly war, northern Republicans were determined to maintain their ascendancy until the military victory had been fully secured. They appeared particularly anxious to ensure the destruction of two tap roots of the war itself—secessionist doctrine and the institution of slavery. Directly related to those goals were lingering fears of the Confederates, a sense of obligation to freed slaves and consistent Unionists in the South, and selfish commitments to northern economic and political interests. For two years the effort to achieve a final peace settlement satisfactory to northern Republicans was frustrated by a variety of well-known factors. The most serious of these included Republican indecision, constitutional restraints on Congress, a continuing commitment to the rights of states, disagreement between Congress and the President, and the intransigent behavior of the defeated South. In June 1866, the North offered the Fourteenth Amendment to the Constitution as a possible final settlement. When all of the former Confederate states except Tennessee overwhelmingly rejected that proposal, northern Republicans sought a new solution with the radical Reconstruction Acts of March 1867.

The essence of this new Reconstruction program was the enfranchisement of the black population of the South. Temporary military control and the disfranchisement of some former Confederates were minor aspects of the program that were intended to assist in its successful implementation. Furthermore, while the enfranchisement of southern blacks was undeniably a new and radical step, this Reconstruction program was in other respects so conservative that it invited ultimate failure. One source of that conservatism was a continuing commitment to states' rights and to a federal government with minimal powers. The right of secession had been killed by the war, but the principles of federalism and states' rights had not. Befuddled by such ideological restraints in meeting the challenges of Reconstruction, Republicans sought a solution to their dilemma by simply combining two very powerful and traditional ideals of the nation— manhood suffrage and states' rights. It was assumed that the promise of the one would cancel out the danger of the other, and that both together would relieve northern Republicans of a perplexing and embarrassing responsibility. The black vote was supposed to ensure the safety of the Union and at the same time provide adequate protection for freed blacks and loyal whites within the South. The most crucial dimension of this new program was, therefore, the extent to which it shifted the burden of determining the ultimate results of the Civil War from the national government to black voters and their allies. It is of course true that the Fourteenth Amendment had been included to assist this effort and that there would be spasmodic northern efforts to sustain the principles involved, but nonetheless the central battleground of Reconstruction had shifted from the halls of Congress to the fields of the South.

This sudden implementation of black suffrage had a revolutionary impact on southern racial relations and political power. Black voters quickly became involved in politics and soon provided the backbone for the new Republican parties that captured control of constitutional conventions that were rewriting the fundamental law of each reconstructed state. This first test of the power and wisdom of black suffrage resulted in extensive and successful political, legal, and social reform. Black-supported Republicans thereafter also controlled newly established governments, for varying lengths of time, in each one of these states except Virginia. In the course of these developments, blacks were elected in significant numbers to important office throughout the South, and they participated equally with whites in party, convention, and legislative affairs.

In response to those developments, in every southern state a powerful white supremacist opposition developed that not only opposed Republicanism but refused to accept its legitimacy and sought to destroy it as a meaningful political force in the South. Unrestrained in their tactics, commanding most of the South's ability and power, and effectively utilizing racist demagoguery, propaganda, intimidation, violence, and fraud, these so-called Redeemers steadily recaptured political power in one state after another. Plagued by the Redeemers' assault and their own mistakes and weaknesses, Republicans were also beset by a factionalism that contributed to their own decline. The sectional compromise of 1877 merely confirmed the obvious. Northern Republicans affirmed principles of home rule that already obtained elsewhere in the nation, and white-supremacist Democrats firmly consolidated their control of the South. Of course, some tacit concessions were made to constitutional law, and recent scholarship has cautioned us against exaggerating the extent of the Redeemers' triumph by pointing to the fact that blacks and Republicans did remain politically significant in the South until the turn of the century. At that time a reaction against the Populist challenge of the 1890s culminated in a far more extensive disfranchisement and the real establishment of the one-party South.[2] Nevertheless, the entire spirit of Reconstruction,

2. J. Morgan Kousser, *The Shaping of Southern Politics: Suffrage Restriction and the Establishment of the One-Party South, 1880–1910* (New Haven, 1974).

as well as significant Republican political power, essentially had come to an end by 1877, and the ten-year period of radical Reconstruction remained unique in the annals of the South.

For many generations thereafter, historical accounts of Reconstruction were dominated by white supremacist accounts that maligned Republicans and justified, even glorified, the so-called Redeemers. Obviously such accounts reflected the nation's abandonment of southern blacks and Republicans, and out of such interpretations grew two of the most influential and enduring stereotypes in our history—those of the carpetbagger and scalawag. This almost totally negative view of Reconstruction was at first challenged by some of the Republican participants themselves, and later by a handful of black, liberal, or radical scholars who found much justice, heroism, and positive accomplishment in Reconstruction and much reaction and injustice in its defeat. By the end of World War II this sympathetic attitude was aided by shifting attitudes respecting race, and over the past two decades there has been a veritable flood of revisionist work on Reconstruction history.[3] At the present time an almost total reversal of attitudes respecting both the northern and southern dimensions of Reconstruction is occurring. The motives of northern Republicans have been legitimized, carpetbaggers and scalawags have achieved a new respectability and applause, southern Republicanism has been praised for its positive accomplishments, and the racism and reaction of the Redeemers has been roundly denounced. (The trend of reinter-

3. For a review of the historiography see especially Bernard A. Weisberger, "The Dark and Bloody Ground of Reconstruction Historiography," *Journal of Southern History*, XXV (1959), 427–47; Vernon Wharton, "Reconstruction," Arthur S. Link and Rembert W. Patrick, eds., *Writing Southern History: Essays in Historiography in Honor of Fletcher M. Green* (Baton Rouge, 1965), 295–315; Larry G. Kincaid, "Victims of Circumstance: An Interpretation of Changing Attitudes Toward Republican Policy Makers and Reconstruction," *Journal of American History*, LVII (1970), 48–66; Richard O. Curry, "The Civil War and Reconstruction, 1861–1877: A Critical Overview of Recent Trends and Interpretations," *Civil War History*, XX (1974), 215–38; Michael Les Benedict, "Equality and Expediency in the Reconstruction Era: A Review Essay," *Civil War History*, XXIII (1977), 322–35.

pretation has become so intense, that some historians have warned against new distortions in the name of equalitarianism and democracy.) More disconcerting, however, has been the fact that despite the proclaimed enlightenment, popular support, and positive accomplishment of radical Reconstruction, it was decisively crushed. This failure demanded an explanation and represented something of a challenge to the nation's continuing faith in the promise of politics and the American party system.

This problem of failure has increasingly absorbed present-day historians. Consequently, although an extensive rehabilitation of Republicanism continues to characterize Reconstruction history, an initial revisionist stress upon the admirable qualities and accomplishments of Republicans has been replaced by a search for new weaknesses and faults. In this somewhat remarkable shift of attitude, a variety of new criticisms have replaced the old. Once condemned for instituting a program that was considered evil and irresponsible in its aims, Republicans are now criticized instead for failing to achieve their admirable goals. In most early accounts northern Republicans were denounced as vindictive extremists who imposed a cruel and harsh punishment on the South. More recently they were commonly lauded for their racial equalitarianism and touches of moderation, but they are now often criticized either for their failure to invoke firmer federal control or for their failure to provide a program of land confiscation and distribution that would have decisively strengthened the blacks and weakened their white political opponents. Along parallel lines, Reconstruction was once attributed, in good part, to the selfish interests of northern free-labor capitalism; today that same capitalism is often viewed as the source of a moderate political and economic ideology that undermined the Reconstruction promise itself.

The authors of the essays that follow seem divided between those who see no hope at all for Reconstruction in the context imposed by the North and those who seem to suggest that southern Republicanism itself might have been more successful if only it had been more radical or clever. There is still wide-spread agreement that the question of race was the most obvious political issue at stake. But there is disagreement over the precise impact and meaning of that issue. Just how is the impact of racism to be measured, and just what is its relative importance compared to the many other apparent issues involved? For example, Reconstruction political rivalry reflected old class and sectional hostilities, as well as recent bitter conflicts over secession and the war. It involved the desire of traditional rulers to maintain their control, and that desire reflected fears of lower-class power, democratic reform, and increased taxation to support that reform. And what of matters of regional pride and the resentment of defeat? Or of the institutional and economic impact of emancipation and the determination to maintain a supply of tractable and cheap black labor? Was racism more important than all of these combined? And just where did racism as a political factor primarily originate? Was it a cause or a weapon of political dispute? Did it rest in a long-standing popular racism that was aggravated by the freeing and the rise of the blacks, or was it a weapon utilized for political purposes by a former slaveholding elite already well accustomed to using it in defense of slavery? Some recent studies of the post-Reconstruction South have reflected similar concerns and found race conflict in that period more of a political weapon of ruling elites than a fundamental issue in and of itself.[4]

Turning directly to the southern Republican party, one encounters similar perplexities. Although capturing practically all of the black vote and a sizeable minority of the white one, and thus initially commanding a majority of the voting population, this party faced incredible difficulties from the very first. Its primary voting base was a despised and long-oppressed race characterized by abject poverty, illiteracy, political inexperience, and a general lack of social influence and power. Effective coopera-

4. Kousser, *The Shaping of Southern Politics*, 250–65; Michael Schwartz, *Radical Protest and Social Structure: The Southern Farmers' Alliance and Cotton Tenancy, 1880–1890* (New York, 1976), 283–87.

tion with this fundamental black base was seriously hindered by a prevalent, if relatively mild, racism that prevailed among most Republican whites. In addition, southern Republicans lacked adequate numbers of skilled or experienced leaders, they lacked a local political heritage, and they lacked solid financial and press support. They also provoked a hatred from their opponents so intense that it soon turned Reconstruction into an age of violence and terror. Republicans were perceived as uppity members of an inferior race, Yankee interlopers, or native traitors to the South and the white race. They were detested for their support of equal rights, their expensive reforms, and their displacement of the former rulers of the South, and they became scapegoats for all the negative aftermath of the Civil War. To be an active Republican in the Reconstruction South was an open invitation to discrimination, intimidation, physical assault, and even murder.

The political party that faced these difficulties was a hastily formed coalition of remarkably disparate ingredients. Among those who have been identified with one degree or another of support for Republicanism are blacks, prewar opponents of secession, consistent Unionists and wartime peace advocates, reform-minded yeoman and artisans, upper-class moderates and realists, regional representatives seeking some shift in state policy and power, and whites especially receptive to some degree of racial equality, nationalism, or the principles of free-labor capitalism. The relative variety of former Whigs and Democrats included in these groups remains a subject of dispute. Some of these Republicans sought more social and political democracy, others hoped to promote economic prosperity and to check the dangers of radicalism. Some sought to achieve social stability by catering to modern reformism, while others sought the rapid restoration of the Union by catering to northern demands. Some sought to oust secessionists or Confederates from office, some merely sought office for themselves, and some sought support for lucrative railroad and other economic projects. Obviously a newly formed party of such diversity in

composition and aim could expect to have difficulty in maintaining its unity.

Whether it was planter or poor white, Democrat or Whig,
who cooperated with this Republican party, each obviously
would expect to play some role in shaping party policy. But perhaps more significant was the willingness of these whites to accept the political and civil rights of black Americans and to
actively cooperate with them in political affairs. The extent to
which many whites, of many different groups, did just that was
impressive indeed and suggests that race relations in the postwar South were far more malleable than has often been assumed.

As the intensity of a white-supremacist opposition came to
bear, however, as programmatic decisions were made, and as
the limitations of northern support became clear, the difficulty
of maintaining Republican unity increased. The allegiance of
blacks was essentially secure because of the Republican record
and the sharpening political division on the race question itself,
but the direction in which Republicans moved on other matters
would readily affect white support. Whenever Republicans catered to one group of whites they were apt to alienate another,
and that possibility was intensified by the general difficulty of
being a Republican in the Reconstruction South. The more the
Republican party differed from the expectations and hopes, or
the desired program, of particular whites, the more they were
encouraged to move out of an embarrassing alliance to join the
forces of white supremacy. Also encouraging such a drift was
the fact that the most apparent and immediate promise of Republicanism to the white population as a whole already had
been achieved by the initial constitutional reforms of 1868.

While Republican factionalism was soon obvious, its precise
significance remains obscure. Was it a basic source of Republican decline, or was it more a reflection of an already hopeless
situation? Was southern Republicanism so radical that it alienated too many whites to succeed? Or was it so moderate and
so tainted by internal racism that it failed to mould the kind
of strength and organization necessary to success? Some of

the suggested dimensions of Republican factionalism have included conflicts of black versus white, of scalawag against carpetbagger, of radical against moderate, of Whig versus Democrat, and of one region of a state against another. The two most popular themes appear to be a rivalry of scalawag against carpetbagger and simply a struggle between rival personalities for patronage and power. We know very little about what specific programmatic issues, if any, were involved, and we have hardly begun to study the importance of intrastate rivalries, the cleavages between moderate and radical strategies, the conflicts between agricultural and business interests, or clashes between the races or among the blacks themselves.

In the search for answers to such questions, some of the most popular new methods of historical study, such as rigorous quantification or in depth social study, have as yet had slight impact. The most obvious exceptions have occurred in the realm of black history and economics. A fresh interest in the neglected history of the black experience has produced many studies enhancing our knowledge of the black community and its role in political affairs; and recent economic studies have effectively utilized quantitative techniques to broaden our understanding of postwar economic developments, although the political implications of this work have remained undeveloped.[5] Quantification and behavioral analysis, which have had such a remarkable impact on national political history, as yet have had little impact on our analysis of southern Reconstruction politics other than in

5. See note 3 for the literature. More recent works include Charles Vincent, *Black Legislators in Louisiana During Reconstruction* (Baton Rouge, 1976); Edward Magdol, A Right to the Land: *Essays on the Freedmen's Community* (Westport, Conn., 1977); Thomas Holt, *Black Over White: Negro Political Leadership in South Carolina During Reconstruction* (Urbana, 1978); Robert Higgs, *Competition and Coercion: Blacks in the American Economy, 1865–1914* (New York, 1977); Roger L. Ransom and Richard Sutch, *One Kind of Freedom: The Economic Consequence of Emancipation* (New York, 1977); Jay R. Mandle, *The Roots of Black Poverty: The Southern Plantation Economy after the Civil War* (Durham, 1978); and Gavin Wright, *The Political Economy of the Cotton South: Households, Markets, and Wealth in the Nineteenth Century* (New York, 1978).

their treatment of the scalawags. Similarly, the study of ideology, which has had a great impact on antebellum history, has been given little consideration as it pertains to Reconstruction, and the in-depth study of such matters as the yeomanry, the postwar elite, and significant class division has only just begun.[6]

To a significant extent, the present state of Reconstruction history reflects the fact that over the past generation the necessity to correct a unique heritage of distortion has stood, quite properly, at the center of professional concern. Correspondingly, a movement beyond that preoccupation has been slow, while the corrective process itself has been more successful in destroying old myths than it has been in creating a satisfying new synthesis. The essays that follow are offered, then, as a first rather than a last word on southern Reconstruction. Although they are intended to provide a sound and stimulating introduction to the political complexities involved, it is also hoped that they will provoke an awareness of persisting interpretive needs. There is still much to be done. Historians have yet to clarify many matters of ideology, class structure, economic interest, and social change. They have yet to analyze satisfactorily many areas of conflict and of common interest respecting a variety of classes and social groups. Divisions within and between the races continue to demand in-depth research and thought, and the conflict between the forces of the Old and the New South remains disturbingly nebulous. Altogether, the full range of human and social dimensions standing at the base of the history of that era cries for study, and the profession still awaits an effective integration of those dimensions into the political history and a general analysis of the Reconstruction South.

6. Among some beginnings are Jonathan M. Wiener, "Planter-Merchant Conflict in Reconstruction Alabama," *Past and Present*, LXVIII (1975), 73–94, "Planter Persistence and Social Change: Alabama, 1859–1870," *Journal of Interdisciplinary History*, VII (1976), 235–60, and *Social Origins of the New South: Alabama 1860–1885* (Baton Rouge, 1978); James L. Lancaster, "The Scalawags of North Carolina, 1850–1868" (Ph.D. dissertation, Princeton University, 1974).

I

Florida

A *Failure of Moderate Republicanism*

JERREL H. SHOFNER

THE FLORIDA government implemented under the 1867 congressional Reconstruction enactments was radical neither in concept nor intent. Republicans occupied the governor's office in Tallahassee from July 1868 until January 1877, but these men differed little in their racial and economic ideas from their native white Conservative-Democratic opponents. If the intent of congressional Reconstruction was to make a secure place in postwar society for freed Negroes, it failed in Florida at its inception. Part of the cause of that inevitable failure lies with the legislative process. Legislation is a product of compromise and concession. The final version of the March 2, 1867 Reconstruction Act was written by John Sherman and not Thaddeus Stevens. Furthermore, it was a great distance from Washington to Tallahassee and the intent of legislation was subject to interpretation at many points.

Union General Israel Vogdes suggested in a report from Jacksonville in June 1865 that there were only two basic avenues for readmitting Florida to the Union. Formerly wealthy planters, who had constituted the dominant minority in antebellum Florida, had been deprived of all their resources except land—

and they were fearful that a victorious Union government might confiscate that. Assure them that they could keep their land, Vogdes wrote, and they would gladly become a loyal nucleus around which the state government could be restored. The alternative, which the general thought inadvisable, was to suppress the white population by vigorous military occupation and to enfranchise the freedmen.[1] Versions of each alternative would be attempted, but only amidst federal indecision, delay, and endless bickering. By the time Congress emerged victorious from its battle with President Johnson, former Confederate Floridians had lost many fears and gained two years experience in resisting northern intervention in their affairs. Events since 1865 had not only given them confidence that they could influence the administration of congressional laws but had also given them a moral justification for their resistance.

The moral advantage came from what the Floridians believed to be a broken bargain. When President Johnson offered restoration in 1865, he sent William Marvin as provisional governor to supervise the calling of a convention that was to repudiate slavery, nullify the secession ordinance, cancel the debt incurred in support of the Confederacy, and recognize all laws enacted by Congress since 1861. After those conditions were met the president agreed to recognize the state as restored. In his addresses to Floridians, Marvin, a longtime federal judge of Key West, repeatedly expressed his belief that Floridians would not be asked to enfranchise Negroes.[2] Then, after the 1865 convention reluctantly met the minimal requirements laid down by the president, Florida was refused readmission by a suspicious Congress. By 1866 Governor David S. Walker and other native Floridians were complaining that they had met the requirements of the victorious Union but were still being denied the

1. Israel Vogdes to Salmon P. Chase, June 7, 1865, in Salmon P. Chase Papers, Library of Congress.
2. Address of William Marvin, August 3, 1865, in Records of the Department of State, Record Group 59, Volume on Provisional Government of Florida, National Archives; *Journal of the Constitutional Convention of 1865 at Tallahassee, Florida,* 132.

readmission they had been offered.[3] However faulty this reasoning might have appeared to northern congressmen, it was satisfying to ex-Confederate Floridians.

The ambivalence of Florida Republicanism was another important factor in the ultimate failure of Reconstruction. Once described as "the smallest tadpole in the cesspool of secession," Florida had a population of about 140,000 people thinly scattered across the northern portion of its thirty-seven million acres of land. Temporarily without adequate transportation facilities and with so much undeveloped land, Florida was ideally suited to the needs of many people looking for places to settle and make their fortune after the Civil War. Numerous individuals who came to the state during and after the war as military or civil governmental officials saw opportunity in the frontier conditions of the state and elected to remain for reasons other than those usually attributed to carpetbaggers. Harrison Reed and William H. Gleason, two of the most influential architects of the 1868 constitution, were from Wisconsin where they had previous experience in community building on the frontier. Reed exemplified those white northerners who had a sincere desire to help the freedmen while at the same time promoting their own personal fortunes by developing transportation and inducing settlement of the frontier state. Gleason was far more interested in economic development than in humanitarian motivations, but he also typified a number of newcomers to the state who recognized that political stabilization was a necessary condition for economic success. These men were anxious to comply with the congressional enactments mostly as an incident to their primary aims.

By the time congressional leaders had won their struggle with President Johnson and enacted the 1867 Reconstruction laws, some of these northerners were harmoniously cooperating with native whites on economic schemes, the success of which depended on a stable and friendly civil government. Thomas W.

3. *Florida House Journal*, 1866, pp. 20, 87–88.

Osborn, assistant commissioner of the Freedmen's Bureau in Florida, for example, was in a law and real estate partnership with McQueen McIntosh, who had led the extreme wing of the Florida secession convention in 1861. Harrison Reed, as a federal mail agent for Florida and Georgia, had won a wide and favorable acquaintance with native Floridians while rebuilding the postal service. He was collaborating on an important railroad project with David L. Yulee, a former United States senator who had left the Union with his state.[4]

Other northerners were contending with local white leaders over problems arising from efforts to define Negro citizenship and a free labor system. These agents of the Freedmen's Bureau were also ambivalent. Most were quite sincere in carrying out their Bureau duties, but also often doubtful of the abilities of freedmen.[5]

A substantial number of white Floridians, some of whom had been Unionists opposed to their Confederate neighbors and others who genuinely wished to see Negroes elevated to full citizenship, joined with the various newcomers in an emerging Republican party. As congressional Reconstruction policy developed, these groups of incipient Republicans, with their diverse and often contradictory goals, joined in opposing former Confederates but also competed for control of the state government. This rivalry would become a central ingredient in the failure of Reconstruction in Florida.

When the March 1867 Reconstruction Acts were announced there was widespread shock and dismay among native whites in Florida. Some threatened emigration; others waited for the Supreme Court to declare the enactments unconstitutional. But

4. Harrison Reed to David L. Yulee, April 18, 1867, in David L. Yulee Papers, P. K. Yonge Library of Florida History, Gainesville, Florida; Tallahassee *Semi-Weekly Floridian*, March 19, 1867.

5. D. M. Hammond to A. H. Jackson, November 14, 1867, W. G. Vance to Jackson, July 31, 1867, A. B. Grumwell to Jackson, October 3, 1867, all in Records of the Bureau of Refugees, Freedmen, and Abandoned Lands, Record Group 105, National Archives.

most influential Floridians recommended compliance with the new laws.[6] Crucial to their belief that they could live with the Reconstruction laws was Governor David Walker's recent victory in a dispute with the Florida military commander over the extent of martial law in the state.

The military reorganizations, which had accompanied President Andrew Johnson's Reconstruction plan in the summer of 1865, ultimately left Major General John G. Foster in command of Florida. A West Point officer with no particular social goals, Foster had cooperated with Provisional Governor William Marvin in implementing President Johnson's plan and had won the praise of prominent native white Floridians for his mild policies.[7] This happy situation deteriorated rapidly in the summer of 1866 as President Johnson and Congress began battling over Reconstruction policy. When congressional legislation, passed over the president's veto, empowered military officials to protect Negroes and white Unionists against unfair civil processes, Johnson retaliated with a proclamation that the insurrection was ended. General Foster and the newly elected governor, David S. Walker, soon found themselves at odds over jurisdictional questions involving local civil officials and Freedmen's Bureau agents. Acting according to General Grant's orders, Foster declared martial law in several northern Florida counties where Negroes and white Unionists were unable to obtain justice in the state courts.[8]

Continuing his battle with Congress, President Johnson issued another proclamation on August 20, making it even clearer that he regarded civil law paramount to military authority in the southern states. This pronouncement further convinced native

6. Tallahassee *Semi-Weekly Floridian*, January 15, 25, March 1, 1867; St. Augustine *Examiner*, March 9, 1867.
7. St. Augustine *Examiner*, March 9, 1867; John G. Foster to Philip H. Sheridan, August 6, 1865, in Miscellaneous Collection, P. K. Yonge Library.
8. John G. Foster to David S. Walker, June 12, 1866, John G. Foster Letterbook, in Miscellaneous Military Collection, Library of Congress; House Executive Documents, 40th Cong., 2d Session, No. 57, p. 11.

white Floridians that they need not tolerate military interference in their internal affairs.[9] The resulting stalemate was best exemplified by a clash in Nassau County.

At Fernandina in Nassau County the property of numerous Confederates had been sold by federal tax officials during the war. These sales and federal ambivalence left many parcels of real estate with two owners, each with a plausible claim, at the end of the war.[10] An elaborate appellate procedure was established by the United States government to resolve the ensuing disputes, but impatient ex-Confederates were enraged at lengthy delays and sought repossession of their property through the state courts. When the Nassau County sheriff began ousting Negroes and white Unionists from property to which they held title by virtue of wartime tax-sale purchases, Foster intervened.[11] General Grant first emphatically supported the Florida military commander, ordering him to assure that no tax-sale purchaser was dispossessed of his property by local officials.[12] But as Johnson's support of the state officials increased, General Foster's instructions were correspondingly limited. On August 19, 1866, Grant authorized state courts to hear appeals regarding property sold for taxes and ordered Foster not to interfere when the sheriff ousted tax-sale purchasers.[13]

This major concession was still insufficient to satisfy Governor Walker and local officials at Fernandina. A series of com-

9. Tallahassee *Semi-Weekly Floridian*, December 11, 1866; James E. Sefton, *The United States Army and Reconstruction* (Baton Rouge, 1967), 79–81.

10. Tallahassee *Semi-Weekly Floridian*, June 8, 1866; St. Augustine *Examiner*, September 29, 1866; Joseph L. Lewis to Florida Direct Tax Commission, May 17, 1865, in Records of the Direct Tax Commission, Record Group 58, National Archives.

11. John G. Foster to George K. Leet, May 7, 1866, in Foster Letterbook; Austin Smith and Daniel Richards to E. A. Rollins, May 31, 1866, J. W. Barlow to Florida Direct Tax Commission, April 10, 1866, Direct Tax Commission to Barlow, April 10, 1866, all in Records of the Direct Tax Commission, Record Group 58, National Archives.

12. John G. Foster to David S. Walker, May 12, 1866, Charles Mundee to John T. Sprague, May 7, 1866, in Foster Letterbook; D. Richards to Elihu B. Washburne, May 14, 1866, in Elihu B. Washburne Papers, Library of Congress.

13. George Lee to John G. Foster, August 19, 1866, in Foster Letterbook.

munications in late October and November culminated in a November 19, 1866 order that "in no case will [the military commander at Fernandina] use the U.S. troops in Civil matters except by Special Orders from these Hd. Quarters."[14] This amounted to a complete reversal of Grant's May order to protect tax-sale purchasers from acts of state officials. General Foster resigned, saying that he could not act effectively without clearer instructions than he had recently received from Washington.[15]

With this series of events in mind, ex-Confederate Florida leaders advised their neighbors not to emigrate until they had first attempted to accommodate to the March 1867 Reconstruction legislation. Governor David Walker, ex-Senator David L. Yulee, McQueen McIntosh, a former federal judge, and a few others worked with Harrison Reed, William H. Gleason, Jonathan C. Greely, a Jacksonville businessman, Thomas W. Osborn, former head of the Freedmen's Bureau in Florida, and other like-minded Union Republicans to establish a coalition party of business-oriented conservatives that could lead the state back into the Union on a platform of compliance with congressional Reconstruction and promotion of the economic development of the frontier state. The coalition movement faltered partially because of differences over civil rights, but more significantly because a few Radical Republicans succeeded in organizing the newly enfranchised freedmen into a cohesive Republican electorate through a series of Union League chapters in the northern Florida counties.[16]

Having mistakenly believed that they could control the political activities of their former slaves, the planters and their ex-Confederate neighbors were first enraged to find that some of

14. J. H. Lyman to A. A. Cole, November 19, 1866, John G. Foster to George L. Hartsuff, November 19, 1866, in *ibid*.

15. John G. Foster to Philip H. Sheridan, November 25, 1866, Foster to O. O. Howard, November 18, 1866, in *ibid*.

16. Jonathan C. Greely to S. N. Williams, May 7, 1867, David S. Walker to David L. Yulee, May 6, 1867, Charles E. Dyke to Yulee, July 22, 1867, all in Yulee Papers; Proceedings, Union Republican Club of Jacksonville, 1867, typescript in P. K. Yonge Library.

their moderate Republican collaborators, especially Thomas Osborn, were attempting to organize the Negroes into a Republican party. But both native Conservatives and their potential collaborators were alarmed when it became clear that the blacks were rallying to a handful of Radical Republicans who appealed to them on issues that neither moderate Republicans nor ex-Confederates had wished to raise. Daniel Richards, a former Illinois state senator and protege of Congressman Elihu B. Washburne; Liberty Billings, a white minister who had served as chaplain and later commander of a Negro regiment; William U. Saunders, a Negro from Maryland who was a Republican party official; and Charles H. Pearce, a Negro sent from Canada by the African Methodist Episcopal Church, were the most important Radical Republican leaders. By the time the constitutional convention met on January 20, 1868, these men had garnered the support of a working majority of delegates. With only twenty-nine delegates present at its opening session, the convention elected Richards as its permanent president. He immediately named Billings, Saunders, and Pearce to a committee with power to rule on the seating of late-arriving delegates.[17]

The early days of the constitutional convention were a low point for the moderate Republicans who had first failed to complete a coalition arrangement with ex-Confederate Conservatives and then watched the Radicals win the support of most of Florida's enfranchised black voters. Neither Harrison Reed, William Gleason, nor Thomas Osborn had been elected to the convention, but they determined to influence it from outside. A few white moderate Republican delegates, notably William J. Purman, Edward M. House, and C. R. Mobley, used dilatory methods to delay the progress of the Radical-controlled convention while a new strategy was being formulated.[18] Meanwhile, Charles E. Dyke, Conservative editor of the Tallahassee *Floridian*, castigated the Radicals for the disorder of the convention, although it was being caused by their moderate adversaries.

17. Daniel Richards to G. W. Atwood, January 13, 1868, Richards to Elihu B. Washburne, November 19, 1867, February 2, 1868, in Washburne Papers.
18. New York *Tribune*, February 5, 8, 10, 1868.

After nearly two weeks of debate over procedural matters, the moderates gained enough strength in the convention to challenge the Radicals on a test vote. The question was called on the seating of a moderate delegate from Santa Rosa County whose credentials were irregular. With forty-three of the forty-six delegates then present and voting, the Radicals mustered a majority of twenty-two to twenty-one. The convention then adjourned for the weekend and the Radicals expected to begin serious consideration of the new constitution when business was resumed. When they met the following week, however, there were only twenty-two delegates present. The moderate faction had seceded and met at Monticello where they closeted themselves with conservative leaders Charles E. Dyke and McQueen McIntosh to write a constitution mutually acceptable to both Conservatives and moderate Republicans.[19]

At Tallahassee, after futilely calling on the military commander to arrest the seceding delegates, the regular convention decided that its twenty-two remaining members constituted a quorum, since only forty-three of the forty-six delegates had ever been seated, and proceeded to draft a constitution. The task was completed in less than two days, the document was dispatched to General George C. Meade, commanding general of the Third Military District, and the convention resolved itself into a nominating convention to name candidates for offices under the new constitution.[20]

While the regular convention was adjourned awaiting further instructions from General Meade, the moderates returned from Monticello and, with the perhaps unwitting assistance of the military authorities, initiated a series of extra-legal actions that resulted in their constitution being adopted instead of the Radical version. They came into town late at night on February 10, 1868, entered the convention hall, held a session of the convention well after midnight, voted to oust Richards, Billings, Saun-

19. *Journal of the Constitutional Convention Begun at Tallahassee, January 20, 1868*, 30; New York *Tribune*, February 2, 1868.
20. Jacksonville *Florida Union*, February 8, 1868; St. Augustine *Examiner*, February 7, 1868.

ders, and Pearce on the grounds that they were ineligible for membership, and replaced them with delegates more amenable to the moderate position. Horatio Jenkins, Jr., a former Union officer acquainted with Benjamin Butler and other influential national Republicans, was elected president of the reorganized convention. The midnight assemblage then voted to expunge the entire record of the convention since January 20, and replace it with a set of notes kept by J. Berrien Oliver, the Conservative editor of a Tallahassee newspaper.[21]

Chaos engulfed Tallahassee on the following morning when the Radicals discovered what had happened. Prevented from entering the convention hall by the moderates who had barricaded themselves inside, Billings called on a crowd of several thousand Negroes who readily agreed to storm the hall. Conservative Governor David S. Walker asked for and received military assistance to prevent this in the name of preserving order.[22] In this way federal power was used to assist the moderates in their usurpation of convention authority.

In Atlanta General Meade was thoroughly confused by the information he was receiving and decided to go to Tallahassee and take command of the situation.[23] Arriving there on February 17, he called for the resignation of both Richards and Jenkins and ordered another reorganization of the convention. Richards meanwhile had lost support and no longer commanded a majority of the delegates, so he vehemently protested this action but reluctantly entered the convention hall.[24]

Horatio Jenkins was now elected president of the convention by a vote of thirty-two to thirteen. The ouster of the four "ineli-

21. *House Miscellaneous Documents*, 40th Cong., 2d Sess., No. 109, p. 2, No. 114, p. 3; St. Augustine *Examiner*, March 7, 1868; John Wallace, *Carpetbag Rule in Florida* (Gainesville, 1964), 58; *Journal of the Convention of 1868*, 42–47.

22. New York *Tribune*, February 17, 1868; General G. G. Meade to H. Jenkins, February 10, 1868, in Records of the Army Command, Third Military District, Record Group 98, National Archives.

23. G. G. Meade to F. F. Flint, February 16, 1868, in *ibid*.

24. Jacksonville *Florida Union*, February 28, 1868; *House Miscellaneous Documents*, 40th Cong., 2d Sess., No. 109, pp. 21–24.

gible" delegates was made permanent and their replacements were seated. The constitution drafted at Monticello was adopted by the reconstituted convention by a vote of twenty-eight to sixteen. After passage of an ordinance denying pay to any delegate refusing to sign, nine more signatures were obtained on the moderate draft. This document was also dispatched to General Meade's Atlanta headquarters. The convention adjourned and again a nominating convention was held.[25] The moderates nominated Harrison Reed for governor, William Gleason for lieutenant governor, and Charles M. Hamilton for Congress.

General Meade forwarded both draft constitutions to Congress for review, but he recommended the approval of the moderate version on the procedural ground that it was signed by a majority of the convention delegates while the Radical one only had twenty-two signatures. There were only three major differences between the documents, but these were crucial. The Radical constitution would have made most state and county offices elective while the moderate draft provided that the governor appoint every official in the state except local constables. The latter provision would enable a governor, if he were so disposed, to limit Negro officials in the black belt counties. The Radical draft excluded from suffrage all persons who had held federal office and subsequently engaged in the rebellion against the United States. It also required a comprehensive loyalty oath which would have barred from office all who had supported the Confederacy. The moderate document made no mention of the rebellion and required a simple oath of future loyalty.[26]

The Radical constitution would have provided representation in proportion to population. The several populous counties in the north-central part of the state with large Negro majorities would have had multiple-member delegations while some of the smaller white counties would have been joined into dis-

<hr/>

25. St. Augustine *Examiner*, February 22, 1868; Harrison Reed to David L. Yulee, February 16, 1868, in Yulee Papers; Jacksonville *East Floridian*, March 5, 1868; Wallace, *Carpetbag Rule*, 57–58.

26. Wallace, *Carpetbag Rule*, 350–358, 362, 393–394.

tricts with single representatives. The Monticello version severely limited proportionate representation; instead it provided that each county must have at least one and no county more than four representatives in the lower house. Senate districts were similarly arranged. It was this feature which led Harrison Reed to write David Yulee that "the apportionment will prevent a Negro legislature." Despite the methods by which his group had managed to control the convention, Reed added that "the destructors have been overthrown and the state saved to 'law and order'." A Conservative newspaper understated the case in declaring that "a strong [bid] was made for Conservative votes."[27]

The moderates, with the beneficent assistance of the United States Army, had made significant gains against their Radical opponents in the weeks since the constitutional convention first met, but the outcome still depended upon which constitution the congressional joint committee selected to send to the people of Florida for ratification. Both groups sent representatives to lobby before that committee. Richards, who was closely associated with Elihu B. Washburne, a committee member, and Saunders both went to Washington with a memorial that bitterly condemned the Monticello draft constitution. They were assisted by Charles H. Pearce, William Bradwell, another Negro minister from Jacksonville, and Calvin L. Robinson, Florida's member of the Republican national committee. Robinson argued that the Monticello document, if implemented, would assist the Conservatives in gaining control of the state.[28]

The moderates were represented by Reed, Gleason, and George J. Alden, all of whom were closely acquainted with congressional and Republican party leaders. Gleason was a friend of Benjamin F. Butler, who also received letters from Horatio Jenkins and John W. Butler, both moderates who had

27. St. Augustine *Examiner*, February 22, 1868; Harrison Reed to David L. Yulee, February 16, 1868, in Yulee Papers.
28. Jerrell H. Shofner, *Nor Is It Over Yet: Florida in the Era of Reconstruction, 1863–1877* (Gainesville, 1974), 186.

served with Butler's command during the war. Reed was acquainted with several men of varying political persuasions. Having been a newspaperman in Wisconsin for more than twenty years before the Civil War, he was on close terms with most of the Republicans of that state, including conservative Republican Senator James R. Doolittle. With easy access to the decision-makers, the moderates presented their case in subdued tones while Daniel Richards was loudly castigating the other side to anyone who would listen.[29]

In April the Congress, which allegedly imposed "Radical Reconstruction" on Florida, voted to send to the people of that state for approval the moderate draft constitution which one of its chief architects declared would "prevent a Negro legislature."

Back in Florida the moderate Republicans campaigned for the election of Reed and Gleason and the ratification of the constitution. Billings, with William U. Saunders for a running mate, campaigned against the constitution. In its ostensibly impartial role of supervising the implementation of the Reconstruction laws, the army once again assisted the moderates. Colonel John T. Sprague ordered Billings arrested for making "incendiary speeches" and held in jail without charge until after the election. He was not released until the state was returned to civil control in July under the constitution he had opposed. The Radical group rapidly disintegrated after Billings' arrest. Jonathan C. Gibbs, an able Negro Radical leader, joined Saunders to campaign for Reed and the constitution. Others followed suit. Horatio Jenkins circulated a letter he had received from Congressman Benjamin Butler endorsing the moderate constitution.[30]

Native white Conservative leaders were generally pleased with the new constitution, but they split over methods of capi-

29. William H. Gleason to Benjamin F. Butler, December 28, 1868, Horatio Jenkins to Butler, March 26, 1868, Butler to Jenkins, April 8, 1868, John W. Butler to Butler, April 13, 1868, Butler to John W. Butler, April 20, 1868, in Benjamin F. Butler Papers, Library of Congress.

30. Shofner, *Nor Is It Over Yet*, 187–88.

talizing on it. With the Republicans battling each other, many native whites wanted to name a slate of candidates and campaign for the governorship. But Charles Dyke of the *Floridian* cautioned against such an audacious plan. Reminding his eager Conservative allies that he had worked diligently "abusing the one side and patting the other on the back" to help bring about the Republican debacle, he argued that native Floridians should be content to ignore the gubernatorial office and concentrate on exploiting the favorable apportionment provisions in order to win as many legislative seats as possible.[31] A Conservative slate was ultimately nominated for the governorship despite Dyke's opposition.

At the mid-May election the constitution was ratified by a vote of 14,520 to 9,491. Reed won the governorship with 14,170 votes to 7,852 for the Conservative candidate and 2,262 for the Radical. When the legislature was organized about one-third of the seats in both houses were held by Conservatives. But former Confederates had not known until a few days before the election whether they would be able to participate in it. Two years later the full significance of the apportionment provision of the moderate constitution manifested itself when Conservatives captured nearly one-half of the membership of both legislative houses.

Since Republican governors sat in Tallahassee until January 1877, longer than in any other former Confederate state except Louisiana and South Carolina, it is easy to overlook the significance of the 1868 constitutional struggle in the ultimate failure of Reconstruction in Florida. Yet the events surrounding the ratification controversy and the substantive provisions of the document itself practically assured that ex-Confederate Conservative Floridians would be able to survive congressional Reconstruction with little impairment of their political or social arrangements.

Anxious to attract support, or at least negate opposition from

31. Ibid., 189.

important native leaders, Reed and the moderates had made major concessions to them. Although no coalition resulted, Reed appointed two Conservatives—Robert H. Gamble and James D. Westcott—to major cabinet offices in his administration. Four of the seven circuit judgeships and numerous lesser offices were filled with Conservatives. These overtures ultimately failed. Having obtained as much as they could reasonably have hoped from the moderate Republicans, Conservatives soon lashed out at the Reed administration with every means they could muster. As Reed's comptroller, Gamble even used his office to embarrass the governor on fiscal matters. At the local level, native whites resorted to intimidation and violence to gain control of their counties while their Conservative allies condemned the governor for his inability to enforce the law at any distance from the state capital. In the legislature, Conservative members used dilatory tactics to disrupt and delay Republican legislation while the Conservative press attacked the Republicans for the disorderly activities in the state house.

The extra-legal methods by which the moderate constitution was implemented provided a poor example for future Republican party harmony. Not only were the defeated Radicals embittered by such blatant tactics, but the entire series of events set a precedent for future factionalism which ultimately discredited the Republican politicians among even their most partisan supporters. With the Radical faction reduced to impotence, the moderates soon divided. Without the stabilizing influences of tradition, aspiring politicians made temporary alliances and broke them freely. The result was chaos and confusion which added substance to the wildly exaggerated charges of the hostile native white population.

A key means of limiting the number of Negro officeholders, the immense gubernatorial powers provided by the 1868 constitution caused continuing difficulty. Not only were these powers a constant threat in the event the Conservatives ever won the governorship and took over the state election machinery, but they were also a major source of friction for the infant Republican party. With the authority to appoint about 450 state and local officials, the incumbent governor had potential control over every aspect of state government as well as the patronage to build a strong personal following. But the difficulty of managing such an extensive officialdom in frontier Florida, with its embryonic and fluid political structure, was more than Harrison Reed, or perhaps any man, could handle. Before his administration was six months old, Reed was engaged in a struggle for survival within his own party. Thomas Osborn, another ambitious moderate Republican, was elected by the 1868 legislature to the United States Senate. He had the longer of the two staggered senate terms and he thus became responsible for federal patronage, which he used to build his own political organization. The governor and Osborn were soon embroiled in a struggle which lasted throughout Reed's four-year term and eventually eliminated both men from party leadership. In the meantime this conflict contributed mightily to the downfall of the Republican party in Florida.

The struggle first emerged at a special legislative session in late 1868. Contrary to a constitutional prohibition against dual officeholding, several state legislators had accepted federal positions. Reed declared their seats vacant and called new elections. When the affected persons retaliated with an impeachment resolution, the Negro legislators, angered by Reed's veto of a civil rights bill, voted with them, and Reed was impeached. A month-long debacle followed during which both Reed and Lieutenant Governor Gleason claimed to be governor. The affair ended with Reed still governor but alienated from many of the white Republicans with whom he had so recently collaborated against the Radicals and their Negro allies. The Conservative press bemoaned the humiliation of the state even as they chortled at the Republican spectacle.[32]

32. *Florida Senate Journal*, Extra Session, 1868, p. 23; *Florida House Journal*, Extra Session, 1868, pp. 41–42; St. Augustine *Examiner*, November 14, 28, 1868; Charles M. Hamilton to George S. Boutwell, December 20, 1869, in Applications for Collector, Record Group 56, National Archives; Tampa *True Southerner*, December 3, 1868.

Reed ousted his secretary of state, who had sided with Gleason in the impeachment affray, and replaced him with Jonathan
C. Gibbs, a distinguished Negro leader, thus gaining an able
and loyal administrative assistant as well as a vastly improved
relationship with Negro Republicans. When the impeachment
charges were revived in the 1869 legislative session, two Negro
Republicans, Emanuel Fortune and Henry S. Harmon, led a
successful move to exonerate the governor. Shortly thereafter
Reed's white Republican opponents, especially William J. Purman and Marcellus L. Stearns, made themselves anathema to
the blacks when they had Charles H. Pearce, the AME church
leader, removed from the senate on spurious bribery charges.[33]

Amorphous, but extremely bitter, Republican factions continued to battle each other throughout Reed's administration. There
were two other lengthy impeachment imbroglios. Still anxious
to complete Florida's lagging railroad system as a means of fa-
cilitating population growth and economic development, Reed
called a special legislative session in 1869 to authorize state financial aid to private railroad companies. Despite the bipartisan support given these measures, legislation enacted by this
and the regular session of 1870 became a major source of the
subsequent allegations of fiscal irresponsibility hurled at the
Republican administrations. Some $4 million in state bonds
were authorized for the support of railroad companies. The bond
issues were at the center of the final two impeachment attacks
on Governor Reed. The last attack occurred in April 1872 just
before the state and national elections.[34]

Elated at the sorry record of the Republican administration,
Conservative-Democrats went into the 1872 gubernatorial election calling for reform in state government and an end to the
waste and corruption they alleged against the incumbent Republicans. So optimistic were they that they nominated for gov-

33. Tallahassee *Sentinel*, January 20, February 6, 13, 1869; Jacksonville
Florida Union, February 11, 1869; Harrison Reed to Columbus Delano, De-
cember 4, 1869, in Applications for Collector, Record Group 56, National
Archives.
34. For a fuller discussion of railroad affairs see Shofner, *Nor Is It Over
Yet*, 208–224.

ernor William D. Bloxham, a straight-out Conservative-Democrat and Leon County planter who had served in the Confederate army, and they initiated a campaign emphasizing white supremacy. This shortsighted campaign strategy did much to heal the serious rifts in the Florida Republican party.

Some Negroes, especially in Leon, Alachua, and Duval counties, and white Liberal Republicans had hoped in 1872 to ally with the Conservative-Democrats against the carpetbagger Republicans. They even called a Liberal Republican convention to meet in Jacksonville at the same time as the Conservative-Democratic convention. Completely ignored at Jacksonville, however, Liberal Republicans had little choice but to attend the regular Republican nominating convention two weeks later. Several of the Leon County Negro leaders refused to attend the convention, however, and those who did attend were determined to block the gubernatorial nominee of those white Republicans affiliated with Senator Osborn.[35]

The two major candidates for nomination were Marcellus L. Stearns, who was closely affiliated with Osborn and thoroughly disliked by most Negroes, and Ossian B. Hart, a native-born former slaveholder who had been a wartime Unionist. The blacks favored Hart despite his background. When the president of the convention declared Stearns nominated by virtue of a questionable counting of the delegate votes, the Negroes disrupted the convention. During the melee, Stearns managed to get to the floor and withdraw his name in the interest of party harmony. After Hart was nominated, a black Duval County delegate moved that Stearns be nominated for lieutenant governor for his magnanimous act. The motion carried.[36]

In the November election, held amid torrential rainstorms in peninsular Florida, the Republicans won the statewide elections. For the presidency Ulysses S. Grant defeated Horace

35. William D. Bloxham to R. H. M. Davison, July 30, 1872, manuscript in P. K. Yonge Library; Tallahassee *Weekly Floridian*, August 13, 20, 27, 1872; Thomas W. Osborn to William E. Chandler, August 17, 1872, in William E. Chandler Papers, Library of Congress.

36. Tallahassee *Weekly Floridian*, August 13, 1872; Wallace, *Carpetbag Rule*, 215.

Greeley in the state by about 2,000 votes, while Hart defeated Bloxham by a slightly smaller majority. The legislative elections were a different matter. The Democrats came painfully close to winning both houses. They would be a minority in the 1873 lower house by only three votes while the state senate would have thirteen Republicans and eleven Democrats.

Hart began his administration with most Republicans calling for and predicting future party harmony. Several important and beneficial financial measures were enacted during the first legislature. For example, a one million dollar bond issue enabled the state to begin operating on a "pay-as-you-go" basis for the first time since 1868. But shortly after this legislature adjourned, Governor Hart became seriously ill with pneumonia and languished until early 1874 when he died. During Governor Hart's long illness Stearns, whom the blacks disliked and distrusted, acted as governor, finally assuming the office in his own right when Hart died. In the meantime, Conservative-Democrats had joined Liberal Republicans to elect Simon Conover to the United States Senate.[37] The Republican party was soon split along lines similar to those of the previous administration.

Once in office, Senator Conover generally allied with the blacks while Governor Stearns found his support among the white officeholding Republicans who dominated the party's central committee. As these two Republican groups assailed each other, the Conservative Democratic minority capitalized on their feud. Continual reports in the Conservative press of factional fighting gradually had their effect. Many new residents were coming into east and central Florida in the 1870s. Although many were northerners who had generally favored the Republican party during the 1860s, they also desired low taxes and inexpensive government. Reports of malfeasance by officials, extra legislative sessions, and frequent bickering among Republicans gradually convinced these new settlers that a change in state government was necessary. By 1873 two influential Republican

37. Shofner, *Nor Is It Over Yet*, 288–91.

newspapers in east Florida called on Republicans to improve
their situation by voting for Conservative-Democrats in state
elections while continuing to support the national Republican
party. One of these, the Jacksonville *New South*, was edited by
John S. Adams, formerly a state immigration official, and the
other, the *Florida Agriculturist*, was edited by Solon Robinson,
who for many years before moving to Florida served as agricultural editor of the New York *Tribune*.[38]

The 1874 off-year elections were highlighted by more Republican intraparty battling, including a furniture-destroying
fight at a convention in the state assembly hall. In that election
the Republicans retained both congressional seats, but the legislature finally went Democratic, at least on joint ballots. The senate was deadlocked at twelve to twelve, but there were twenty-
eight Democrats to twenty-five Republicans in the lower house.
The 1875 legislature was to elect a United States senator to replace the obscure Abijah Gilbert whose term was expiring.[39]

The 1875 senatorial election was a difficult one because the
Democrats, with a majority of only three, could not unite on a
candidate until Charles W. Jones, a comparatively obscure Irish-
born lawyer from Pensacola, was nominated. Elected on the
twenty-fourth ballot, Jones was applauded by both Democrats
and independent Republicans. The Democratic Tallahassee
Floridian admitted that Jones was not its choice but exulted
that native Floridians had finally outvoted the "Radicals" on
a matter of such importance. "The real cause [for losing the
United States senate seat to the Democrats]," wrote Adams in
the *New South*, "was the years of disgraceful squabbling within
the party."[40]

38. Tallahassee *Weekly Floridian*, July 15, 22, 1873; Henry A. L'Engle to Edward M. L'Engle, August 2, 1874, in L'Engle Papers, Southern Historical Collection, University of North Carolina; William J. Purman to B. H. Bristow,
September 15, 1874, in Applications for Collector, Record Group 56, National
Archives. Edward King, "Pictures from Florida," *Scribners' Monthly*, IX (November, 1874), 30; Edward King, *The Southern States of North America* (London, 1875), 419.

39. Jacksonville *New South*, July 15, 18, August 15, 17, 1874; *Florida House
Journal*, 1875, p. 9; *Florida Senate Journal*, 1875, p. 19; Tallahasse *Weekly
Floridian*, February 16, 1875.

40. Tallahassee *Weekly Floridian*, February 9, 1875; Thomasville *Times*,

In 1876 the Florida Republicans still possessed the governor's office, with its vast appointive powers, and two of the three Supreme Court seats. But Governor Stearns was an original member of the group that had opposed the Radicals in 1868, and he had consistently opposed Governor Reed and his black supporters. Although he had built up strong support among the white officeholders of the party, Stearns remained unpopular with the Negro leaders and he had done nothing to bring harmony to the strife-torn party. As the 1876 election approached the newspapers were filled with charges of corruption and inefficiency, most of which were levelled by high Republican officials against each other. Congressman Purman accused Governor Stearns of dishonesty, while Stearns alleged that Purman had accepted bribes in making recommendations for federal appointments. Senator Conover was accused of embezzlement and, worst of all, collusion with Democrats. The senator was even arrested on the embezzlement charge although he was soon exonerated. The Conservative press gleefully reprinted these charges and called on the people of Florida to reform their government by electing Conservative-Democratic officials.[41]

As the parties prepared to nominate candidates for the 1876 election, the Republican Tallahassee *Sentinel* declared that "Party unity must and shall be preserved! Just how we are not prepared to say." The state executive committee, largely controlled by Governor Stearns, attempted to unify the party and assure the governor's renomination by including in its call for a state convention a premature announcement of its temporary organization. Realizing the disadvantage of a convention controlled by Stearns supporters, Senator Conover, who was also running for governor, refused to accept the committee's action. Despite a vigorous campaign on the senator's part, however, delegates pledged to Governor Stearns were elected in most of the counties. Refusing to accept the situation, contesting Con-

February 27, 1875; Jacksonville *New South*, February 10, 13, 1875.

41. Tallahassee *Sentinel*, May 13, 27, April 1, 1875; Fernandina *Observer*, January 1, 1876; Jacksonville *Tri-Weekly Sun*, March 30, 1876; Tallahassee *Weekly Floridian*, April 4, 1876.

over delegations from several populous counties appeared at the convention in Madison.[42]

Stearns' control of the temporary organization was decisive and, after a bitter and destructive floor fight, the pro-Conover delegates were excluded. Stearns was renominated for governor and David Montgomery of Madison County was named as his running mate. Conover delegates from about twenty-six counties then held their own convention in a nearby wooded area and nominated the senator for governor and Joseph A. Lee, a southern Unionist, for lieutentant governor. Understating the situation considerably, the Tallahassee *Sentinel* concluded that "entire unity was not secured at the convention."[43]

Having tried unsuccessfully to defeat the Republicans in 1872 with a native born, ex-Confederate planter, the Conservative-Democrats were determined in 1876 to nominate a candidate who would appeal to the new settlers in east Florida as well as the native voters. An ideal candidate was available. George F. Drew was a New Hampshire-born businessman who had lived for many years in Georgia before settling at Ellaville, Florida after the Civil War, where he operated a prosperous lumber mill. Drew had been a Unionist during the war, had voted for Grant in 1868, and became a Liberal Republican in 1872. By 1876 he was a Conservative-Democrat, but he was much more palatable to conservative northerners who were dissatisfied with the wasteful and quarrelsome Republican regime in Tallahassee than a straight-out southern Democrat such as Bloxham would have been. The Republicans were alarmed and furious at Drew's nomination. "He must have been nominated to give the 'Lost Cause' a Union flavor," the *Sentinel* surmised. "His nomination is a wicked fraud to catch Union men and Northern Republicans coming into the state. We would rather have the most bitter Bourbon."[44]

42. Tallahassee *Sentinel*, May 13, 1875; Tallahassee *Weekly Floridian*, June 6, 1876.
43. Tallahassee *Sentinel*, June 3, 1876; Quitman, Georgia *Reporter*, June 8, 1876; Tallahassee *Weekly Floridian*, June 6, 1876.
44. Tallahassee *Sentinel*, June 10, 24, 1876; Ocala *East Florida Banner*,

The Republicans held two separate congressional nominating conventions in August. Both Stearns and Conover eagerly sought their endorsements. With the *Sentinel* warning that "the Florida Republicans must 'Unite or Die'," both conventions ultimately endorsed the governor. Purman was renominated for Congress from the first district and began making peace with Stearns with whom he had only recently been engaged in a bitter name-calling duel. The second district convention passed by Congressman Josiah T. Walls of Alachua County, the only Negro elected to a high office in Florida during Reconstruction, and named Horatio Bisbee, Jr., a white Jacksonville attorney, to replace him. Except for one presidential elector, there was not a Negro on the Republican state ticket in 1876.[45]

Conover announced that he would remain in the race even after both congressional district conventions rejected him in favor of Stearns, and the persistent factionalism alarmed Republican leaders. There had been such divisions before but they had always been resolved before the elections. Because a close race was obviously developing for the presidency, the national Republicans felt compelled to intercede in the Florida struggle. Not only were there two slates of candidates for the state governorship, but there were also competing electoral tickets. One disgusted Florida Republican warned that many Republicans had already resolved to vote for George F. Drew for governor, but were still willing to vote for Hayes for president if they were given the opportunity. To make this possible the national committee needed to ensure that only one Republican electoral ticket was offered on election day. In response to pressure from the national committee, Conover finally withdrew in early September. He did not campaign for Stearns but he did call on Republicans to support the regular party candidates.[46]

June 10, 1876; Key West *Key of the Gulf*, July 1, 1876; File GJ 3309, in Records of the Court of Claims, Record Group 123, National Archives.

45. Tallahassee *Sentinel*, July 15, 1876, Quincy *Journal*, August 4, 1876; Tallahassee *Weekly Floridian*, August 29, 1876; Wallace, *Carpetbag Rule*, 333.

46. John F. Rollins to William E. Chandler, August 9, 1876, in Chandler Papers; Jacksonville *Daily Florida Union*, August 24, September 8, 1876; Tallahassee *Sentinel*, September 16, 1876.

For some Republicans there had been too much hurried peacemaking. John Wallace and other Leon County Negroes continued to oppose Stearns and determined to vote the Democratic ticket. In the latter days of the campaign, Wallace and J. Willis Menard, a Duval County Negro leader, announced as independent candidates for first and second district congressional seats. Ex-Governor Harrison Reed came out of retirement and joined them as a candidate for governor. William U. Saunders, an original member of the Radical faction of the 1868 constitutional convention, campaigned for these independent candidates. Solon Robinson, editor of the *Florida Agriculturist*, called on his Republican readers to join him in voting a split ticket for the Republican Hayes and the Democratic Drew. Henry Sanford, an influential national Republican with large landholdings in Orange County, contributed financially to the Hayes campaign in Florida, but ignored the state ticket.[47]

There were threats of violence, some minor altercations, heated verbal exchanges, fraud, and economic intimidations surrounding the election of November 7, 1876, but no serious violence occurred. Fraudulent practices were limited by diligent poll watchers from both parties at every precinct. Because Florida's election subsequently became embroiled in the lengthy dispute over the presidential election of that year, nearly every irregularity was ultimately reported, often in exaggerated terms. Both sides claimed victory by as much as 2,000 votes, but it was soon clear that a few votes would decide the Florida election, and the uncertainty would not end until the state canvassing board had counted the votes and certified the election results. It was also clear that disruptive Republican factionalism was finally taking its toll. Split ticket voting in several counties caused the state ticket to run several hundred votes behind the Hayes electors.[48]

47. Note from Harrison Reed, October 6, 1876, in L'Engle Papers; Tallahassee *Sentinel*, September 16, 1876; Henry S. Sanford to John Friend, December 31, 1876, in Sanford Papers, Sanford, Florida.

48. For a full account of the election and the resolution of the dispute that followed see Shofner, *Nor Is It Over Yet*, 311–27.

With "visiting statesmen" from both national parties crowding into Tallahassee, the canvassing board agreed to count the presidential votes first and then turn to the state elections. With a membership of two Republicans and one Democrat, the board declared that Hayes had defeated Tilden by a majority of 43 of the more than 48,000 votes cast. Since Stearns had trailed Hayes by about 400 votes the Republicans at Tallahassee now faced a dilemma. The small Hayes majority had been obtained by counting a questionable return from Baker County. In order to increase the Republican majority by enough votes to elect Stearns, the board would have to throw out a large number of votes. While it had authority to rule on the validity of county returns and reject those it considered erroneous, the Republican managers were afraid that a wholesale alteration of the returns could not be sustained. But when Stearns and his allies in Florida informed the "visiting statesmen" that they had little interest in a Republican presidential victory in which they did not share, it was agreed that the effort should be made. The Republican majority of the returning board then rejected as irregular about 2,000 votes to elect Stearns over Drew.

Attorneys for Drew then asked the Republican-dominated state supreme court to reverse the board's decision for Stearns, which it did. The court decision alarmed the national Republicans who feared that it also might upset Hayes' claim to Florida's electoral vote and throw the presidential election to Tilden. But the federal electoral commission which was created to resolve the dispute over conflicting returns from Florida, South Carolina, and Louisiana decided that it had no power to investigate the peculiar circumstances of the Florida election and gave Hayes the state's electoral votes. While this debate continued, George F. Drew was peacefully inaugurated as Florida's governor on January 2, 1877.

Possessed of the powerful governor's office bequeathed by moderate Republicans, the Conservative-Democrats quickly tightened their control of the state government. Governor Drew appointed county officials who could be depended upon to control election results, and in 1880 William D. Bloxham, who had lost to Hart in 1872, won the governorship. The "redemption" of Florida by native whites was thus completed. In 1885 a new constitution was drafted which provided for the permanent disfranchisement of most Negro voters. Florida became a dependable component of the "solid south," and Negroes were relegated to a political, social, and economic position not very different from their bonded servitude before 1865.

Negroes had participated more fully in politics during the Republican years than they would for many decades. They had enjoyed a measure of freedom under the tutelage of the national government which was infinitely greater than had been possible before emancipation. They had more opportunity to move about, to bargain with their employers or sometimes become landowners themselves, to vote for officials who would govern them, and to hold many minor offices as well as a few important ones. Negro legislators learned to bargain with their white colleagues, and several measures were enacted which were directly beneficial to their race.

Yet blacks never received full support from the white Republicans for legislation they deemed essential to their well-being. Civil rights bills repeatedly failed to pass because Republican votes were cast against them. When a civil rights act providing for equal access to public accomodations, but allowing segregated schools, finally passed by a narrow majority, three Conservative-Democratic senators voted for it.[49] And despite the fact that a number of blacks held local offices, they were always a minority at all levels of government. Only Congressmen Josiah T. Walls and Jonathan C. Gibbs, who served as secretary of state and then superintendent of public instruction, ever held high offices. Both were well qualified for their positions and were so acknowledged by white members of both parties.

Although it lost control of the state legislature in 1874, the Republican party managed to hold the Florida gubernatorial office until 1876 when the state election became entangled in the presidential election dispute, the resolution of which has become known as the "end of Reconstruction" and the "restora-

49. *Florida Senate Journal*, 1873, pp. 52–53.

tion of home rule." Because of this timing and Conservative-Democratic propaganda both before and after 1876, it has often been assumed that the Republican party dominated the state in the interests of propertyless Negroes at the expense of a powerless native white population until the "redemption" in 1876. But that is not true except in the narrowest sense. Dominant Republicans catered little to the blacks, and native white Floridians were never entirely without influence. Having learned during President Johnson's Reconstruction efforts in 1865–1866 that there is a great disparity between policy formulated at Washington and its implementation in the states, opponents bargained effectively with the Republicans at every opportunity. Whether they were collaborating on railroad construction schemes with moderate Republicans, advising constitutional convention delegates on ways to make the 1868 constitution palatable to native Floridians, using economic intimidation to regain control of their counties, or blocking Republican legislation with dilatory tactics in the state legislature, the Conservative-Democrats were always a limiting factor on the Republican party's power.

Nor were the white Republicans who dominated their party particularly sympathetic toward Negroes. No group played a more significant role in the failure of congressional Reconstruction than those moderate Republicans who used extra-legal tactics to take control of the 1868 constitutional convention away from Billings, Richards, and their Radical allies. While it is likely that congressional Reconstruction would have been a failure in any event, the outcome of the 1868 constitutional struggle made it certain that there would be little radicalism in Florida.

The 1868 constitution was not imposed on a helpless native white population as Conservative-Democrats subsequently claimed. Nor was it intended to place Negroes in control of the state. Rather it was the product of intense maneuvering by groups of men with widely differing goals. The contest occurred within the context of congressional legislation, but Congress had allowed ample room for internal decision. The Radicals who first controlled the constitutional convention would not

modify their demands for Negro equality and the punishment of
ex-Confederates, and they were unable to win without doing
so. Although they had not obtained much representation in the
convention of 1868, native white Conservatives remained the
most vocal and economically influential part of the population.
From the equivocation of the Washington government during
1865–1867 they had learned many ways of thwarting or twist-
ing laws enacted in distant Washington. They were unwilling to
accept subjection to northern Radicals supported by a Negro
electorate as long as there was any alternative.

The pragmatic Republican moderates were more interested
in an alliance between government and business to develop the
raw frontier lands of Florida than they were in Negro rights.
They had more in common with the native white Conservatives
than they did with Liberty Billings and Daniel Richards who
were intent on restructuring the society of the state. Many of
them recognized the need for protecting Negroes under the law
but they had little sympathy for racial equality. They believed
that a state government would have a better chance for success
if it met the legal requirements of congressional laws regarding
Negro rights without going so far as to alienate the native white
leadership. Harrison Reed, Ossian B. Hart, William H. Gleason,
and Thomas W. Osborn all had economic ideologies similar to
those of such Conservatives as Governor David Walker and
David Yulee. With communications already established between these groups, they tried to work out an acceptable compromise. A coalition ultimately failed because the basic issue,
what to do about freedmen who now had political power, could
not be resolved. But that does not detract from the importance
of the effort. Reed frankly admitted the degree of his commitment to Republican principles in an 1869 address to the legislature: "It was only as a Republican that I could get measures for
the benefit of the State from the dominant party at Washington.
We would have been paralyzed without it."[50]

50. Jacksonville *Florida Union*, May 20, 1869.

Unable to control the convention of 1868 by parliamentary procedure and unwilling to submit to the Radicals, the moderates used extra-legal measures to achieve their ends. The United States army, knowingly or not, gave them crucial assistance in doing so. Once the Radicals were defeated the moderates believed that the Negroes would be left leaderless. There would be time enough to win them over after the framing of a constitution which invited acquiescence from the powerful native Floridians.

Once in possession of the convention hall the moderates were able to claim compliance with the letter of the law. It was Conservative Governor Walker who asked the Tallahassee commander to place a guard in front of the convention hall in the name of law and order, but only *after* the moderates had taken illegal possession of it. Upon arrival in Tallahassee, General Meade was favorably impressed by the harmonious relations displayed between native white leaders and the moderate Republicans. Primarily concerned with maintaining order rather than promoting a particular social goal, he was disposed to solve the convention dilemma by the least disruptive method. This support of the moderates was decisive. Having built a small majority in the convention by attracting two Negro defectors from the Radical group, the moderates were elated when Meade called for new elections for convention officials. With two draft constitutions before him, the general forwarded both to Congress but recommended the moderate version on mere procedural grounds.

The joint congressional committee also assisted the moderates. Despite the significant differences between the two constitutional drafts, members of the joint committee accepted the moderate version without serious discussion of how it might affect Reconstruction developments in Florida. That the committee ultimately accepted the moderate constitution, apparently on the narrow procedural ground that it had the approval of General Meade, emphasizes the limited goals of the "Radical" architects of Reconstruction.

The Conservatives received more than they gave. The advantage of the apportionment provisions favoring the white counties has already been mentioned. The extensive gubernatorial appointive power was beneficial to them as long as the Radicals could be prevented from obtaining the governor's office. Reed's earlier appointment of Conservative-Democrats to cabinet and judicial offices was helpful. When George F. Drew became governor in 1877, this power proved to be an exceedingly effective means of destroying the Republican party.

Reed and his moderate allies had hoped their concessions to the Conservative-Democrats might provide an enduring basis for cooperation. But the native whites did not see the 1868 situation as a permanent compromise settlement. Rather, they viewed it as a partial victory from which they might work toward their basic goal of ousting from their society the unwelcomed intruders who had forced Negro suffrage on them. In the long run, the moderate overtures to the Conservatives enhanced the ability of the opposition to disrupt and destroy Republican efforts, while it also provided a poor foundation on which to build future party harmony.

Unable to overcome the factional bitterness engendered by the 1868 constitutional battle, the moderate Republicans spent much of their energies fighting each other during the following eight years. Negro leaders attempted with limited success to exact a price for their continued support of the Republican party while Conservative-Democrats used their minority membership to disrupt the legislative process and blame the resulting inefficiencies on the majority party. With their legislative strength declining and northern zeal for Reconstruction waning, it was only a question of time until the Republicans lost the governorship, the citadel on which the moderate Republicans had counted so heavily.

Without basic changes in the social attitudes of nearly all southern whites—attitudes which they shared with most northern whites—there was scant likelihood that any solution to postwar problems in the United States could have been found.

Lacking strong agreement on the goals of Reconstruction and with the diffusion of power both at the national level and between levels of government, Congress was unable to enact and implement a program which had much chance of success. But the critical point at which that program faltered in Florida was the 1868 constitutional convention. Drew's inauguration in 1877 was the logical outcome of that convention struggle and the subsequent factionalism in the Republican party.

As a final gratuity several economy measures were enacted during the Hart-Stearns administration which eventually brought important budgetary savings to Florida government. But these laws were not effective until after the Conservative-Democrats had won the governorship. They were thus able to claim credit for the resulting economies and convince Florida voters that they had "redeemed" the state from the wasteful and corrupt Republicans. Native white Floridians had never been dominated by a Negro-oriented party, and Conservative-Democrats had contributed tremendously to the confusion, violence, and waste that marred the Republican record. They were then able to convince white Floridians that Negro suffrage forced on the state by a hostile Congress had caused the turbulence of the Reconstruction years and that whites must unite to prevent a return to such conditions. This became a compelling purpose in Florida politics. White supremacy and a united Democratic party were imperative for the well-being of the state. For many decades after 1877, Democratic party leaders were able to use such racially charged issues to prevent consideration by the voters of vital social and economic problems confronting the state. This was the real failure of Reconstruction and both black and white Floridians paid a heavy price for it.

Bibliographical Essay

THE FIRST SCHOLARLY HISTORY OF FLORIDA RECONSTRUC-
tion is William Watson Davis, *Civil War and Reconstruction in
Florida* (New York: Columbia University Press, 1913), one of
the best of the state studies produced by the students of William Archibald Dunning at Columbia University. One of Davis'
major sources was John Wallace, *Carpetbag Rule in Florida*
(Jacksonville: Da Costa Printing and Publishing House, 1888),
a critical treatment of the Republicans in Reconstruction Florida by a Negro politician who was present and active at the time.
Although some historians have discounted his work because of
his close association with Conservative-Democrat William D.
Bloxham, Wallace had broken with the Republican officeholders during the administration of Marcellus L. Stearns and campaigned against the governor in the 1876 election.

An important revisionist work dealing with Florida blacks
during Reconstruction is Joe M. Richardson, *The Negro in the
Reconstruction of Florida, 1865–1877* (Tallahassee: Florida
State University, 1965). For a general study of the Reconstruction period from the viewpoint of recent scholarship, see Jerrell
H. Shofner, *Nor Is It Over Yet: Florida in the Era of Reconstruction, 1863–1877* (Gainesville: University Presses of Florida, 1974). Some of the Florida Republican leaders are discussed
in David H. Overy, *Wisconsin Carpetbaggers in Dixie* (Madison: State Historical Society of Wisconsin, 1961). A brief sketch
of Harrison Reed and his beleaguered administration may be
found in Richard N. Current, *Three Carpetbagger Governors*
(Baton Rouge: Louisiana State University Press, 1967).

Despite their propensity for error and distortion, the newspapers of the period contain invaluable information about political activities and attitudes as well as the social and economic affairs of post-Civil War Florida. Of those that have been preserved, the most significant include the Tallahassee *Floridian*, edited by Charles E. Dyke, one of the most astute Conservative-Democrats of the time; the Tallahassee *Sentinel*, which under several editors was consistently Republican although it was often forced to take sides in the party's factional struggles; the Jacksonville *Florida Union*, a moderate Republican journal devoted as much to development of Jacksonville and the Florida peninsula as to Republican political hegemony; and the Jacksonville *New South*, a reform Republican paper edited by J. S. Adams who revolted against the Republican officeholders during the Stearns administration. Others include the *St. Augustine Examiner*, a Conservative-Democratic paper that remained comparatively aloof from politics; the Jacksonville *Florida Agriculturist*, edited by Solon Robinson, former agricultural editor of the New York *Tribune* and a Republican who also broke with the Stearns administration; and the Savannah *Morning News*, a Conservative-Democratic paper that carried much information about Florida.

Personal manuscript collections relating to Florida Reconstruction are scarce and scattered, but a few important ones have been preserved. The Edward M. L'Engle papers at the University of North Carolina and the David L. Yulee papers at the P. K. Yonge Library of Florida History at the University of Florida contain a large volume of information relating to the political and economic activities of these two men and their Conservative-Democratic associates. The papers of moderate Republican William H. Gleason at the P. K. Yonge Library were helpful. The Henry Shelton Sanford papers at Sanford, Florida, a microfilm copy of which is in the P. K. Yonge Library, is a voluminous collection of a conservative Republican with whom many Floridians of all political persuasions corresponded. The Elihu B. Washburne papers in the Library of Congress contain a series of letters from Daniel Richards, one of the Florida Radical Republicans.

The legislative journals and the proceedings of the 1868 constitutional convention were indispensable. Also valuable were the records of the Florida secretary of state, now housed in the recently created Division of Archives, History, and Records Management.

Several documents of the 40th Congress, all of which have been reprinted in Wallace, *Carpetbag Rule*, along with Senate Report No. 611 and House Report No. 35 of the 44th Congress, 2nd Session, cast considerable light on the failure of Reconstruction in Florida. Also useful were the records of the Freedmen's Bureau, Army Commands, and Department of Justice in the National Archives.

Individuals involved in Florida Reconstruction deserve more biographical study than they have received. In addition to Current's work on Harrison Reed, Peter D. Klingman has recently completed a dissertation on Josiah T. Walls, Florida's only black Congressman. Lewis Cresse has written a dissertation on William H. Gleason. But David L. Yulee, Edward M. L'Engle, and perhaps Charles E. Dyke are proper subjects for book-length biographies. Others, including William D. Bloxham, Ossian B. Hart, William J. Purman, Jonathan C. Greely, Jonathan C.Gibbs, Henry S. Harmon, and Charles H. Pearce, might be adequately treated in articles.

II

Alabama
Democratic Bulldozing and Republican Folly
SARAH WOOLFOLK WIGGINS

HORACE MANN BOND once observed about Alabama Reconstruction that "certain facts add piquancy to the general notion that Reconstruction in Alabama was a tightly drawn struggle between Virtue, as represented by the Democrats, and Vice, as represented by the Republicans."[1] Bond was correct in perceiving that Alabama Reconstruction had been viewed in terms too simplistic to be very accurate. Truthfully, Democrats and Republicans in Alabama were in many respects far more alike than different, and neither party had a corner on vice or virtue. One Northern traveler in Alabama in the 1870s wryly observed that the Democratic governor during Reconstruction was "little, if at all, more economical" than either his Republican predecessor or successor and that wherever "conspicuous financial jobbery" had occurred Democrats oftener than not, had been "parties in interest."[2]

The author wishes to acknowledge assistance from The University of Alabama Research Committee.

1. Horace Mann Bond, "Social and Economic Forces in Alabama Reconstruction," *Journal of Negro History*, XXIII (July, 1938), 333.
2. Charles Nordhoff, *The Cotton States in the Spring and Summer of 1875* (New York, 1876), 89.

Democrats played an important part in the Reconstruction of their state, unlike their role in some other former Confederate states in that era, and Alabama had a viable two-party system in operation soon after it was readmitted to the Union in 1868. This two-party system ended with the 1874 election when Alabama Democrats so thoroughly demolished their opposition that they remained virtually unchallenged in their political control of the state until the twentieth century. With the collapse of the Republican party as a power in Alabama came the collapse of Reconstruction. Some of the seeds for the Republican disaster of 1874 were present at the outset of Reconstruction; others were sown along the way.

An important reason for the failure of Reconstruction in Alabama, as elsewhere in the South, was the fact that the freedmen remained economically dependent on the white population. Without some degree of economic independence, subsequent efforts in politics were doomed almost from the outset. Unquestionably, any gesture that resembled redistribution of land would have met screaming opposition from whites, but the only possible chance for success in establishing black economic independence in this state existed in the first six months of the postwar period. At that time Alabamians were relieved that the long war was finally over, and they seemed ready to accept whatever peace terms the federal government offered. A college president observed that there was "entire acquiescence," and a soldier said Alabamians were "thoroughly whipped and own it," and "ready to do anything . . . for a return to the prosperity of old."[3] The alternative to accommodating to existing circumstances was "to make issue with the victors" which would result in the state remaining indefinitely under military rule. One newspaper advised its readers that it was their duty to save themselves from further loss and trouble and realize that the federal government would protect the freedmen in their legal rights. There was, as yet, no boasting about the glory of the lost

3. J. L. M. Curry to E. B. Washburne, January 11, 1865, in Elihu B. Washburne Papers, and F. W. Kellogg to Zachariah Chandler, June 19, 1865, in Zachariah Chandler Papers, both in Library of Congress.

cause. But as months passed, arrogance replaced acquiescence in Alabama, and, like the opportunity to end slavery immediately after the American Revolution, once the opportune time had passed, attitudes were not again conducive to solving a controversial problem.[4] Blacks in Alabama remained subject to the economic pressures of their white employers, and their political prospects were no more independent.

Another of those seeds of failure present in 1865 was the attitude of whites toward blacks, an attitude which colored Reconstruction in Alabama from its very beginning. Ultimately, political success or failure in the state hinged largely on how a party coped with the race issue. Throughout the postwar period Alabama whites, regardless of political affiliations, remained convinced of the fundamental racial inferiority of blacks. In 1865 many regarded blacks as so socially and intellectually inferior and so weak in character that no legislation would make them into good citizens. White Alabamians saw their government as "made by white men, for the benefit of white men, to be administered by white men, and nobody else, forever," and they were willing to grant blacks no more than minimum legal and civil rights. Alabamians presumed that they would be left considerable freedom to manage the race question with little outside interference. Such assumptions reflected a lack of a thorough realization of what it meant to lose a war, as a favorite plea by spring 1866 was "all we ask is to be let alone."[5]

Presidential Reconstruction in Alabama reflected the racial views of Alabamians; it was certainly no threat to them in 1865. President Andrew Johnson appointed Lewis E. Parsons, a respected Talladega lawyer and Douglas Democrat in 1860, as provisional governor. Parsons declared in force all Alabama laws enacted before January 11, 1861, except those regarding slav-

4. Huntsville *Advocate*, July 19, August 31, 1865; Livingston *Journal*, August 5, 1865; *House Reports*, 39th Cong., 1st Sess., No. 30, Pt. 3, pp. 9, 12, 15, 28.

5. J. L. M. Curry to E. B. Washburne, January 11, 1865, in Washburne Papers; Benjamin F. Saffold to L. E. Parsons, August 2, 1865, in Governor Lewis E. Parsons Papers, Alabama State Department of Archives and History; Livingston *Journal*, August 5, 1865; Montgomery *Daily Advertiser*, April 4, 1866.

ery, continued in office those there at the war's end, and announced the opening of voter registration. The Freedmen's Bureau in Alabama generally cooperated with the governor, especially in using the judicial machinery Parsons reorganized to administer justice to the freedmen. Subsequently, the bureau had misgivings because blacks encountered many opportunities to be oppressed, but since there seemed no better immediate alternative, the courts continued to operate as they had in the past.[6]

The actions of the 1865 constitutional convention embodied the attitudes of white Alabamians during presidential Reconstruction as they made the transition from the old era to the new. Instead of apportioning representation according to the whole population of the state, representation was based on the white population alone, thus putting into law the concept of a "white men's government."[7]

The new governor elected later in 1865 was Robert M. Patton, prosperous north Alabama merchant and Douglas Democrat who sat out the war at home. The most significant and far-reaching legislation of his administration was the decision in February 1867 to allow the state government to endorse a railroad's first mortgage bonds for construction of intrastate or interstate roads. Unwisely the law made state aid available to any railroad project regardless of its merit; but before any company could take advantage of the act, Congress suspended Patton's government with the passage of the first of the Reconstruction Acts.[8]

Both the Republican and the Democratic-Conservative par-

---

6. Proclamation of Governor Lewis E. Parsons, July 20, 1865, in Governor Lewis E. Parsons Papers; Wager Swayne to O. O. Howard, August 21, November n.d., 1865, in Reports of Swayne to Howard, and Wager Swayne to J. S. Fullerton, June 13, 1866, in General Letters Sent, Headquarters Assistant Commissioner for Alabama, No. 5, Records of Bureau of Refugees, Freedmen, and Abandoned Lands, Record Group 105, National Archives.

7. *Journal of the Proceedings of the Convention of the State of Alabama, 1865*, 104–105.

8. *Acts of the General Assembly of Alabama*, 1866–67, pp. 686–94.

ties were formally organized in Alabama in 1867. When the Republicans organized in June, the discomfort of white Alabamians who found themselves in a political party with blacks was immediately obvious. The prospect of black suffrage was difficult for native white Republicans to swallow, as they privately described blacks in their new role as voters as new and "unwelcome allies" and black suffrage as a "bitter pill."[9] The Democratic-Conservative party organized in September and was equally ambivalent about how to meet the issue of black suffrage. They obviously expected to lead these new voters politically and urged blacks to trust men whom they knew and to beware of strangers, "who bear no evidence that they were honored where they are better known." Speakers were appointed to instruct black voters about the Conservative party.[10] Both parties faced the same dilemma: How to create a biracial political party without driving away white constituents.

Voter registration under congressional Reconstruction occurred in July and August when 74,450 whites and 90,350 blacks were enrolled. Obviously a substantial number of white Alabamians were able and willing to swear the "iron-clad" oath in order to register. The new electorate chose a constitutional convention of ninety-seven Republians and three Democrats to meet in November. The Republican members included forty-eight whites who had been in Alabama before 1860, twenty-six white northerners, and nineteen blacks.[11]

The suffrage issue provoked the most bitter disagreement during the convention. Violent wrangling both in the franchise committee and on the floor of the convention ultimately produced a suffrage article which enfranchised blacks, disfranchised those unable to hold office under the proposed Fourteenth

9. Joseph C. Bradley to Wager Swayne, April 6, 12, 1867, and Joshua Morse to Swayne, April 17, 1867, in Papers of Bureau of Refugees, Freedmen, and Abandoned Lands, Alabama State Department of Archives and History.
10. Montgomery *Daily Advertiser*, September 6, 1867.
11. Sarah Woolfolk Wiggins, *The Scalawag in Alabama Politics, 1865–1881* (University, Ala., 1977), 25–26, 151–52. The 1860 census reported 526,431 whites and 437,770 blacks in the state.

Amendment, and disfranchised those men who had applied for pardons under presidential Reconstruction. Such disabilities exceeded the minimum requirements under the Reconstruction Acts, but despite the severity of these restrictions many Democrats were still eligible to vote. The convention also reapportioned the legislature, this time on the basis of the whole population of the state.[12] Other than extending suffrage, the convention did little for Alabama blacks. Native white delegates were obviously uncomfortable with the race issue and went no further than political necessity under the Reconstruction Acts demanded.

Of tremendous importance to the future course of Reconstruction was the disfranchisement of those unable to hold office under the proposed Fourteenth Amendment. Alabamians who had taken an oath to uphold the U.S. Constitution and then held even a minor post under the Confederacy were now disfranchised, although many of these men had opposed secession and the Confederacy and had held such positions to avoid conscription into the Confederate army. Although the convention did authorize the Alabama lesiglature to relax suffrage disabilities in the future, the failure to offer amnesty to this group at the outset of congressional Reconstruction embittered many who sympathized with the ideas of the Republican party.[13]

The campaign for ratification of the new constitution saw both Democrats and Republicans attack the document for the same racial and economic reasons. Some Republicans were outraged at the "disfranchisement of so many of our best people and the enfranchisement of a whole race of ignorant stupid negroes." Other Republicans urged colonization of blacks outside the

12. *Official Journal of the Constitutional Convention of the State of Alabama, 1867*, 30–35, 44–46, 96, 99–101.
13. William Byrd to George S. Boutwell, December 15, 1868, and David P. Lewis to J. J. Giers, November 26, 1870, in Records of the Select Committee on Reconstruction, 40th and 41st Cong., Records of the U.S. House of Representatives, Record Group 233, National Archives; Wager Swayne to Salmon P. Chase, June 28, 1867, in Salmon P. Chase Papers, Library of Congress.

South, claiming that if they were allowed to remain, they would "ultimately be extirpated, as self-preservation is above all human codes."[14] The Democrats, like some Republicans, believed the suffrage clause of the constitution would make the blacks the ruling class in Alabama, and they were outraged that ignorant, propertyless, half vagabonds incompetent to comprehend politics would be allowed to tax, humiliate, and subordinate whites. As they saw it, the crux of the question of ratification was not black suffrage or black civil rights. The real issue was "shall the white man be subordinate to the negro? Shall the property classes be robbed by the no property herd?"[15] In short, the issue was white supremacy, both economic and social.

Enough Democrats had been able to register to vote in 1867 to encourage a belief that they could block the ratification of the constitution. Basing their plans on the provisions of the Reconstruction Act of March 23, 1867, they hoped to exploit the requirement that a majority of the registered voters must vote on the proposed constitution. They decided to organize a boycott of the ratification election, set for early February 1868, by neither running candidates nor participating in the election. They hoped to defeat the constitution by staying home from the polls themselves and by intimidating others from voting through the terror of the Ku Klux Klan.

The boycott was successful in that only 71,817 of the 170,631 registered voters turned out. Those in favor of the constitution were 70,812, those against 1,005.[16] However, success was only temporary as the Reconstruction Act of March 11, 1868 provided for the adoption of the constitution by a majority of those

14. Samuel Dixon to R. M. Patton, December 1, 1867, in Governor Robert M. Patton Papers, Alabama State Department of Archives and History; A. W. Dillard to Andrew Johnson, January 24, 1868, in Andrew Johnson Papers, Library of Congress. See also C. S. G. Doster to Joseph Hodgson, November 16, 1867, in Montgomery *Daily Mail*, November 21, 1867; Huntsville *Advocate*, January 7, 1868.

15. Montgomery *Daily Advertiser*, January 7, 1868.

16. Original Manuscript Election Returns, in Papers of the Secretary of State of Alabama, Alabama State Department of Archives and History.

voting. Although Alabama's election had occurred under the old law, Alabama was readmitted to the Union in June 1868 because a large majority of the votes cast in the election had favored the constitution.

Republican candidates had been unopposed for all offices under the new constitution when they ran in February, and in July 1868 they assumed control of the state government. Scalawag William Hugh Smith of Randolph County, a lawyer and Douglas Democrat who left Alabama in 1862, became the new governor.

During Smith's two-year administration, 1868–1870, Republican policies unwittingly contributed to the party's political collapse in 1874. Racial attitudes lay behind two of the most important Republican failures in this period. When the Ku Klux Klan harassed Republicans, appeals to the governor brought only verbal support because he feared activation of a militia would alienate native whites; a militia raised in Alabama would be predominately black because there was no large white Republican stronghold as existed in nearby east Tennessee.[17] The governor's assurances were little comfort to those living under the Klan's reign of terror, although the alternative held the potential for a race war. The second failure was a legislative one, as white Republicans did little in the general assembly in behalf of their black members. When black legislators pushed for a common carrier bill, white Republicans used delaying tactics to kill a proposal that would have assured blacks equality in transportation and public accommodations.[18]

The most ambitious project of Governor Smith's administration was an economic one which, despite enthusiastic bipartisan support in 1868, also unwittingly contributed to the ultimate

17. Montgomery *Daily Alabama State Journal*, October 2, 1868; Montgomery *Daily Advertiser*, September 22, 1868; Allen W. Trelease, *White Terror: The Ku Klux Klan Conspiracy and Southern Reconstruction* (New York, 1971), 81–88, 123–24. See also Governor William H. Smith Papers, October 1868 through August 1869 and Letterbooks, 11, 12, 13, in Alabama State Department of Archives and History.

18. Montgomery *Daily Advertiser*, July 14, 17, 18, 24, 27, 30, 31, August 4, 5, 6, 13, 15, 1868.

defeat of the Republican party. The legislature broadly expanded the 1867 law whereby the state endorsed railroad bonds to stimulate the construction of internal improvements. Consolidation of existing lines and plans for completion of missing links in a north-south rail network quickly appeared. The Republicans' Alabama and Chattanooga Railroad and the Democrats' South and North both benefited from the lesiglature's financial generosity, which was hastened by well-placed bipartisan bribes. As governor, Smith did not carefully follow the letter of the law in his broad endorsement of railroad bonds, but during 1868 and 1869 the Democratic-Conservative party did not mount any hue and cry about what was going on as they later would.[19]

The policy of Congress on the amnesty question early in congressional Reconstruction also had serious consequences for Alabama Republicanism. Alabamians caught by the officeholding disabilities of the Fourteenth Amendment had their franchise restored by the 1868 Alabama lesiglature, but some faced continued exclusion from office because they believed they had not been disloyal and refused to apply to Congress for a removal of disabilities. It was therefore suggested that men who had opposed secession, cooperated with the Confederacy only so far as safety demanded, and now accepted Reconstruction be exempt from the disabilities of the Fourteenth Amendment. With such a policy, said Wager Swayne, commissioner of the Freedmen's Bureau, it would be possible to convert "many of our friends from passive well-wishers into serviceable candidates and efficient helpers."[20] Unfortunately, Congress did not act on the matter in 1868, and many sympathetic Douglas and

19. *Senate Reports* 42nd Cong., 2nd Sess., No. 22, Vol. VIII, 232, Vol. X, 1411, 1417–18; *Alabama* vs. *Burr* (1885), 115, *U.S. Reports*, 416–21; Bond, "Social and Economic Forces," 321–26; "Reports of Col. James L. Tait, Receiver of Lands, of the Alabama and Chattanooga R.R. to the Governor," *Alabama Public Documents*, 1873, No. 16, p. 507.

20. David P. Lewis to J. J. Giers, November 26, 1870, and David P. Lewis to Benjamin F. Butler, June 23, 1870, in Records of the Select Committee on Reconstruction; Wager Swayne to Salmon P. Chase, June 28, 1867, in Chase Papers.

Bell men of 1860 in Alabama abstained from politics because they were barred from officeholding until the passage of the General Amnesty Act of 1872. The Alabama Republican party could ill afford such losses.

While Republican policies both in Washington and Alabama undermined the future of the party in the state, the behavior of the party's personnel created further trouble. A quarrel opened in 1869 between Governor Smith and one of Alabama's two carpetbagger U.S. senators, George E. Spencer. Smith and Spencer agreed on nothing, and each accused the other of thoughtlessly endangering the future of the Republican party in Alabama. Other Republicans soon took sides in the quarrel, which lasted throughout the Reconstruction years, and carpetbaggers and scalawags were included in both groups.[21] The Spencer-Smith feud saw Republicans so busy attacking one another that little energy was left for the opposition.

Republican dissension was aggravated by the bitter resentment of opponents of secession and the Confederacy toward the appointment of newcomers or blacks to office. Having survived wartime persecution, they were stung at being ignored and unrewarded for earlier loyalty. One outraged scalawag complained to Governor Smith that the carpetbaggers had "already landed everything that is Republican in Hell."[22]

While Republicans wrangled among themselves, Alabama Democrats debated how they might take advantage of the political disorder among Republicans and win the 1870 election. After the relaxation of suffrage requirements in 1868, Democrats registered to vote in increasing numbers, and they were

21. Wiggins, *The Scalawag in Alabama Politics*, 57–61. For accounts of Spencer's notorious political and financial activities see Sarah Van V. Woolfolk, "George E. Spencer: A Carpetbagger in Alabama," *Alabama Review*, XIX (January 1966), 41–52, and "Carpetbaggers in Alabama: Tradition Versus Truth," *Alabama Review*, XV (April 1962), 133–44.

22. David P. Lewis to W. H. Smith, August 12, 1868, A. W. Dillard to John Hardy, August 24, 1868, William Bibb Figures to W. H. Smith, August 24, 1868, D. C. Humphries to W. H. Smith, September 5, 1868, all in Governor Smith Papers.

now optimistic about their election prospects. In 1870 they again faced the fundamental problem of Reconstruction politics in Alabama—how to cope with black suffrage. Many Democrats believed further criticism of black suffrage was futile flaying of a dead issue and that it would be wiser to convince blacks that their best interests lay with those whites whose lands they farmed.[23] Other Democrats disagreed, believing that "mixing up with negro suffrage" would "drive away ten votes to every negro vote" gained.[24] Ultimately, those Democrats who favored efforts to attract the black vote prevailed in the 1870 campaign. For governor they nominated Robert Burns Lindsay of Tuscumbia, a native of Scotland who was an Alabama legislator and Douglas Democrat before the war. Under his leadership, Democrats sought the black vote to supplement their white support, and they carried Alabama in 1870 in a disputed election. The Democratic margin statewide was less than 2,000 votes out of a total of 157,430 votes cast. Dramatic Democratic gains in four black counties, Greene, Sumter, Macon, and Russell, which were normally Republican were the key to the Democrats' narrow victory. If Republicans had carried these four counties by the vote they had received there in 1868, Republicans would have won the election. It was no accident that these counties were the scene of most of the Klan's terror in 1869 and 1870. Clearly, where peaceful encouragement to vote Democratic failed, the heavy hand of the Klan was called upon, but the effect was the same: black counties that were normally Republican suddenly voted Democratic.[25]

23. Albert Elmore to John W. A. Sanford, June 8, 1870, in John W. A. Sanford Papers, Alabama State Department of Archives and History; Montgomery *Daily Advertiser,* January 25, 29, February 2, 5, 22, 24, 27, March 4, 31, April 3, 9, 1870; Montgomery *Daily Mail,* June 11, 1870.

24. Montgomery *Daily Mail*, February 17, May 7, 21, 1870; Tuscaloosa *Independent Monitor*, March 8, 15, April 5, 1870.

25. Original Returns, 1868, 1870; *Senate Reports*, 42nd Cong., 2nd Sess., No. 22, Vol. VIII, 183–84, X, 1822. Klan activities prior to the 1870 election are detailed in Trelease, *White Terror*, 246–73. A "black" county is one where blacks represent over 50 percent of the country's population. A "white" county is one where blacks represent less than 25 percent of the county's population.

Once in control of the state for the first time since congressional Reconstruction began, Democrats set the stage for their own defeat in 1872. They assumed that there would be no difficulty in retaining power, and they dropped the debate over black suffrage. They also had financial troubles, as they found that they were no more able to resolve the state's problems than the Republicans before them. When the day of financial reckoning came with the default of the Alabama and Chattanooga Railroad on the interest due on its bonds, Democratic mismanagement was severly attacked even by its own party. Ultimately, the Democrats saw the Louisville & Nashville Railroad absorb and stabilize their South and North Railroad, while the state seized its Republican competitor the Alabama and Chattanooga. Subsequent legislative investigation criticized both Republican Governor Smith and Democratic Governor Lindsay for lack of sound financial leadership and for inadequate record keeping.[26]

By 1872 the Democrats considered the record of their incumbent governor such a political liability that they chose another candidate for governor. They also blindly nominated a ticket entirely of ex-secessionists, provoking some of the party to wonder if this ticket would alienate black voters.[27]

Meanwhile, the Republicans, sobered by their defeat in 1870, moved with extraordinary unity to prepare for the 1872 election. Although the Liberal Republican movement was organized in Alabama, it did not materialize as a serious threat to the regular Republicans. Republican factionalism died down, and the party nominated men who would appeal to the Conservatives of 1860, many of whom had been recently relieved by the Amnesty Act of 1872.[28] One such man was nominated for gover-

26. *Alabama House Journal*, 1871–72, pp. 303–19, 354.
27. Charles S. Scott to Robert McKee, June 10, 1872, and J. G. Harris to Robert McKee, July 9, 1872, in Robert McKee Papers, Alabama State Department of Archives and History.
28. John G. Stokes to W. E. Chandler, October 12, 1872, in William E. Chandler Papers, Library of Congress.

nor, David P. Lewis of Huntsville, a lawyer who opposed secession, left the state in 1864, and became a postwar Democrat. In November 1872 the Republicans easily swept the state, winning back the black counties which had gone Democratic two years earlier. The so-called Democratic redemption of 1870 had been short-lived. Truthfully, the record of the Democrats, as much as Republican unity and the black vote, gave the Republicans the 1872 election.

Once back in office, Republicans returned to their old ways as if they had learned nothing from their defeat in 1870 or from their victory in 1872. Bickering over patronage resumed as Republicans competed for federal and state offices and for the federal printing contract.[29] In the legislature in 1873, when black legislators pushed for passage of civil rights bills, white Republicans once again hedged, for fear of alienating their white constituents. Democratic legislators, favoring civil rights bills no more than white Republicans, proposed to cut off amendments and to force a vote on the issue in "its most odious form." Such a move would compel leading Republican legislators to take the bill "pure et simple which will kill [them] in the Northern counties or vote against it which will throttle them in the nigger counties." The civil rights bill eventually passed the Democratic state senate and failed in the Republican house.[30]

A few months later, before the uproar over the civil rights bills in the Alabama legislature could fade, the same issue appeared in Congress. During the six-month debate in Congress, Alabama black Republicans urged Republican support for the measure much to the embarrassment of their white colleagues.[31] Alabama Democrats, sobered by their defeat in 1872, reevaluated the basis for their earlier victories and now realized that they had an issue for their 1874 assault on the Republicans. An

29. For a full discussion see Wiggins, *The Scalawag in Alabama Politics*, 88–90.
30. Montgomery *Daily Advertiser*, February 25, 26, March 1, 27, 1873; R. K. Boyd to Robert McKee, February 18, 1873, and B. B. Lewis to Robert McKee, May 14, 1874, in McKee Papers; Selma *Southern Argus*, February 14, 1873.
31. Selma *Southern Argus*, July 17, 1874; Talladega *Our Mountain Home*, July 29, 1874.

appeal to racial prejudices might alienate more whites from the Republican party. Democrats interpreted the proposed federal civil rights bill of that year as an effort to legislate social equality and the upcoming 1874 election as involving the question of white or black supremacy in governing Alabama. It was time that all understood that Alabama was a "white man's state" and that white men were determined to rule it. Since blacks had voted overwhelmingly Republican since their enfranchisement, white Democrats announced that their race must also unite politically.[32] In line with their efforts to attract the north Alabama white vote, the Democrats nominated for governor George S. Houston, a former United States senator and Douglas Democrat who sat out the war at home in the Tennessee Valley. Republicans responded with a slate of white moderates to check Democratic wooing of the white vote.

The campaign methods of both political parties in 1874 verify Bond's comment that neither party had a corner on vice or virtue. Determined to win the election, Democrats resorted to intimidation, ostracism, violence, and murder. They hoped to drive off white Republicans and discredit those who remained. Democratic meetings organized economic and social pressures against white Republicans, denouncing them as enemies of their race deserving "warfare" on their business activities and exclusion from all "social relations with white men or their families."[33]

Economic pressures against potential black Republican voters were widespread. Employers in several sections of the state fired black laborers who refused to vote Democratic, and such groups as "white men's clubs" in Mobile published resolutions that as individuals they would not employ Republicans. Democrats compiled economic "Black Lists" of those who intended to vote Republican and organized "pledge meetings" where

32. R. K. Boyd to Robert McKee, June 1, 1874, and B. B. Lewis to Robert McKee, May 14, 1874, in McKee Papers; Selma *Southern Argus,* July 10, 1874.
33. Montgomery *Daily Alabama State Journal,* July 1, 1874; Talladega *Our Mountain Home,* June 28, July 1, 1874. See also Sarah Woolfolk Wiggins, "Ostracism of White Republicans in Alabama During Reconstruction," *Alabama Review,* XXVII (January 1974), 52–64.

blacks had to pledge to vote Democratic or risk losing their jobs.[34]

Violence supplemented economic pressures. In Sumter County "secret plans" were reported at work which could create a five-hundred-vote Democratic majority. Later that summer the assassinations of two prominent Republicans, a black and a carpetbagger, had a chilling effect on local Republicans. To sustain this fear among the blacks, squads of thirty to forty white men armed with shotguns rode the rounds of the county almost nightly. Elsewhere, armed Democrats disrupted Republican rallies and burned buildings where meetings had been held. They threw rotten eggs at an associate justice of the Alabama Supreme Court as he spoke at the Butler County Courthouse, chased a Republican congressman out of Tuskegee, and attempted to disrupt the meeting of the Barbour County Republican Convention. Intimidation by the "white league" in Conecuh County successfully convinced Republicans not to meet in the county.[35]

While Democrats tried to terrorize their opposition, Republicans busied themselves trying to buy support. In August 1874 rations for flood relief were allotted for counties in central and west Alabama. Republican Governor D. P. Lewis chose members of his party as local agents to distribute the provisions and added counties in areas that had not been flooded earlier that year. Confusion resulted, and some blacks believed that all were eligible for rations whether or not they had suffered flood damage. Reputedly, some Republicans told blacks that they must vote the straight Republican ticket or lose their rights under the law.[36]

Despite the Republican vulnerability to charges of inepti-

34. *House Reports*, 43rd Cong., 2nd Sess., No. 262, vi, xi, xiii, xvi.

35. *Ibid.*, i–xlviii; J. G. Harris to Robert McKee, May 13, 1874, in McKee Papers; William Mills to Assistant Adjutant General Department of the South, September 22, 1874, and William P. Miller to "Sir," September 28, 1874, in File 3579 AGO 1874, Records of the Adjutant General's Office, Record Group 94, National Archives.

36. *House Reports*, 43rd Cong., 2nd Sess., No. 262, pp. 1285, 1288, 1290–92, 1294, 1296; Selma *Southern Argus*, June 25, 1875.

tude in office, race was the issue in the 1874 campaign and provoked the largest voter turnout in Alabama during Reconstruction, as well as some of the worst election-day violence. In Mobile, a group of armed and mounted Democrats rode through downtown streets near the polling places about two o'clock in the afternoon. At the same time some two or three hundred black Repulican voters left the seventh ward to vote in the fourth ward, a practice which was legal under state election laws. Democratic couriers spread the news of this move, and whites gathered to meet them. As the blacks came to Government Street, a volley of pistol shots greeted them. They retreated, leaving one dead in the street and carrying off four wounded. From that time until the polls closed, not a black man was seen near the polls in Mobile.[37]

At Eufaula in Barbour County armed white Democrats assembled in the streets near the polls and awaited unarmed black voters who came in from the country to vote. About noon most of the blacks had arrived but had not yet voted. A fight began, a black man was stabbed, and firing started in the crowd and from a row of adjacent buildings. The whites secured more guns from an armory nearby, and, as in Mobile, many blacks fled without voting. Six whites were wounded, one fatally, while two blacks were killed and thirty-five to forty were wounded.[38] The Democrats carried both Mobile and Barbour counties.

There were also nonviolent but irregular efforts to discourage Republican voters. Some polls controlled by Democrats in strong Republican precincts in Russell County did not open at all. Approximately three hundred voters left the closed polls at Hurtville and went to Seale to vote only to discover they had arrived too late in the day. In other towns polls opened briefly but closed before all who were waiting had voted.[39]

37. *House Reports*, 43rd Cong., 2nd Sess., No. 262, p. 451; Montgomery *Daily Alabama State Journal*, November 8, 1874.
38. *House Reports*, 43rd Cong., 2nd Sess., No. 262, xxiii; Montgomery *Daily Alabama State Journal*, November 6, 1874.
39. Montgomery *Daily Alabama State Journal*, November 5, 1874; F. B. Taylor to Assistant Adjutant General, November 4, 1874, Records of the Adjutant General's Office, Record Group 94, National Archives.

Elsewhere, Republicans voted only to have their ballots destroyed. At Spring Hill in Barbour County Democrats stormed the polling place, smashed the lamps, and fired at a Republican judge who was counting the votes. He and his sixteen-year-old son ducked behind a store counter for safety. In the darkness the boy was fatally wounded, and the ballot box with an estimated 450 or 500 Republican majority disappeared. In Opelika in Lee County, Democrats voted at box one, Republicans at box two. When the Democratic board of supervisors counted the votes, they threw out box two, which one Republican manager claimed contained 1,252 Republican votes. Election supervisors in Bullock County threw out 732 ballots, predominately Republican, because the poll lists were uncertified.[40] The Democrats carried Lee as well as Barbour County, but they lost Bullock to the Republicans.

Such election-day fraud and violence represented a final outburst of racial fears and emotions which had built steadily throughout the campaign. The election itself provided a catharsis for nerves worn raw, and aroused Democrats poured to the polls. Their gubernatorial candidate, George S. Houston, polled 107,118 votes compared to the 78,521 Democratic votes of 1872. In contrast, David P. Lewis, the Republican candidate, obtained 93,934 votes in 1874 compared to 89,020 in 1872. Democratic gains were dramatic across the state. In the white counties their support almost doubled from 18,402 in 1872 to 32,341 in 1874, while in the black counties they moved from 33,905 to 38,429. Republican growth was minimal by comparison. In the white counties they polled 9,546 votes in 1872 and only 9,895 in 1874. In the black counties Republicans did somewhat better, increasing from 59,409 to 61,593.[41]

Although throughout Reconstruction Republicans repeatedly requested the stationing of federal troops at the polls, soldiers in Alabama did not intimidate voters for the benefit of the Republican party. In fact, in several areas federal troops main-

40. Montgomery *Daily Alabama State Journal*, November 8, 22, 1874; *House Reports*, 43rd Cong., 2nd Sess., No. 262, xix, xxviii–xxix.
41. Original Returns, 1874.

tained such a hands-off attitude during the election that Democrats carried some normally Republican counties by fraud, intimidation, and violence. The order governing the role of troops in Alabama at this time was General Order No. 75 issued by the Headquarters of the Department of the South in Louisville, Kentucky, stating that troops were to aid civil officers to enforce writs of the federal courts and that while enforcing one law, troops were not to be allowed to violate others. Simultaneously, the U.S. attorney general instructed his marshals and attorneys that troops in Alabama were not to interfere with "any political or party action not in violation of the law."[42]

On election day, November 3, 1874, officers commanding troops in Alabama executed these instructions in different fashions. A literal interpretation was followed in Russell, Mobile, and Barbour counties. The officer in charge in Russell County refused a request from a deputy U.S. marshal for soldiers to supervise a crowd at the ballot boxes at the courthouse with the reply that troops were not there to take part in the election nor to regulate the manner in which it was conducted. When a riot was rumored, he repeated that he could not move except "for and in the execution of the 'Writs of the U.S. Courts.'"[43]

On election day in Mobile and Barbour counties, troops on alert awaited the appropriate summons from a U.S. marshal. The commanding officer in Mobile dismissed the local uproar as no more than a "drunken brawl" which the local police could handle. Although he was ready to comply with legitimate calls for assistance, he saw no reason to act in this instance "in the light of General Orders on this subject." Too late did he learn how serious the disturbance in downtown Mobile had been.[44]

42. Enclosure in E. D. Townsend to Irwin McDowell, September 23, 1874, Records of the Adjutant General's Office, Record Group 94, National Archives; George H. Williams to R. W. Healy, September 3, 1874, in Source Chronological Files, Alabama, Records of the Department of Justice, Record Group 60, National Archives.

43. F. B. Taylor to Assistant Adjutant General, November 4, 1874, in Records of the Adjutant General's Office, Record Group 94, National Archives.

44. Loomis L. Langdon to Assistant Adjutant General Department of the South, November 3, 5, 1874, in *ibid.*

In Barbour County the federal commander at Eufaula nervously telegraphed the day before the election for reassurance from headquarters in Louisville: "Owing to the delicate situation here, I have instructed detachment commanders that in case of urgent necessity they may assist Sheriffs as a *posse comitatus*. Am I right?" The assistant adjutant general shot back an immediate answer. "No! You are not right. General Orders No. 75 fully set forth your duty. You are stationed at Eufaula to aid the U.S. Civil officials to execute processes of the U.S. Courts." After this telegram arrived on the afternoon of the election day, the officer in Eufaula wired a detachment lieutenant at nearby Spring Hill to keep his troops away from the crowd and "to have nothing whatever to do with the Sheriff and State Officers." The message reached the lieutenant in an unsealed envelope. The lieutenant feared at this time that others had seen the wire before it reached him and that knowledge of its contents would encourage the Democrats.[45] That evening his worst fears materialized in the attack on the polls at Spring Hill.

The deputy U.S. marshal later testified that in Eufaula itself sporadic shooting drove four or five hundred voters from the polls, but when he reported this intimidation to the federal commander, the latter retorted that "if the whole town was burned up, and everybody killed," he could do nothing under his orders. Barbour County Republicans could justifiably complain that the execution of army orders resulted in a "license to the armed mob present to murder at will."[46]

While General Order No. 75 was read literally in Russell, Mobile, and Barbour counties, it was interpreted loosely in Opelika. The deputy U.S. marshal and the Lee County sheriff requested that troops aid them in keeping order during the

45. A. S. Daggett to Assistant Adjutant General Department of the South, November 2, 1874, Chauncey McKeever to A. S. Daggett, November 3, 1874, A. S. Daggett to W. J. Turner, November 3, 1874, E. Schriver to the Adjutant General of the Army, December 22, 1874, all in *ibid.*

46. E. Schriver to the Adjutant General, December 22, 1874, E. M. Keils to W. W. Belknap, December 1, 1874, in *ibid.*

election in the county courthouse. Troops were sent to guard the polls all day, and they also organized voters into lines to facilitate balloting. The federal officer feared a "bloody riot" would have occurred had he and his men not interfered. The department commander condemned the troops' action in Opelika and rebuked the captain responsible: "You should have had nothing to do with the State officers nor should you have quartered your troops in the County court-house."[47]

A congressional committee later investigating this election heard extensive testimony on the activities of the troops in Alabama, and although the committee as a whole rarely agreed, the majority and the minority discovered little direct military interference in the election. They concluded that the troops kept away from the polls except in Opelika. Troops stationed in Alabama at this time numbered only 679, and they were scattered at thirty posts in twenty-two counties on election day.[48] Republicans carried only nine of these twenty-two counties. In general, it was Alabama Republicans, not Democrats, who complained about the role of the federal troops in the 1874 election.

The election over, Democrats did not relax their attacks on Republicans. They applied economic pressures to the black population and in some areas made good their earlier threats to discharge those who voted Republican. Angry blacks, resentful of the meager gestures in their behalf by white Republicans, met in Montgomery after the election and recapitulated the grievances of Alabama blacks, grievances which had grown particularly serious in the last two years as a "cry of down with the negro, commonly known as the 'race-issue,'" had spread across the state. They also created "The Emigration Society" to plan a black colony in the far West and chose commissioners to seek northern financial support.[49]

The few Republicans remaining in office despite the Demo-

47. E. R. Kellogg to Assistant Adjutant General Department of the South, November 4, 1874, Chauncey McKeever to E. R. Kellogg, November 16, 1874, in *ibid.*

48. *House Reports*, 43rd Cong., 2nd Sess., No. 262, xxxiv, xxxviii, 1284.

49. *Ibid.*, xxxix–xl, 1113–18.

cratic landslide soon found that even they were not safe. Democrats made it as difficult as possible for Republicans to make bond for their offices, expecting them to resign and leave the positions to the Democrats. One scalawag who was elected treasurer of Montgomery County owned $38,000 in real estate and therefore expected no trouble about his bond. Once elected, however, he found that men who had promised to be his bondsmen reneged, saying the Democrats had threatened them with economic and social ruin if they kept their promise.[50]

In Talladega County a scalawag was elected probate judge and soon made his bond. Nevertheless, the Democratic governor declared the post vacant and appointed the defeated Democratic candidate to the position because, he claimed, the Republican's bond had been approved by a state supreme court justice whose term had expired prior to the act of certification. Yet, Governor Houston had been administered his oath of office by another supreme court justice whose new term had not yet begun. In Macon County, as in Talladega, the governor declared the probate judgeship vacant and appointed the defeated Democratic candidate to the position.[51]

Republicans in offices that required no bonds did not escape harassment. The most notable example of this was the effort in 1875 to oust George E. Spencer from his seat in the United States Senate. The Alabama legislature appointed a committee of four Democrats and one anti-Spencer Republican to investigate the mechanics of Spencer's reelection in 1872. The committee easily uncovered outlandish examples of the senator's unscrupulous wheelings and dealings to get himself reelected, and they recommended that the United States Senate also investigate the election. The Senate did investigate and after weeks of hearings ruled in favor of Spencer.[52]

50. *Ibid.*, xli; Tuskegee *Weekly News*, April 1, 1875; Montgomery *Daily Alabama State Journal*, January 26, March 9, 1875.

51. Talladega *Our Mountain Home*, January 20, 1875; Montgomery *Daily Alabama State Journal*, February 27, 1875.

52. *Ibid.*, March 21, 30, April 6, 11, 12, 23, 1876; *Report of the Joint Committee of the General Assembly of Alabama in Regard to Alleged Election of*

Less important Republican officeholders were not overlooked. Democrats in the Alabama House of Representatives successfully challenged the election of Republicans from Russell and Barbour counties and replaced them with Democrats. The legislature abolished the Dallas County Criminal Court because the judge was a Republican who refused to resign. Other vindictive efforts were less successful. Defeated were proposals to abolish various county offices held by Republicans, to repeal fees and commissions of tax assessors and collectors for certain Republican counties, and to eliminate a Republican judge from office by cutting his home county out of the district and requiring judges to live in the district in which they presided.[53]

Appointed Republicans also felt the Democratic pressures. A Republican clerk of the Alabama Supreme Court, appointed in 1868 and reappointed in 1873, found himself under pressure to resign in January 1875. Sensing the direction of the political wind in Alabama at the time of his reappointment in 1873, he had consulted with the one Democrat then on the court who assured him of personal support. But in 1875 the now Democratic court found the clerk "not agreeable," and in the face of mounting pressures he resigned, although his term ran until 1878.[54]

While these efforts were underway to oust Republicans in office, Democrats also acted to minimize Republican strength in future congressional elections. Because the state's eight congressmen had been elected from six districts plus two elected from the state-at-large, Republicans had carried two seats from the black belt in 1874 despite the general Democratic landslide. Now the Democratic legislature gerrymandered five

George E. Spencer as United States Senator, together with Memorial and Evidence (Montgomery, 1875). For a full discussion of the details of Spencer's reelection efforts see Woolfolk, "George E. Spencer: A Carpetbagger in Alabama," 41–53.

53. Montgomery *Daily Alabama State Journal*, November 29, December 5, 1874, January 31, March 9, 12, 1875; Mobile *Daily Register*, February 4, 1875.

54. Montgomery *Daily Alabama State Journal*, April 15, 1875.

heavily populated Republican counties into the fourth district so that it was composed entirely of the black counties of Dallas, Hale, Lowndes, Wilcox, and Perry. The remaining black counties of central Alabama were distributed into districts where white voters predominated.[55]

Despite these steady assaults on Republicans, the Democrats were aware that they must restrain the zealots in their ranks lest Congress intervene and overthrow the Democratic government in the state. This concern was more than an idle worry. At the urging of a Republican congressman from Alabama, a congressional investigation committee studied the 1874 Alabama election and produced damaging evidence about the conduct of both parties but especially regarding the tactics of the Democrats. When Congress adjourned in March 1875 without acting on the Alabama question, Democrats rested more easily.[56]

Simultaneously with the congressional investigation of the 1874 election, state Republicans fought back on another front. An Alabama representative in Congress introduced a bill to enforce guarantees contained in earlier civil rights acts. This proposal included an authorization for the president at his discretion to declare four specified states in rebellion, to impose martial law, and to suspend the writ of habeas corpus. Alabama was one of the four states which could be affected. The bill failed to pass, but Alabama Democrats understood that the bill had the potential to provide the machinery to overturn the Democratic state government.[57]

By summer of 1875 Democrats felt less insecure in office and began plans for a constitutional convention to implement some reforms that had been widely discussed for the last six months, including a compromise of the state debt, elimination of unnecessary state and county offices, legislative reapportionment, and

55. *Acts of the General Assembly of Alabama*, 1874–75, pp. 115–16.
56. *House Report*, 43rd Cong., 2nd Sess., i–lxxii.
57. Linden *Marengo News-Journal*, March 25, 1875; Montgomery *Daily Alabama State Journal*, February 18, 1875; *Congressional Record*, 43rd Cong., 2nd Sess., Part 3, Appendix, 15–24.

general economy in the operation of the state government. In August, Alabamians voted to call a convention to convene the next month. The convention, which included twelve Republicans, eighty Democrats, and seven Independents, drafted a constitution which was not radically different from that drawn by the Republicans in 1868. Most of the new features of the 1875 constitution reflected a concern for economic retrenchment and political entrenchment of those in office. The convention left the solution of the state debt to the legislature and the governor but reduced the state bureaucracy. Jobs were combined or eliminated and salaries lowered to reduce costs; and to entrench its party in power, the predominately Democratic convention reapportioned the legislature at the expense of the Republican counties of the black belt and required individuals to vote in the beat in which they resided.[58] This latter measure would prove a great blow to Republican hopes for a revival of their political fortunes in Alabama.

Republicans were divided on whether or not to favor ratification of the new constitution. Some prominent Republicans endorsed the document because it guaranteed all citizens equality before the law, prohibited the use of the state's credit for private enterprises, limited the rate of taxation, and provided economy measures in state government.[59] This Republican division about the constitution added to the ease with which it was approved. Only four counties voted against it; all were Republican counties in the black belt.

The 1876 election, a year after the constitution had been revised, represented a last chance for Alabama Republicans in the nineteenth century. The Spencer-Smith feud which had so damaged the party in the 1870 election worsened after the Republican defeat in 1874. Natives, newcomers, and blacks were included in both factions, and unfortunately, the party was now more seriously divided than at any period during Reconstruc-

58. *Journal of the Constitutional Convention of the State of Alabama, 1875*, pp. 198–201.
59. Montgomery *Daily Advertiser*, October 23, 24, 1875.

tion. In November 1875 the Smith faction had begun an effort to reform the party and reduce the influence of Senator Spencer. Over the next seven months factionalism worsened until in May 1876 two Republican state tickets were nominated, one reflecting the Spencer wing of the party and the other representing the Smith wing. The competition between the two tickets was not resolved until just prior to the August election, when both Republican tickets were withdrawn and an Independent ticket of political unknowns substituted.[60]

Little time remained for a successful campaign, and neither faction really made much effort. To no one's surprise the Independent ticket was soundly beaten. The Democratic gubernatorial candidate received 95,837 votes compared to the Independent candidate's 55,586. The total vote in 1876 noticeably declined from a high of 201,052 in 1874 to 151,423 in 1876, despite the fact that it was a presidential election year. As in earlier elections, Republicans accused the Democrats of carrying the state by fraud, and Senator Spencer called in vain for a congressional investigation.[61]

Republicans could justifiably complain of fraud. In the black counties Republicans won 61,593 votes in 1874 but only 34,295 in 1876. Meanwhile, the Democratic vote in the black counties in these two elections remained rather stable: 38,429 in 1874 and 36,544 in 1876. At least part of the reason for the sharp drop in Republican votes in 1876, while the Democrats showed only a small loss, lay in Democratic use of the seemingly innocent provision of the 1875 constitution which required individuals to vote in the beat in which they resided. Democrats controlled the state government, and they were able to appoint their strongest partisans as election managers. On election day some polls opened and closed at the whim of election officials while other polls moved several times during the day. Some election officials refused to open the polls at all, and others announced that they were not going to remain at the polls all day to permit

60. Wiggins, *The Scalawag in Alabama Politics*, 108–14.
61. Original Returns, 1876.

blacks to make "radical majorities." The failure to open polls in Republican strongholds in Hale, Perry, Marengo, Bullock, Barbour, Greene, Pickens, Wilcox, and Sumter counties undermined Republican strength as effectively as the earlier terror of the Ku Klux Klan, and it involved no bloodshed.[62] The Democrats successfully minimized the black Republican vote, and the election of 1876 ratified the Republican defeat of 1874.

Democrats learned from their political successes and failures during Reconstruction in Alabama. The first success in 1870 reflected a delicately contrived campaign to solicit the votes of both blacks and whites to create a biracial party. The landslide redemption of 1874 was based upon a white supremacy campaign to win whites and the use of economic pressures and outright violence both to intimidate and to win black votes. In the late 1870s Democrats well remembered the short-lived first redemption of 1870, and once they hit upon an overwhelmingly successful formula by which to control the state, they applied it consistently in Alabama for the next quarter century.

One Republican explained his party's failure as the result of "Democratic 'Bulldozing' supplemented by Republican folly and knavery." He blamed the personnel, not the principles, of the party for its failure.[63] He would have been more correct to blame both personnel *and* principles. For it was not only ineptitude in office and party factionalism that killed the Republicans; it was Republican inability to master their racial prejudices, work out an economic program acceptable to the interests of the party's diverse membership, and go beyond half-a-loaf gestures to blacks. Alabama Democrats and Republicans were much alike in their economic and racial attitudes during Reconstruction, and Alabama Republicans particularly exemplified what W. R. Brock has observed about Republicans in general. They were "children of their age" who were "bound by its assumptions

62. Montgomery *Daily Alabama State Journal*, August 9, 11, 1876.
63. Willard Warner to John Sherman, June 10, 1876, in John Sherman Papers, Library of Congress.

and inhibitions." [64] It was this bondage that allowed Democrats to seize the initiative that was the basis for the Democratic overthrow of the Republican party and of Reconstruction in Alabama.

64. William R. Brock, *An American Crisis: Congress and Reconstruction, 1865–1867* (London, 1963), 302.

Bibliographical Essay

FOR OVER A HALF CENTURY THE BASIC STUDY OF RECONstruction in Alabama has been Walter Lynwood Fleming, *Civil War and Reconstruction in Alabama* (New York: Columbia University Press, 1905). Unfortunately, its pro-Democratic bias hampers an objective analysis of the Republican and Democratic parties in Alabama and the causes for the failure of the Reconstruction experiment. The same bias mars John W. DuBose, *Alabama's Tragic Decade, Ten Years of Alabama, 1865–1874*, James K. Greer, ed. (Birmingham: Webb Book Company, 1940). The most valuable early study of the period is Ethel Armes, *The Story of Coal and Iron in Alabama* (Birmingham: Chamber of Commerce, 1910), which impartially details the financial and railroad activities of Democrats and Republicans in the Reconstruction era.

Revisionist work on Alabama began with Horace Mann Bond, "Social and Economic Forces in Alabama Reconstruction," *Journal of Negro History*, XXIII (July 1938), 290–348. Bond raises as many questions as he answers about the period, and the essay unfortunately includes numerous minor errors. Nevertheless, the article is a vital improvement over the simplistic views of Fleming and DuBose about Reconstruction.

Recent revisionist scholarship seems to be concentrating on blacks and Republicans. Peter Kolchin, *First Freedom: The Responses of Alabama's Blacks to Emancipation and Reconstruction* (Westport, Conn.: Greenwood Press, 1972), studies the postwar adjustment of blacks to mid-1868. Loren Schweninger, *James T. Rapier and Reconstruction* (Chicago: University of

Chicago Press, 1978) is a study of one of Alabama's three black congressmen. Sarah Woolfolk Wiggins, *The Scalawag in Alabama Politics, 1865–1881* (University, Ala.: University of Alabama Press, 1977), focuses on the origins of and the role of the scalawag in the leadership of the Republican party. The best bibliography of recent work is Robert Reid, "Changing Interpretations of the Reconstruction Period in Alabama History," *Alabama Review*, XXVII (October 1974), 263–81.

Other valuable studies are several volumes that focus on subjects other than Alabama Reconstruction but incidentally include some aspect of the Reconstruction problem in Alabama. Horace Mann Bond, *Negro Education in Alabama: A Study in Cotton and Steel* (Washington, D.C.: Associated Publishers, 1939), sheds valuable light on economic matters and on black Republicans. Allen Johnston Going, *Bourbon Democracy in Alabama, 1874–1890* (University, Ala.: University of Alabama Press, 1951), briefly summarizes the Reconstruction years before concentrating on post-Reconstruction Democrats. Malcolm C. McMillan, *Constitutional Development in Alabama, 1798–1901: A Study in Politics, the Negro, and Sectionalism* (Chapel Hill: University of North Carolina Press, 1955), is essential for an understanding of the backgrounds as well as the contents of the Alabama constitutions of 1868 and 1875. Although Allen W. Trelease, *White Terror: The Ku Klux Klan Conspiracy and Southern Reconstruction* (New York: Harper & Row, 1971), is a general study of the klan in the South, it is extremely valuable for information about Alabama. The volume provides a detailed analysis of the activities of the klan in Alabama and also is the first effort to evaluate the role of federal troops in Alabama elections, in this case the 1870 state election.

Both federal and state government publications are important: the *Congressional Globe*, the *Congressional Record*, the Alabama legislative *Journals* and *Acts*, and the *Journals* of the 1868 and 1875 constitutional conventions. Essential for accurate appreciation of the 1874 election in Alabama is the report of the congressional committee that investigated the election,

Affairs in Alabama, February 23, 1875, *House Reports*, 43rd Cong., 2nd sess., no. 262 (Washington, D.C., 1875). The testimony before the committee details information on every aspect of the campaign and the election, and significant reports and correspondence are included that shed much light on the role of federal troops in Alabama. *The Report of the Joint Committee of the General Assembly of Alabama in Regard to the Alleged Election of George E. Spencer as United States Senator, together with Memorial and Evidence* (Montgomery: W. W. Screws, 1875), not only provides insight into Democratic efforts to evict Republican officeholders remaining after 1874 but also bares a devastating picture of Republican factionalism throughout the Reconstruction years.

Alabama newspapers are extremely valuable, especially the Montgomery Republican papers, the *State Sentinel* and the *Alabama State Journal*. Important as a balance to the views of the Republican press are the Democratic Selma *Southern Argus*, Montgomery *Advertiser*, Mobile *Register*, and Tuscaloosa *Independent Monitor*.

Of all the sources available for studying why Reconstruction failed in Alabama, the most valuable material is found in manuscript collections. While Alabama Republicans left few extensive individual collections, they were incessant letter writers, and Alabama material turns up like needles in widely scattered haystacks. Outstanding is the information found in the papers of Rutherford B. Hayes in R. B. Hayes Library, Fremont, Ohio, and Andrew Johnson, William E. Chandler, and John Sherman, Library of Congress. Many Alabama Republicans were close personal friends of Hayes, Chandler, and Sherman and regularly sent them lengthy accounts of Alabama affairs.

Often overlooked is the enormous amount of Alabama material in collections in the National Archives. The party quarrels about distribution of offices are reflected in Applications for Collectors of Internal Revenue, Applications for Appraisers of Customs, and Applications for Collectors of Customs, in the Records of the Treasury Department, Record Group 56; Source

Chronological Files and Appointment Papers, in the Records of the Department of Justice, Record Group 60; Papers Pertaining to Presidential Nominations to Civil and Military Positions in the U.S. Government, in the Records of the U.S. Senate, Record Group 46. The role of U.S. troops in the 1874 Alabama election is traced in File 3579 AGO 1874 Records of the Adjutant General's Office, Record Group 94, National Archives.

Manuscript collections in the Alabama State Department of Archives and History, Montgomery, are also siginificant. The papers of the Reconstruction governors, Lewis E. Parsons, Robert M. Patton, William Hugh Smith, David P. Lewis, and George S. Houston, are valuable, especially those of Governor Smith. Also useful are the papers of Robert McKee, editor of the Democratic Selma *Southern Argus*. The papers of the secretary of the state of Alabama contain the Original Returns for Presidential, Congressional, and State Elections in Alabama. These election returns make possible analysis of centers of Republican strength and evaluation of the importance of the black vote.

III

Mississippi

Republican Factionalism and Mismanagement

WILLIAM C. HARRIS

LASTING FOR almost a decade (1867–1876), Republican Reconstruction provided Mississippi with a new political order that was radical only in its implications. To be sure, the congressional Reconstruction Acts of 1867 imposed military rule, enfranchised black male adults, and opened the door for a new ruling element in the state. But the Reconstruction laws stopped short of confiscating property, imposing advanced rights for blacks, or permanently disqualifying former Confederates from voting and holding office, all of which had been advocated by true Radicals in Congress. Indeed, congressional policy anticipated a quick restoration of Mississippi and other southern states to their full rights in the Union provided only that they accept the political changes produced by the war as expressed in the three postwar amendments to the Constitution. Military rule under the benevolent Generals Edward O. C. Ord and Alvan C. Gillem was not harsh and affected the citizenry in a generally unoffensive fashion. Civil officials, many of whom had served in the conservative government under presidential Reconstruction, continued to perform most of the regular functions of government during the three-year period of military supervision.

The so-called Black and Tan constitution, framed by carpet-baggers, scalawags, and blacks in 1868, was progressive, not radical. The provision that "Taxation shall be equal and uniform throughout the State" was a drastic change from antebellum practice, but with the destruction of slave property, it could hardly be considered radical or threatening to the old citizens. Assessments for tax purposes, as before, would be in the hands of local authorities. Many of the provisions in the constitution, such as the article providing for "a uniform system of free public schools," were built on an antebellum foundation. The main difference now was that blacks as well as whites would be the beneficiaries of the law. The old citizens feared that the new political order would insist on the racial integration of public facilities, but when white Republicans and black leader James Lynch displayed no taste for a clause in the new constitution requiring that all schools be open to both races, white apprehensions were allayed.[1]

Nevertheless, on the matter of political rights for former Confederates radicalism won a temporary victory in the constitutional convention. Antagonized by the abusive language of the conservative press, the Republican majority adopted a clause that, if ratified, would have barred former Confederates from holding office in the state. The intense opposition that this clause generated provided the impetus for the defeat of the constitution at the polls and a continuation of military rule. The next year, when the new president, U. S. Grant, announced his displeasure with the "proscriptive" features of the constitution, moderates, led by James Lusk Alcorn, a wealthy Delta planter, supplanted the Radicals as the dominant faction in the state Republican party. In addition to Alcorn, the moderate leadership included James Lynch, the leading black politician in the state, and carpetbagger Ridgley C. Powers, who would become governor in 1871. In the fall election of 1869 the constitution of 1868, shorn of its disabling features, was ratified, and the re-

1. Jackson *Clarion*, March 11, 21, April 28, 1868; Forest *Register*, April 1, 1868; Vicksburg *Weekly Republican*, April 7, May 26, 1868.

vamped Republican party with Alcorn as its candidate for governor swept to an easy victory over an aberrant Republican ticket that had the reluctant support of Mississippi conservatives.

At the heart of moderate Republicanism in the state was the belief that the new political order could not be sustained for long without the backing of a large number of whites. Moderates insisted that Republican dependence upon black voters to maintain the party's ascendancy was a slender reed that might be broken at the first sign of trouble. Only a racially balanced party, including, as Lynch said, "an element of the hitherto governing class," could lay the foundation for "a peaceful and prosperous commonwealth" that would survive Reconstruction.[2]

When the moderate Republicans assumed power in 1870, they launched a program that was designed to give confidence to the old citizens while protecting the fundamental political and civil rights of blacks. The economic upswing of 1870, which moderate Republicans identified with their political success, worked to their advantage in the campaign to win white support and launch the new government on a sound footing. Some moderates even envisaged the disappearance of racial prejudice and political intolerance after they had had a chance to demonstrate the soundness of their policies.[3]

But trouble soon developed. During the winter of 1870–1871 the agricultural economy plummeted, precisely at the time when the first taxes under the new order fell due. Unable to pay their taxes, thousands of farmers and planters lost property to the sheriff's hammer. As many conservatives had feared from the beginning, the levies to support the new government seemed so heavy as to preclude all hope for economic rehabilitation as long as the Republicans held power.[4]

2. New York *Times*, August 2, 1869 (Lynch quote); Jackson *Weekly Pilot*, December 11, 1869; James Lusk Alcorn to Elihu B. Washburne, December 5, 1868, in Elihu B. Washburne Papers, Library of Congress.

3. Jackson *Weekly Pilot*, January 15, April 2, 9, 1870; Vicksburg *Times and Republican*, August 4, 1870; *Annual Message of Gov. Jas. L. Alcorn to the Mississippi Legislature, Session of 1871* (Jackson, 1871), 29–30.

4. C. Byrd to Oscar J. E. Stuart, January 22, 1871, in John B. S. Dimitry Pa-

These social and economic conditions contributed to the wave of violence that swept the state in 1870–1871, culminating in the Ku Klux Klan terror in the eastern counties. Federal authorities, however, acting under the Enforcement laws, suppressed the violence, and in the local elections of 1871 the Republicans retained control of the state government even while losing most of the white counties. Significantly, the election returns reveal that the moderate Republican strategy of appealing to the old citizens, principally the old-line Whig element, had not borne fruit. Probably no more than five thousand whites had been persuaded by the moderates to defy conservative opinion and cast Republican ballots.

Within the Republican party factionalism flared as a result of Governor Alcorn's failure to provide security for the party faithfuls, his appointment of non-Republicans to office, and his "war on carpetbaggers" of the Radical wing. Radicals, led by United States Senator Adelbert Ames and scalawag Robert W. Flournoy, charged that the moderates in their attempt to build a biracial party had grievously compromised Republican principles and had undermined the Reconstruction settlement in the state. Radicals insisted that the strength of the party rested with its black vote, and the efforts to attract a large number of former Confederates would be at the expense of black rights and the political ascendancy of true Republicans. They claimed that from the beginning the moderate strategy was an illusion born of conservative intrigue and the gullibility of wayward Republicans.[5]

Nevertheless, the departure in late 1871 of the "disorganizer-in-chief," as the Radicals labeled Alcorn, for the United States

pers, Duke University Library; Vicksburg *Times and Republican*, August 15, 1871; Jackson *Weekly Clarion*, January 19, 26, 1871; *Hinds County Gazette*, May 17, November 29, 1871.

5. Adelbert Ames to his wife Blanche, October 26, 1871, in Blanche Butler Ames (comp.), *Chronicles from the Nineteenth Century: Family Letters of Blanche Butler and Adelbert Ames* (2 vols.; Clinton, Mass. 1957), I, 344–45; Vicksburg *Times and Republican*, July 19, 1870; Jackson *Pilot*, January 26, July 31, 1871.

Senate, and his replacement as governor by Powers renewed moderate Republican hopes that the Radical revival could be checked and a racially balanced party could still be developed in Mississippi. Powers immediately announced that his administration would place top priority on reforming the financial structure of the government and assisting the material development of the state. Claiming that the age of political intolerance and opposition to the fundamental rights of blacks had ended, this carpetbag governor declared that "the people are now free to devote their entire attention and energies to bettering their material condition."[6] Specifically, the state administration by reducing taxes and reining in the extravagant local governments could restore confidence in business and in the agricultural economy. By implication, such a program of reform would placate the white masses and attract many to the Republican party. Only by the adoption of a reform platform, Powers insisted, could Republicanism be saved from the ignoble fate that it was experiencing in other southern states.

Despite earlier reverses for the moderate Republican cause, Governor Powers and his associates believed that solid reasons existed in 1872–1873 for the success of their plan. Bourbonism or die-hard opposition to Republican Reconstruction appeared doomed in the state. The New Departure arguments of Albert Gallatin Brown, John F. H. Claiborne, Ethelbert Barksdale, and others, calling on whites to accept in good faith the postwar amendments to the Constitution and respect all of the rights of blacks, seemed at last to be having a significant influence on the old citizens. Primarily from the state's plantation districts, the New Departurists reflected the insecurity of whites living in a sea of blacks where political power for the former slaves was a reality. To them, accommodation was essential if they were to retain any influence in public affairs and avert the radicalization of the local governments. These conservatives maintained

6. *Annual Message of Gov. R. C. Powers to the Legislature of Mississippi, Session of 1872* (Jackson, 1872), 1, 3–4; Vicksburg *Times and Republican*, January 17, 1872.

that in counties where "Radical adventurers" had already gained control, redemption could only be achieved with the cooperation of independent blacks.[7] Accommodationists were also vitally concerned with the need for labor stability, which, they believed, would be significantly advanced by a cessation of racial agitation and an acceptance of black rights. Even in white counties many conservatives were tired of political and racial strife and were anxious for a state government that would reduce taxes and promote material development.

A major improvement in white attitudes toward the new public school system gave moderate Republicans additional cause for optimism. Viewed by Republicans as the cornerstone of the new order in the state, the school system had had a fitful beginning in 1870–1871 mainly because of conservative opposition to the principle of black education and the unfounded white fear that the schools would be racially integrated. But as the schools were organized, whites began to see the benefits of a comprehensive system of education, and by 1872 county superintendents, most of whom were Republicans, were flooding state Superintendent Henry R. Pease's office with reports of increasing popular support for the schools. From the plantation districts, superintendents reported that planters were aiding black laborers in the establishment of schools for their children. Even in the predominantly white eastern counties, where the Ku Klux Klan had recently roamed, school officials informed their superiors of a remarkable change in sentiment toward the biracial system of schools. Pease, a carpetbagger who would soon be elected to the United States Senate, concluded from these reports that "irrational prejudices and passions are gradually giving way to reason and an enlightened conservatism." Like many other Republicans in 1872–1873, Pease associated this development with a broader change occurring in Mississippi. "The masses of the people, including a large proportion of the wealthy

7. *Hinds County Gazette*, November 30, 1870; Natchez *Democrat*, September 20, October 25, 1871; Jackson *Weekly Clarion*, August 14, 21, September 4, 1873.

and intelligent classes, are beginning to demand a conforma-
tion to the great fundamental changes in our state and nation,
particularly with reference to popular education."[8]

The decline of opposition to the Republican order was also
evident in the virtual abandonment in 1872–1873 of the shrill,
"billingsgate" style of journalism that had been the standard
fare of the Bourbon press. Although Horace Greeley was a bitter pill for conservatives to swallow, the national Democratic
party's endorsement of the Liberal Republican candidate for
president and its acceptance of the New Departure platform
contributed to the benign change in white Mississippian attitudes toward biracial democracy. By 1873 former Governor
Brown and other New Departure leaders were calling for the
disbandment of the decrepit state Democratic party and the
organization of a moderate or "reform" coalition that would include blacks as well as white Republicans and conservatives.[9]
Even though most whites might refuse to cooperate with a carpetbagger like Powers, or even with an old citizen like Alcorn,
the moderate Republican emphasis on the harmony of material
progress and reform offered considerable promise that conservatives would at least be weakened by division on Reconstruction issues and that the Bourbon spirit of political intolerance
and racist vituperation might remain mute. A prolonged period
of political quietude was essential to the success of the Republican party and the Reconstruction settlement. Republicans
needed time to deal with the difficult problems of the postwar
period and to demonstrate that their program and leadership
were not hostile to the interests of the whites.

Despite hopeful signs of political and racial conciliation from
conservatives, the moderate Republican strategy failed. Governor Powers proved incapable of providing the leadership for a

8. *Mississippi Educational Journal*, I (April 1871), 133–37; *Mississippi
Senate Journal*, I (1873), 709–10, 822, 860, 877.
9. Natchez *Weekly Democrat*, March 20, April 10, May 29, 1872; Vicksburg
Times and Republican, March 15, 24, April 9, 1872; Greenwood *Times*, August 16, 1873; Jackson *Weekly Clarion*, September 25, 1873.

program of reform and conciliation. At the same time, the strong-
willed Alcorn was in Washington and unable to play a direct role
in the affairs of the state. Furthermore, the political eclipse of
James Lynch and his death in late 1872 removed from the scene
an important moderate force in the black community. Lynch
was replaced by a group of young, militant black leaders who
had won election to the legislature in 1871. Although not opposed to reform per se, these young men, including the new
speaker of the House, John R. Lynch, and William H. Gray of
the Delta, with a large black minority behind them in the legislature, refused to cooperate with Governor Powers, insisting
that his emphasis upon financial reform and material progress
would divert attention from the unfulfilled black demands for
civil rights legislation. The moderate effort to bring whites into
the party also threatened to cut short the black drive for more
influence and power in the state, while President Grant's lop-
sided victory over Greeley in the election of 1872 convinced
many Republicans of both races that the party's ascendancy in
the state was safe behind its bloc of black voters and the support
of the federal government.

In the state campaign of 1873 moderate Republicans suffered
a final defeat at the hands of the Radicals. The Republican con
vention adopted a platform calling for the racial integration of
the public schools and the university at Oxford. At the same
time Ames easily defeated Powers for the gubernatorial nomination. Black delegates, who probably constituted a majority in
the convention, demanded and received three of the six positions on the state ticket for members of their race. However,
Ham Carter, their first choice for lieutenant governor, was defeated for the nomination by a combination of white Republicans and discordant blacks. Instead, Alexander K. Davis, a
nondescript black of Noxubee County who would prove corrupt in office, was nominated for the position.[10]

Die-hard moderate Republicans reacted in cold fury to the

10. Washington *New National Era*, September 11, October 23, 1873; Jackson *Weekly Clarion*, September 4, 1873.

triumph of the Radicals. Alcorn held his own Republican convention, which nominated him for governor on a platform denouncing the "corrupt" Ames ticket and calling for retrenchment and reform in government. Spurred to action by fear of a Radical victory in the election, New Departure conservatives seized control of the state Democratic-Conservative convention and secured the approval of a resolution disbanding the party and freeing its members to vote for the moderate Republican ticket. But as Greeley had been in 1872, Alcorn was a bitter pill for conservatives to swallow. In addition to long-standing reasons for opposing the "Eminent Man," Alcorn's refusal to inject the race issue into the campaign damaged his chances for winning support among many conservatives, particularly those of the Bourbon persuasion.[11] The coalition of Alcorn Republicans and New Departure conservatives could not stop the Radical juggernaut, and Ames defeated his rival by a margin of nineteen thousand votes in the election. Radicals also captured control of the new legislature, although many of the members shunned the Radical label, preferring instead to be identified simply as Republicans.

Actually, the old distinctions between Radicals and moderate Republians on Reconstruction issues had become blurred and had lost most of their force in the intense factional struggle of 1871–1873. When the Ames Radicals assumed control of the state government in January 1874, they were more concerned with consolidating their power and punishing Alcorn Republicans than in advancing the cause of black rights or any other radical program. The 1873 platform committing the party to the integration of the public schools was quickly forgotten. Even in the legislature, where blacks were within four votes of having a majority in the lower house and had assumed a powerful influence in the Republican caucus, the Radical leadership was content to ignore the issue.

11. Vicksburg *Times and Republican*, September 23, 27, October 14, November 2, 1873; New York *Times*, September 21, 1873; Washington *New National Era*, October 2, 1873; Ames to his wife Blanche, September 30, 1873, in Ames (comp.), *Chronicles* I, 583.

At first Governor Ames took a page from the moderate Republican past and sought to convince the old citizens that he was a dedicated reformer and a promoter of racial conciliation. In his inaugural address he decried the old charges against the Radicals that if given power they would act mainly for the blacks of the state and would tolerate corruptionists in office. He announced that one of the highest goals of his administration would be to remove "all causes of distrust, real, or imaginary, which may exist between the different classes of our citizens."[12] On the matter of corruption, the carpetbag governor promised that where malfeasance was suspected he would see that it was "mercilessly investigated, let the consequences of exposure fall upon whom they may."[13]

Conservatives seemed to have recognized that the Radical quest for "social equality" for blacks had spent its force. During the next two years they rarely raised the old bugaboo of racial amalgamation against the Ames Radicals. Faced with still another economic crisis, white Mississippians were more concerned by 1874 with the effect on their livelihood of Republican tax policies and financial management than with the issue of black civil or political rights. The two issues, at least temporarily, had been separated in the minds of a large number of whites, and Ames' commitment to reform held out the hope that racial passions could be kept out of politics, or at least kept within controllable bounds. Ames' promise in his inaugural address to institute a "rigid economy and a strict accountability" in the expenditures of public funds produced a wave of relief throughout the state and conservative expressions of support for his effort to bring Mississippi out of "the mire of financial ruin and social despondence." Even some Bourbons hailed his "declaration of war against corruption and extravagance."[14] At the same time moderate Republicans told Ames that Republicanism could

12. *Inaugural Address of Gov. Adelbert Ames to the Mississippi Legislature, Thursday, January 22, 1874* (Jackson, 1874), 4–5.
13. *Ibid.*, 8.
14. Pascagoula *Star*, February 1, 1874; Jackson *Weekly Clarion*, February 12, 1874; J. D. Barton to Governor Ames, February 27, 1874, in Governors' Records, Vol. 91, Mississippi Department of Archives and History, Jackson.

not be saved from disaster unless he "fearlessly applied" his promise of economy and reform. These Republicans insisted, as they had before, that a policy of retrenchment and reform would reduce political tensions and keep the conservatives divided, thus continuing their incapacity to do harm.[15]

Like Powers before him, Governor Ames proved unequal to the task of hammering through the legislature a significant program of reform. Moreover, Ames rejected any important reductions in state expenditures, although he secured legislative approval for measures to retire depreciated state warrants and adjust inequitable property assessments. Ames and his friends in the legislature specifically ignored proposals to reduce the excessive costs of the judiciary, which at approximately $250,000 per year was by far the largest item of expense in the state budget. The legislature not only refused to cut the expense of public printing, as a number of reform Republicans had urged, but it increased these costs by establishing an elaborate system of legal publishing for the chancery court districts of the state.[16]

The carpetbag governor's promise not to tolerate corruption and favoritism soon developed a hollow ring. He early surrounded himself with a coterie of northern cronies whom he relied upon for information and advice, much of which was narrowly partisan and frequently unwise. Although himself free of improbity, Ames permitted the shady O. C. French to remain in his close circle of advisers even after he was implicated in a scheme to defraud the state of thousands of acres of valuable timberlands along the Pearl River.[17] He also refused to take action against state Superintendent of Education Thomas W. Cardozo, who soon after taking office found himself "shingled all over with indictments for embezzlement and fraud" that he had

15. Vicksburg *Times*, January–March 1874.

16. *Ibid.*, March 28, April 19, 1874; *Mississippi House Journal*, 1874, pp. 694–95.

17. *Mississippi in 1875: Report of the Select Committee to Inquire into the Mississippi Election of 1875, with the Testimony and Documentary Evidence* (2 vols.; Washington, 1876), I, 326; Vicksburg *Times*, March 13–15, 26, 1874.

accumulated while serving as circuit clerk of Warren County. The Jackson *Pilot*, which was managed by friends of the governor, charged that the indictments were a political move to harass Cardozo and, by implication, the Ames administration. Circuit court officials in Warren County, all of whom were Ames appointees, delayed bringing Cardozo to trial until after the fall of the Republican government. The dishonest conduct of Lieutenant Governor Davis also brought discredit to the Radical administration, although Ames made an effort to check his activities.[18]

At the local level charges of mismanagement and malfeasance became rife in 1874–1875. Though not an unusual practice during the Alcorn-Powers years, a number of party faithfuls simultaneously held two or three offices by virtue of the governor's appointment. Nevertheless, the most frequent complaints, as before, were against the county supervisors, who were elected officials and in many cases had been in office since 1871. Most of these charges had a partisan ring about them and were exaggerated or completely false. But even Republicans admitted that an unusually large number of tax collectors and county treasurers, whether for corrupt reason or not, were defaulters, and in most cases were still holding office. Furthermore, county supervisors were acting in a more irresponsible way than ever before. In one case, O. S. Lee, a carpetbag associate of Ames and deputy treasurer of Holmes County, absconded with $57,000 in public funds after killing two blacks in a local factional dispute. The situation became so bad in the counties that Ames obtained legislative approval in 1875 for the appointment of nine special revenue commissioners, at least six of whom were carpetbag friends, to investigate charges of defalcation and recover as much of the taxpayers' money as possible.[19] Little real

18. Jackson *Pilot*, July 28, 1875; Jackson *Weekly Clarion*, July 19, 1876; Ames to his wife Blanche, August 27, 1875, in Ames (comp.), *Chronicles*, II, 148.

19. F. Heiderhoff to Ames, September 14, 1874, Wilson Hood to Ames, December 19, 1874, both in Governors' Records, Vol. 99; George E. Harris to President U. S. Grant, November 24, 1875, printed in *Issues of the Canvass of*

progress toward reform, however, had been made when the Ames government fell in 1876.

The governor's favoritism and his failure to act vigorously against officials charged with malfeasance contributed not only to a revival of conservative assaults on the Reconstruction regime but also refueled the factional conflict in the Republican party. Despite an initial demonstration of good will toward prodigal Republicans who returned to the party after Alcorn's defeat in 1873, Ames and his associates seemed determined to nail them to the wall. When United States Senator Henry R. Pease, a leading Radical, refused to use his influence in Washington to block the reappointment of federal District Attorney G. Wiley Wells, a carpetbag antagonist of the governor, Ames, in typical fashion, denounced the senator as "a tricky double dealing fellow" and sought his political destruction.[20] By the summer of 1874 Ames' war against Pease, Alcorn, and other "sorehead" Republicans had seriously widened the split in the party and had cost the governor the support of a number of prominent Republicans, several of whom had earlier supported him in his conflict with the moderate faction of the party.

Under attack from all sides by late 1874, Ames, who privately expressed an intense dislike for Mississippi, turned even more to his carpetbag friends in Jackson, who, according to state Attorney General George E. Harris, a scalawag, "were a close corporation of mercenary men."[21] The governor's basis for making decisions had become tragically limited. As a result, when confronted with a political crisis, as he soon would be, Ames was unable to assess properly the complexities involved and act realistically to control the situation. Equally significant, his decisions no longer carried the full weight of the Republican party in the state. With the Radical regime severely weakened inter-

---

1876 (Jackson, 1876), 5–6; Ames to his wife Blanche, September 5, 11, 1875, in Ames (comp.), *Chronicles*, II, 125–26, 175; *Laws of Mississippi, Regular Session, 1875*, p. 30.

20. Ames to Pease, May 15, 1874, Ames to A. R. Howe, June 1, 1874, Ames to C. F. Harris, August 4, 1874, all in Letterbook D of Governor Adelbert Ames, Mississippi Department of Archives and History.

21. Harris to President Grant, November 24, 1875, in *Issues of the Canvass of 1876*, p. 5.

nally, a successful conservative challenge appeared, for the first time since the Republican triumph in 1869, to be a distinct possibility. It remained to be seen, however, if the conservatives, whose demoralization and divisions were accentuated by the abandonment of the Democratic party in 1873, could take advantage of Republican troubles and unite on a common ground for the "redemption" of the state from Radical rule.

Mississippi conservatives at first approached their new political opportunity with considerable wariness. They had been burned previously by a strategy based on the belief that Republican factionalism had fatally weakened the party's control. The twenty-thousand Republican majority at the polls, protected by federal might, still seemed a formidable barrier to overcome. In spite of their differences, blacks and most white Republicans in the past had rallied to the regular party standard on election day; in 1874–1875 conservatives had no assurance that this pattern would be soon broken.

Nevertheless, the failure of the Ames regime to develop a significant program of retrenchment and reform and the increasing tax burden on the great majority of the people emboldened conservatives in their opposition to the Republicans. The national Democratic success in winning control of the House of Repre sentatives in 1874 promised an early end of federal intervention to protect the discredited Republican governments in the South, although President Grant, whose term would not expire until 1877, appeared determined to provide for their security, as indicated by his continued use of federal power in Louisiana. Bourbon strength in the state, which had fallen to a low point during the Powers years, revived in 1874 and increased as Republican weaknesses became more apparent. In an effort to win control of the conservative movement, Bourbons denounced the New Departure policy of accommodation with blacks and called for a militant, white-line strategy to redeem Mississippi from the "Ames plunderers."[22]

Most conservative leaders, however, still rejected the Bour

22. Vicksburg *Vicksburger*, February 15, 1874; *Hinds County Gazette*, September 23, 1874; Pascagoula *Star*, November 29, 1874, January 2, 1875.

bon demand for an assault on the black vote and the raising of racial passions in the state. Led by former Democrat Albert Gallatin Brown in the south and former Whig John W. C. Watson in the north, moderates continued to insist that the New Departure, which was primarily designed to attract reform-minded Republicans of both races to the conservative cause, offered the only mode for overcoming the Radical majority at the polls. In the heart of the Delta, John S. McNeily of the Greenville *Times* declared that the "mistaken and desperate policy" of the Bourbons was "pregnant with evil and misery" for Mississippi. The adoption of the Bourbon strategy "would constitute quite a dilemma for the white people of communities like [ours] where the very opposite of this 'color line' policy has been beneficially and successfully practiced for several years past."[23] The Port Gibson *Standard*, also published in a predominantly black county, decried the revival of Bourbon militancy on the ground that it would result in a war of the races. "The color line bids fair to be a line of battle, and battle is not the thing we want," the *Standard* announced.[24]

Other moderate leaders argued that a cessation of federal intervention to prop up Radical regimes in the South depended on the continued growth of accommodationist sentiment. Deliverance from Republican rule will come soon, the Jackson *Clarion* assured its readers, "if the Northern mind is not disturbed by apprehension of a 'new rebellion,' which Southern whites can prevent if they exercise patience and forebearance." Nothing should be done by southerners to give a new lease on life to northern Republican "demagogues whose stock in trade is the manufacture of outrages." At the same time L. Q. C. Lamar's famous eulogy in Congress for Charles Sumner was designed, he admitted, to encourage northern sympathy for southern conservatives in the struggle to overcome Republican rule. [25] A prom-

23. Greenville *Weekly Times*, September 12, 26, 1874.

24. As reported in the Vicksburg *Vicksburger*, August 7, 1874. See also the Jackson *Weekly Clarion*, September 10, 1874.

25. Jackson *Weekly Clarion*, October 22, 29, 1874; James B. Murphy, *L. Q. C. Lamar: Pragmatic Patriot* (Baton Rouge, 1973), 119.

nent north Mississippi conservative succinctly summarized all of the moderate objections to the color-line program of the Bourbons when he wrote: "A white man's party . . . would be foredoomed to certain and overwhelming defeat, and its results would be to check the rising sentiment in our favor at the North and [produce] countless riots and murders in our midst."[26]

Instead of raising the race issue against the Radicals, New Departure spokesmen focused their attacks on the increasing burden of Republican taxes and expenses. In late 1874 they organized local taxpayers' leagues that ostensibly were nonpartisan associations designed to influence the Republican administration to reduce taxes and aid in restoring the land to productivity. "The great cardinal principle of the [taxpayers'] movement is this," the Natchez *Democrat* informed its readers, "that the Senate and county taxation to which our people have been and are now subjected is enormously excessive, unequal, unjust, oppressive, and incompatible with good government and the natural rights of men."[27] People simply could not pay their taxes, the *Democrat* announced, and the list of tax forfeited property was growing by leaps and bounds. In explaining the local need for the tax reform movement, the Greenville *Times* claimed that in 1874 Delta plantations assessed at $20,000 had to pay taxes that ranged between $3,000 and $4,000, despite the meager income realized from the land after debts for supplies had been settled. As a result "over two-thirds of the most valuable plantations in Washington county were sold [recently] for taxes, . . . and not a bid was made for one."[28] The numerous resolutions adopted by local taxpayers' leagues also graphically expressed the problems that property holders experienced as the time for paying new taxes approached in early 1875.

For a time the taxpayers' leagues were able to maintain their nonpartisan facade. A correspondent for the New York *Times* reported in December 1874, at the height of the movement, that in the "manifestoes" of the leagues he saw "none of the old

26. Jackson *Weekly Clarion*, September 10, 1874.
27. Natchez *Democrat*, December 2, 1874.
28. Greenville *Weekly Times*, November 7, 1874, March 27, 1875 (quote).

twaddle about white men's governments and the interests of the Caucasian. On the contrary, an effort has been made to bring such colored citizens as have property, and are of consequence in the State, into the movement for tax reform; and there are evidences that it will succeed."[29] By this time several prominent Republicans and four party journals, but not including the stalwart Jackson *Pilot*, had endorsed the taxpayers' movement. An important convert to the taxpayers' cause was the Radical Republican Robert W. Flournoy. In an open letter "To the People of Mississippi," "Old Osawatomie" Flournoy asserted that despite what Ames Republicans had claimed the people of the state "are taxed beyond endurance." He thundered: "It is a fallacious and comtemptible subterfuge to attempt to palliate a great wrong," as Ames partisans had done, by comparing the rate of taxation in Mississippi with that of other states, which almost invariably had greater wealth than the Magnolia State. Mississippi, he pointed out, had the third highest tax rate in the nation, but was the seventh poorest in per capita wealth. Furthermore, Flournoy said, the tax rate in the state continued to rise; it had almost doubled during the past year, and no relief appeared in sight for oppressed taxpayers, unless the legislature of 1875 could be persuaded to make drastic cuts in expenditures. He specifically called for the abolition of the chancery court system, the adoption of biennial sessions for the legislature, and the end of the registration requirement for voting, which he asserted, in addition to reducing state expenses, would increase the number who voted.[30]

The enthusiasm of Flournoy and other reform Republicans for the taxpayers' movement waned considerably when the crusade lost its elevated tone and became largely a diatribe against Republican profligacy. In the Delta, the Greenville *Times*, a moderate journal in politics but a militant advocate of retrenchment and efficiency in government, averred that "in this State

29. New York *Times*, December 19, 1874.
30. As reported in the Jackson *Weekly Clarion*, July 16, 1874, and the Vicksburg *Times*, July 18, 1874.

the fact that the cloak and machinery of taxation has been diverted to purposes of confiscation is undeniable." Claiming that "the present system of taxation is a robbery which the people are morally and religiously justified in resisting, short of revolution," Ethelbert Barksdale encouraged the taxpayers' leagues to pursue an aggressive policy to rid the state of the "Republican corruptionists."[31] "The wrongs for which our English ancestry brought the head of Charles the First to the block are trivial compared to these we now suffer," the Natchez *Democrat* exclaimed. Nevertheless, the *Democrat* cautioned the people against violent methods to obtain relief, advising that "the people present their grievances to the Legislature, and ask that they be redressed."[32]

Revisionist historians of southern Reconstruction have contended that conservative complaints of tax extortion at the hands of the Republicans were exaggerated, and no doubt there is much truth in this assessment. In Mississippi the state and county tax rates, which together rarely exceeded fifty dollars on the one thousand dollars of assessed property, were not very high by modern standards nor did they depart drastically from those then prevailing in the North. But when other factors are considered—such as the heavy indebtedness of the people, the high rates of interest required to obtain essential provisions, the dearth of income from the land, and the absence of a diversified economy in the state—it is clear that the taxes imposed by the Republicans were burdensome and added to the hardships that the people experienced during Reconstruction. Impecunious planters and farmers could not afford to pay even the relatively modest levies required to sustain the expanded public programs of the postwar period. As a result hundreds of thousands of acres fell annually to the sheriff's hammer for delinquent taxes. When the Republicans came to power in 1870, two million acres were held by public authorities for this reason; by

31. Greenville *Weekly Times*, March 27, 1875; Jackson *Weekly Clarion*, November 9, 1874.
32. Natchez *Democrat*, December 8, 1874.

1875 approximately six million acres, or one-fifth of the land area of Mississippi, had defaulted to the state.[33] The fiscal and tax policies of the Republicans did not create the hard times of the 1870s, but the failure of the new political order to act realistically on the complaints of taxpayers and those who had lost their lands contributed to the continuation of the agricultural depression and ultimately to the undoing of Republican authority in the state.

The climax of the taxpayers' movement occurred in January 1875 when a state convention of protestors met in Jackson. Although it was hailed as a nonpartisan affair, few Republicans attended. Brown, Watson, and other moderates dominated the proceedings and kept the debate focused on the concrete issues of retrenchment and reform. The "Petition and Appeal of the Tax-Payers to the Legislature," adopted by the convention, refrained from the usual polemics against the Republicans. Mainly, it pleaded with the lawmakers to adopt the policy of biennial sessions for the legislature, abate past taxes, and reduce expenditures for public printing, schools, and salaries. The Petition and Appeal also urged the legislature to bridle the authority of the county boards of supervisors, which, it charged, were largely composed of men who "are totally unfit to discharge their duties and are without respectability or accountability."[34]

Despite the support of reform Republicans, the Petition and Appeal received short shrift in the legislature. Dominant Radicals in the legislature, buffeted by a torrent of abuse from Bourbons and outraged by racial disorders that convulsed Vicksburg in December 1874, glibly dismissed the Taxpayers' Convention as the stalking horse for the revival of the "Ku Klux Democracy" in Mississippi. In fact, the editors of the Jackson *Pilot*, the organ of the Radical Republicans in the legislature,

33. Report of the state auditor, in *Mississippi Senate Journal*, 1870, Appendix, 108; report of the state auditor, in *Mississippi House Journal*, 1875, Appendix, 40.

34. The membership and proceedings of the convention may be found in the Jackson *Weekly Clarion*, January 7, 1875.

found reason to gloat over the misfortunes of the old citizens who were behind the taxpayers' movement. For the first time in the history of the state, these carpetbag editors gleefully announced, the landowner had felt the heavy hand of taxation— and he bitterly resented it. "Let him squirm. We mistake the tendency of affairs [greatly] if real estate will ever get back to the happy condition it experienced in the good old Democratic days, when the 'mud-sills' and 'poor white trash' staggered under burdens of taxation that the ruling class might wallow in inglorious ease and increase in unearned wealth."[35]

The hardening of Republican attitudes against reform worked ineluctably in favor of the Bourbons as they sought to gain control of the conservative movement before the 1875 political campaign. Although in agreement with the white-line doctrine of the Bourbons, the white masses were not easily convinced that their opposition to the Republicans would make a difference in the near future. They had heard racist harangues before, which had only dented the Republican armor and had led to demoralizing compromises by conservative leaders. What Bourbons needed to convince wary and still apathetic whites of the soundness of their strategy for redemption was an early and striking demonstration of its viability in a Republican controlled locality. Such a demonstration occurred in Warren County (Vicksburg) in late 1874.

The process of redemption in Warren County began in the summer when Vicksburg whites organized the "People's," or "White Man's" party on a militant, white-line basis. Their immediate objective was to depose the reputedly corrupt Republican administration of the town in the August municipal election. Despite mounting fears of racial violence and the refusal of the Grant regime to intervene, no violent confrontation between the two sides occurred during the campaign. Nevertheless, enough blacks had been intimidated to keep down the Republican vote, and with whites united and turning out in

35. Jackson *Weekly Pilot*, February 13, 1875. See also the issue of February 20 and the Vicksburg *Times*, March 21, 1875.

large numbers, the Bourbons won by 250 votes.[36] Emboldened by this success, Bourbons acted to force black Sheriff Peter Crosby out of office. An aggressive crowd of five hundred "tax payers," inflamed by the Bourbon press' charges of corruption against Crosby, marched on the courthouse on December 2 and demanded his resignation. Under these threatening circumstances, Crosby complied and rushed to Jackson where he sought Governor Ames' assistance in regaining the office.[37]

The governor hurriedly summoned a number of leading Republicans to the Governor's Mansion for consultation on the crisis in Warren County. Several recommended that Ames request federal troops to restore Crosby to his office and suppress the lawlessness in Vicksburg. Unlike the unsuccessful call for federal intervention in August, Grant appeared disposed to honor such a request now. The national elections of the fall had been held and Grant, instead of being subdued by the Democratic success in winning control of the House of Representatives, had shown a new determination to protect southern Republican governments by intervening in Louisiana to suppress the latest threat to the Kellogg regime. Furthermore, racial tension in the Hill City was more foreboding in December than it had been at the time of the municipal election.

Ames, however, rejected the recommendation and sent Crosby home with vague instructions to organize a *posse comitatus* consisting of plantation blacks for the purpose of restoring his authority. The governor promised Crosby state assistance, but the dispatch of two militia officers was the extent of his aid. A bloody racial clash was now inevitable. Rallying several hundred confused blacks to his standard, Crosby marched on Vicks-

36. Ames to President Grant, July 29, 1874, in Letterbook A of Governor Ames; New York *Times*, August 4, 5, 1874; Vicksburg *Times*, July 31, August 10, 1874.

37. An extensive collection of source materials on the disorders in Vicksburg may be found in *House Reports*, 43d Cong., 2d Sess., No. 265. Perhaps the most objective and informed account of the violence is the report of a correspondent to the Cincinnati *Commercial* that appeared soon after the event. The Vicksburg *Times*, January 8, 1875, carried this account.

burg. Whites, including a relatively large number of former federal soldiers who had settled in the county after the war, opened fire on the rag-tag black legions on the outskirts of town and drove them in panic from the scene. During the next few days armed bands of whites swept the county attacking and, in a grievous number of cases, killing those whom they suspected of having participated in the march on Vicksburg. When the racial excitement had run its course, probably about three hundred blacks and only two whites lay dead. Planters, however, in a deliberate attempt to conceal from their tenants the large number of blacks killed lest labor relations suffer, reported to the press that only twenty-five insurgents had died in the outbreak.[38]

Shaken by the violence, Governor Ames and the legislature finally asked for federal assistance and obtained the dispatch of a company of troops to Vicksburg. Only a formal demonstration of military power was needed to reinstate Crosby in the courthouse, reopen the courts, and dissolve the armed bands of whites in the county. Although peace had been restored to Vicksburg and Warren County, events there had inflamed racial passions throughout the state, inspired the cause of Bourbon, white-line militancy, and set an ominous stage for the campaign and election of 1875.

Conservatives prepared for the fall campaign with an intensity seldom seen in American political contests. The cup of conservative bitterness toward the Ames regime overflowed. In an editorial entitled "The Dirtiest Despotism on Earth," George W. Harper of the *Hinds County Gazette* exclaimed that "Radicalism in the hands of Ames and his negroes has swept away every vestige of republican government in Mississippi."[39] Radical adventurers, the Bourbon editor of the Meridian *Mercury* thundered, "have brought the State to the verge of ruin, trampling order, thrift, decency, property, feeling, religion, morality, and

---

38. J. M. Gibson, *Memoirs of J. M. Gibson: Terrors of the Civil War and Reconstruction Days* (n.p., 1966), 81.

39. *Hinds County Gazette*, March 31, 1875.

all that constitutes good government and refined society, under foot of their herded cattle."[40]

Moderate spokesmen, whose numbers and influence thinned as the political and racial excitement intensified, began to manifest a shrillness and militancy in their opposition to the Republians that belied their professions of moderation and concern for black rights and political conciliation. Moderates like Barksdale and Lamar focused their attacks on the failure of the Radical government to provide tax relief and on the militia law of 1875 that gave Ames $65,000 to create a military force, including the purchase of several dreaded Gatling guns. Conservatives naturally expected Ames to raise a black militia with this authorization. Lamar expressed the somber belief that "the future of Mississippi is very dark. Ames has it dead. There can be no escape from his rule. His negro regiments are nothing. He will get them killed up, and then Grant will take possession for him. May God help us!" The moderate Natchez *Democrat* asserted that the "standing army" measure, whose author was a madman, was "concocted to produce disorder and precipitate a race war for political effect."[41]

At last, Bourbons appeared to be in the ascendancy in the anti-Republican movement. Still, neither the reorganizational committee of the state Democratic-Conservative party, which met in May, nor the state convention, held in August, endorsed the color or white-line position of the Bourbons. The delegations sent to the state convention represented a mixture of young, ex-Confederates, who generally stressed the color line, and the surviving leadership of both antebellum parties, who as a rule favored moderation. Because of their experience in debate and maneuver, the old leadership won control of the convention. With Civil War Governor Charles Clark presiding, Watson

40. As reported in the Jackson *Times*, June 8, 1875.
41. Lamar to his wife, February 15, 1875, in Edward Mayes, *Lucius Q. C. Lamar: His Life, Times, and Speeches, 1825–1893* (Nashville, 1896), 211; Natchez *Democrat*, February 11, 1875; Vicksburg *Herald*, January 27, 1875.

chairing the important committee on resolutions, and Lamar delivering the main address, the moderates, although probably outnumbered, defeated the Bourbon effort to place the party on record as favoring the white-line position. They also secured the adoption of a platform affirming "the civil and political equality of all men as established by the Constitution of the United States and the amendments thereto." In addition, the platform emphasized the need for retrenchment in government and tax reform.[42] As the Democratic candidate for state treasurer, the only state office to be filled by the fall election, the delegates chose William L. Hemingway, master of the Grange in Mississippi. The selection of the Grange leader to head the Democratic-Conservative ticket in the election took into account the significant work of the farm organization, some 30,000 strong, in arousing whites to political action against the Radicals.

It was soon clear that the mild platform of the state Democratic-Conservative party—as well as the New Departure resolutions of a number of county conventions—would not be honored in the campaign. The organization of conservatives into militant white clubs or leagues for the purpose of intimidating blacks, however, was slow and probably never occurred in most counties. But the spirit of Bourbon intolerance and belligerence affected almost every community in the state. Some conservative spokesmen were open in their racialist appeal. During the campaign the Forest *Register*, whose editor was a former Klansman, carried at its masthead the slogan: "A white man in a white man's place. A black man in a black man's place. Each according to the eternal fitness of things."[43] Nevertheless, a number of conservative spokesmen, including James Z. George, the state Democratic campaign manager, continued to appeal to

42. Jackson *Times*, May 17, August 5, 1875. The membership and proceedings of the Democratic-Conservative Convention may be found in the Jackson *Weekly Clarion*, August 4, 1875. See *Appleton's Annual Cyclopaedia*, 1875, for the party platform.

43. As quoted in Vernon Lane Wharton, *The Negro in Mississippi, 1865–1890* (Chapel Hill, 1947), 184.

black voters and express the belief that many could legitimately be persuaded to vote the party ticket in the election.[44]

Republicans entered the critical contest of 1875 in sad disarray. The party was convulsed by factionalism at all levels and by a dissatisfaction with Governor Ames. Republicans seemed more anxious to fight each other than to checkmate activities of the Democratic party and the militant white leagues. "Like a nest of vipers, girdled with fire," a conservative reported, "the Mississippi Radicals are striking their poisonous fangs into each other in a way that portends the destruction of the whole brood."[45] "Never before has the strife among our friends been so bitter," lamented Ames on the eve of the campaign that would decide the fate of his party in Mississippi.[46]

The weakness of the Republicans and the Ames administration became apparent early in the campaign. On September 4 a race riot erupted during a Republican rally at Clinton, leaving between twenty and thirty blacks dead at the scene and in the countryside. Although only fifteen miles away, Governor Ames was helpless to halt the retaliation by armed bands of whites against suspected black rioters. At the same time Yazoo County fell to a white vigilante force. Ames raised two companies of black militia to reinstate Republican authority in the county, but when the deposed sheriff, perhaps wisely, refused to leave Jackson, he abandoned the military operation.

Despite his willingness to use force in Yazoo County, Ames had waited until it was too late to organize units to maintain order. The governor had earlier refused to form military companies partly because he believed that few reliable whites could be found who would accept commissions to lead black militiamen. He also reasoned, correctly, that the creation of an all-black militia would incite whites to organized violence against the

44. Jackson *Weekly Clarion*, September 15, 1875; Natchez *Democrat*, October 6, 26, 1875; James Z. George and Ethelbert Barksdale to Committee of Citizens, October [?], 1875 (telegram), in Governors' Records, Vol. 99.

45. As reported in the Jackson *Weekly Pilot*, September 11, 1875.

46. Ames to his wife Blanche, August 5, 1875, in Ames (comp.), *Chronicles* II, 126.

Negroes. Moreover, he preferred to believe that the Grant administration would intervene to preserve order during the election. In March Benjamin F. Butler, Ames' powerful father-in-law in Congress, had written him on behalf of the president that if the need arose the full force of the federal government would be used to put down revolutionary groups in the state.

When the Clinton and Yazoo troubles occurred, Ames put Grant's promise to the test. Declaring that "domestic violence prevails in various parts of this State, beyond the power of the State authorities to suppress," he applied on September 8 for federal troops to maintain order in Mississippi.[47] Alarmed by the threat of federal intervention, Democratic leaders and a few anti-Ames Republicans, notably former Senator Pease and state Attorney General Harris, rushed dispatches to Washington in an effort to persuade federal authorities that peace prevailed in the state. When Ames' request for troops and the statements disputing his claims reached Washington, President Grant was vacationing at Long Branch, his summer home in New Jersey. Attorney General Edwards Pierrepont, in charge of Southern affairs in Grant's absence, rushed the documents to the president and "made a full report" to him which evidently contained a recommendation of the policy that the president would soon adopt. Meanwhile, the northern press, including the New York *Times*, the Chicago *Tribune*, and influential Republican politicians denounced Ames' call for troops as unwarranted and urged the Grant administration to deny his request.[48]

A great deal of printer's ink was spilled in the North in an attempt to justify a nonintervention policy in the Mississippi crisis, but the main reason for the Republican reluctance to act did not appear in the party journals. Northern Republicans, including powerful figures in Grant's administration, were convinced that if troops were sent to Mississippi the party would lose to

47. *Appleton's Annual Cyclopaedia*, 1875, p. 516.
48. New York *Times*, September 13, 16, 1875; New York *Tribune*, September 21, 1875. For excerpts from other northern newspapers on the issue of intervention, see the Jackson *Weekly Clarion*, September 15, 22, 1875.

the Democrats in important fall elections in the North, particularly in Ohio. The climate of opinion in the North had swung decidedly against armed intervention in the southern states, regardless of the seriousness of the situation there. Grant, who was not oblivious to political consideration, agreed with this sentiment, thereby sealing the fate of the Republican order in Mississippi.[49] Nevertheless, the president promised Ames that if conditions further deteriorated he would dispatch troops, but first he wanted the governor to exhaust his own resources.[50]

Left to his own devices, Ames began the organization of a predominantly black militia. A torrent of conservative denunciation greeted the governor's action. "Ames is organizing murder, civil war, rapine, a war of races, in our otherwise peaceful State," the Jackson *Clarion* thundered. Visions of black insurrection swirled through the minds of many whites. During the night, as one Republican reported, "they nervously clutch at their Winchester rifle at the head of the bed. The day-time is spent mainly in cursing Ames."[51] Conservatives intensified their efforts to organize irregular companies for "self-defense." Deadly clashes between armed forces of the two races were narrowly averted in three counties, and in several areas of the state both blacks and whites, a Republican observed, "feel that they are slumbering upon a volcano, which may burst forth at any time and engulf them all in ruin."[52]

Faced with this explosive situation, Ames agreed to a "treaty of peace" with Democratic leaders that produced a degree of racial quiet for the remainder of the election campaign. In the treaty the governor promised to send home the two militia units

49. Ames to his wife Blanche, September 9, 1875, in Ames (comp.), *Chronicles*, II, 169; John A. Carpenter, *Ulysses S. Grant* (New York, 1970), 144; John R. Lynch, *The Facts of Reconstruction*, ed. William C. Harris (Indianapolis, 1970), 150–51.

50. Edwards Pierrepont to Ames, September 14, 1875, in Governors' Records, Vol. 99.

51. Jackson *Weekly Clarion*, September 29, October 13, 1875; Jackson *Pilot*, October 6, 1875.

52. Jackson *Pilot*, October 7, 1875.

in the Jackson area and to encase their arms. No additional companies were to be mustered; but those already organized could still be called out in case of an emergency. On their part, the Democrats promised to preserve the peace and permit a fair election in November.[53]

As a result of the peace agreement a feeling of relief swept across Misissippi, followed by an eerie racial calm that was broken only by a few instances of violence and physical threats. White leaguers, however, had already accomplished their objective of virtually paralyzing the Republican party in a number of counties and communities. The chilling news of Democratic depredations in white-league afflicted counties, along with reports of Governor Ames' inability to provide security for Republicans, spread rapidly through the black communities of Mississippi, creating alarm and causing blacks to fear for their lives if they continued to support the Republican party.[54]

Racial passion and conflict only partly explain the outburst of white enthusiasm and militancy during the campaign of 1875. In a dramatic fashion the campaign witnessed a white democratic uprising against the perceived existence of Republican corruption, tax oppression, and governmental mismanagement. In an October editorial, Barksdale marveled at the spirit of the revolution that was sweeping the state and also attempted to explain its source. He wrote:

When a government is oppressed with very bad rulers, and national affairs are tending toward corruption, the people (being patient and forebearing), as a general rule, bear these grievances for a long time hoping that a reformation may come, through a returning sense of justice on the part of their oppressors. Finally, when hope begins to fade, by the constant increase of wrongs, a few bold and vigilant lovers of liberty become leaders in the work of reformation; and, as soon as the

53. Ames to his wife Blanche, October 14, 1875, in Ames (comp.), *Chronicles*, II, 217; Ames to Attorney General Pierrepont, October 16, 1875, in Governors' Records, Vol. 99.

54. Testimony of scalawag Thomas Walton in *Mississippi in 1875*, I, 56; Ames to his wife Blanche, October 12, 1875, in Ames (comp.), *Chronicles*, II, 216; Jackson *Pilot*, October 15, 1875.

standard is raised, the masses . . . rise up in irresistible multitudes and rally under the revolutionary standard.[55]

Mississippi, Barksdale claimed, "had inaugurated a peaceful revolution" that was "deep-seated and wide-spread. The spirit of this revolution is resistance to corruption and misrule. . . . Such revolutions never go backwards!" This surge of white democratic fervor required little in the way of direction from the conservative leadership; it was spontaneous and usually intolerant. Leaders like George served more to check the excesses of the crusade—and thereby avoid a blood bath or federal intervention—than to rally whites to the Democratic standard. It is impossible to determine where the concern for democracy and freedom from "Radical tyranny" left off and unadulterated racism took over in the political motivation of whites in 1875. But, as Professor George M. Fredrickson has demonstrated for Jacksonian Democracy, these two impulses can exist side by side, and they did in the Mississippi contest of 1875.[56]

The campaign climaxed in late October with the staging of hundreds of parades, barbecues, and rallies, usually sponsored by the Democrats. In the larger towns immense torchlight processions highlighted the festivities. Democrats and "faithful negroes" frequently wore a uniform shirt, usually red, as they marched down the main streets to the cheers of onlookers. In the hotbeds of white-league activity, the campaign processions assumed a martial and menacing air. The conservatives went to the rallies in clubs, each one with its musical band, flags, and regalia. In many cases a cannon boomed in the background as the rally began.[57] When Democratic clubs or white leagues

55. Jackson *Weekly Clarion*, October 13, 1875. For a similar expression, see the Natchez *Democrat*, August 5, 1875.
56. George M. Fredrickson, *The Black Image in the White Mind: The Debate on Afro-American Character and Destiny, 1817–1914* (New York, 1971), 61–62, 66, 84.
57. Fred M. Witty, "Reconstruction in Carroll and Montgomery Counties," *Publications of the Mississippi Historical Society*, X (1909), 127; Natchez

threatened to apply a more direct form of intimidation against their opponents, George intervened to prevent violence that might result in federal intervention.

Remarkably, in view of the steamroller tactics of the Democrats, Republican leaders were able to canvass for the party. Outside of the white-league counties, intrepid Republicans frequently held joint debates with conservatives at rallies that were usually peaceful and free of intimidation, but not of recrimination. Black Congressman John R. Lynch even campaigned in the predominantly white piney woods of south Mississippi where he reported that "perfect order and decorum was preserved" at the rallies despite Democratic threats.[58] Other Republican leaders, including Governor Ames, remained at home and inveighed against the Democrats. Desperately, fourteen black leaders issued a printed address to their followers, pleading with them to persevere in the face of white-line tactics and go to the polls on election day. "The success of the Democratic party," these black stalwarts warned, "will, to all intents and purposes, sound the death knell of all the hopes that the colored man has indulged of educating, elevating and improving his race in this State. Once under the iron heel of Democracy, the colored man will at once sink back to the status he held in 1865—free in name, but not in fact—poor, ignorant and helpless, hedged in by unfriendly laws, which he will have no power to circumvent, a 'hewer of wood and a drawer of water' forever."[59]

Election day, November 2, passed with only a few incidents to disturb the peace. The campaign tactics and efforts of the

Democrat, October 1, 1875; Susan Dabney Smedes, Memorials of a Southern Planter, ed. Fletcher M. Green (New York, 1965), 249, 251–52.

58. Jackson Pilot, October 3, 8, 12, 15, 1875; Pascagoula Star, August 21, 1875; Jackson Times, October 8, 19–22, 29, 1875; entries for October 22, 24, 1875, in Jason Niles Diary, Southern Historical Collection, University of North Carolina.

59. This address was circulated in most of the Republican newspapers of the state. It can be found in the Jackson Pilot, October 4, 1875, and the Jackson Times, October 4, 1875.

conservatives, however, had produced the desired results at the polls. Democratic-Conservatives won the state treasurer's office by a margin of 31,544 votes, captured four of the six seats in Congress, "redeemed" all but a handful of the plantation counties, and gained a comfortable majority in the legislature.[60] Amazingly, the Democratic program of intimidation still fell short of keeping most Republicans from the polls in a majority of the counties. Only twenty-one of the seventy-two counties experienced a major loss in Republican strength in the election of 1875. The Democratic victory turned on the suppression of the black vote in a handful of large black counties (mainly Yazoo, Claiborne, Noxubee, and Hinds) and the outpouring of white voters throughout the state. A Republican policy of fusion with the conservatives in Madison, Washington, and Lowndes, three populous black counties, also provided the Democrats with a large bloc of voters in the contests for the key offices and membership in the legislature. In a demonstration of white participation that has never been matched in Mississippi history, more than 90 percent of the registered white voters went to the polls and overwhelmingly cast Democratic ballots.

When the legislature met on January 4, exuberant conservatives acted to consolidate their victory and arrange a redemption settlement for the state. Threatened by an impending investigation of the election by the United States Senate, the Democratic majority moved cautiously in dismantling the Republican order. After impeaching and removing from office the corrupt lieutenant governor, the Redeemers hesitated in taking action against Ames, who was hardly guilty of an impeachable offense. But in March momentum for the governor's impeachment revived and, rather than face certain removal, Ames resigned from office. Republican Reconstruction had ended, and Mississippi in terms of political tolerance and black rights reverted to a situation hardly better than the one existing in 1865.

60. State and congressional election returns may be found in *Mississippi in 1875*, II, Documentary Evidence, 144–45.

Bibliographical Essay

THE STANDARD DUNNING-SCHOOL ACCOUNT OF THE POST-war decade in the state is James W. Garner, *Reconstruction in Mississippi* (New York: Macmillan Company, 1901). A valuable secondary work, especially for the role of blacks, is Vernon Lane Wharton, *The Negro in Mississippi, 1865–1890* (Chapel Hill: University of North Carolina Press, 1947). William C. Harris, "The Reconstruction of the Commonwealth, 1865–1870," and David G. Sansing, "Congressional Reconstruction," in Richard A. McLemore (ed.), *A History of Mississippi* (2 vols.; Hattiesburg: University Press of Mississippi, 1973) provide a convenient survey. A comprehensive account of all aspects of the so-called Radical period is William C. Harris, *The Day of the Carpetbagger: Republican Reconstruction in Mississippi* (Baton Rouge: Louisiana State University Press, 1979). The only account dealing specifically with the overthrow of Republican authority is John S. McNeily, "Climax and Collapse of Reconstruction in Mississippi, 1874–1876," *Publications of the Mississippi Historical Society*, XII (1912), 283–474. Written years after Reconstruction by a conservative editor who participated in the stirring events of 1875, this essay is a rambling, distorted history. John R. Lynch's *The Facts of Reconstruction* (New York: Neale Publishing Company, 1913), although valuable on some phases of Reconstruction, provides only a brief account of the fall of Republicanism.

Biographies of the leading men of the era are relatively scarce. Lillian A. Pereyra, *James Lusk Alcorn, Persistent Whig* (Baton

Rouge: Louisiana State University Press, 1966) is a solid account of the life of this powerful scalawag. A sympathetic assessment of Ames's career is found in Richard N. Current, *Three Carpetbag Governors* (Baton Rouge: Louisiana State University Press, 1967). Somewhat dated is James B. Ranck's *Albert Gallatin Brown: Radical Southern Nationalist* (New York: D. Appleton-Century Co., 1937). A long-awaited revisionist biography of Lamar has recently appeared, James Murphy, *L. Q. C. Lamar: Pragmatic Patriot* (Baton Rouge: Louisiana State University Press, 1973). William C. Harris in "James Lynch: Black Leader in Southern Reconstruction," *Historian*, XXXIV (November 1971), 40–61, and in his introduction to John R. Lynch, *The Facts of Reconstruction* (2nd ed.; Indianapolis: Bobbs Merrill, 1970) provides brief accounts of the careers of the two most powerful black politicians in Mississippi. Biographical studies, perhaps in article form, are still needed for Ridgley C. Powers, Henry R. Pease, Alexander Warner, and James Hill (all Republicans) and Ethelbert Barksdale, John W. C. Watson, William H. McCardle, George W. Harper, and John M. Stone (Conservatives).

Collectively, Mississippi scalawags have received careful attention, though no consensus has been reached on their political backgrounds, motives, or performance in office. David Donald's "The Scalawag in Mississippi Reconstruction," *Journal of Southern History*, X (November 1944), 447–60, first challenged the traditional interpretation. The reassessment continued with David G. Sansing's "The Role of the Scalawag in Mississippi Reconstruction" (Ph.D. dissertation, University of Southern Mississippi, 1969); Allen W. Trelease, "Who Were the Scalawags?" *Journal of Southern History*, XXIX (November 1963), 445–68; William C. Harris, "A Reconsideration of the Mississippi Scalawag," *Journal of Mississippi History*, XXXII (February 1970), 3–42; and Warren A. Ellen, "Who Were the Mississippi Scalawags?" *Journal of Southern History*, XXXVIII (May 1972), 217–40.

The essay in this volume is based mainly upon primary sources, many of which have been used only slightly if at all by other historians. The most significant source was Blanche Butler Ames (comp.), *Chronicles from the Nineteenth Century: Family Letters of Blanche Butler and Adelbert Ames* (2 vols.; Clinton, Mass.; Colonial Press, 1957). Of outstanding value also were the papers of Governors Alcorn, Powers, and Ames in the Mississippi Department of Archives and History, Jackson. In addition, the printed legislative journals, laws of the state, and reports and messages of the Republican governors were extremely useful. A virtually untapped source of valuable information on state finances and taxation is the printed reports of the state auditor and state treasurer. Private manuscript collections for this period are fairly numerous but small in volume, with the exception of the massive William N. Whitehurst Papers, Mississippi Department of Archives and History.

Because of the partisan bias of the editors, newspapers were used with considerable care. Nonetheless, newspapers contain a mine of information on attitudes, apprehensions, and expressed public policies, all of which are quite relevant to the disintegration of Republican authority in the state. The most significant of these journals are: Jackson *Pilot* (Radical Republican), Vicksburg (later Jackson) *Times and Republican* (moderate Republican), Jackson *Clarion* (moderate Democrat), Greenville *Times* (moderate Democrat), Raymond *Hinds County Gazette* (sometimes Bourbon), Pascagoula *Star* (Bourbon), Vicksburg *Vicksburger* (Bourbon), and New York *Times*

Although congressional documents also have their limitations, a wealth of materials on the disorders of 1874 and 1875 is contained in "Vicksburg Troubles," *House Reports*, 43rd Cong., 2nd Sess., no. 265; and *Mississippi in 1875: Report of the Select Committee to Inquire into the Mississippi Election of 1875, with the Testimony and Documentary Evidence* (2 vols.; Washington, D.C.: Government Printing Office, 1876).

Two valuable and largely unbiased impressions of late Reconstruction developments are Edward King, *The Great South* (Hartford: American Publishing Company, 1875), and Charles Nordhoff, *The Cotton States in the Spring and Summer of 1875* (New York: D. Appleton and Company, 1876).

IV

Virginia
The Persistence of Centrist Hegemony

JACK P. MADDEX, JR.

VIRGINIA stood out as an exception to the prevailing characteristics of southern politics during Reconstruction. As late as 1873, eight of the nine other "reconstructed" states still had Republican governors—but Virginia never elected a Republican governor during the era. The Republican party won a majority in the convention which wrote the state's Reconstruction constitution, but its rival, the Conservative party, elected the succeeding governors and majorities in the legislature. Paradoxically, the state which never chose a Republican governor or legislative majority during Reconstruction elected both in the "Bourbon" year 1881. Virginia never sent a black member to Congress during Reconstruction, but it did in 1888. Its mountainous southwestern corner, which returned large Conservative majorities during Reconstruction, became a Republican stronghold by 1900.

Virginia stood out also from the political turbulence which characterized the Reconstruction South. John S. Wise, who spent those years as a Conservative lawyer in Richmond, later denied that there had been "any period in which negroes or alien and degraded whites were in a position to oppress" Virginians.[1] On the other hand, the black Louisianian Henry Adams concluded from his inquiries in the early 1870s that blacks received milder treatment in Virginia than in the other southern states.[2] Relatively moderate leaders won control of both parties.

The reasons for Virginia's uniqueness were not simple. The political center did not succeed by default, for alternatives to its left and right enjoyed popularity in the late 1860s. Moderates occupied the seats of power, but the way they gained them did not show that most Virginians preferred moderate policies. Nor did demography dictate that the Conservative party would outnumber the Republican. In the South as a whole, Republicans looked principally to blacks and mountain whites for political support. In 1870, 41.9 percent of Virginians were black, a proportion closer to the Deep South than to the Upper South norm. Another 21.2 percent were whites who lived in western mountain counties (including the Shenandoah Valley). The remaining 36.9 percent displayed enough social and economic diversity to afford hope that a Republican minority might emerge even in its ranks. Virginia was not inevitably destined to be either centrist or Conservative. The elements of the body politic and the federal rules for Reconstruction allowed room for several possible political alignments. It was a complex interplay of forces and a succession of experimental efforts which brought about the paradoxical result.

I

The death of the Confederacy and the emancipation of the slaves broke up the political and social framework of antebellum Virginia. While the fugitive Confederate "Extra Billy" Smith impotently claimed that he was still governor, federal bayonets

1. John S. Wise, *The Lion's Skin: A Historical Novel and a Novel History* (New York, 1905), 195–96.
2. *Senate Reports*, 46th Cong., 2nd Sess., No. 693, Pt. 2, p. 103.

installed the Unionist war governor Francis H. Pierpont in the executive mansion at Richmond.[3] Pierpont and his tiny legislature revolutionized their regime, which had spent the later war years in Alexandria, by sponsoring an amendment to their constitution enfranchising former Confederates who would fulfill the terms of President Andrew Johnson's amnesty program. While the rules and presuppositions of politics changed, a number of factions began groping to formulate policies and organize constituencies. In the two years before Congress set down its Reconstruction Acts, however, none went far in building a viable political movement.

The immediate beneficiaries of Johnson's Reconstruction program were antebellum moderates—former Whigs who had initially resisted secession but reluctantly embraced it after the war broke out. In an election in October 1865, former Whigs won a large majority in the new legislature and selected as speaker of the house John B. Baldwin, who with his brother-in-law Alexander H. H. Stuart controlled the influential Augusta County Whig clique. The adherents of the "Baldwin legislature" strode into the new era with consummate certitude that they were entitled to be its rulers. They claimed that Confederate defeat vindicated their hesitation in 1861, that former Whigs in the national Republican leadership would welcome their ascendancy, and that their social and business prominence made them the natural spokesmen for Virginia. In the Richmond *Whig* they announced their ambition to modernize the economy and attract northern investment, and more Virginians heeded them than ever before. In speaking for "the people of Virginia," they evidently felt free to ignore freedmen, wartime Unionists, and unreconstructed rebels. The Baldwin legislature was the only statewide political gathering of former Confederates to meet during presidential Reconstruction, except for

3. At that time the governor spelled his name "Peirpoint." By common consent historians identify him as "Pierpont," following the spelling he adopted in 1881.

a small Whig-dominated meeting of antebellum leaders who chose delegates in 1866 to the conservative National Union Convention.

Despite its self-confidence, the Baldwin group did not enjoy a very broad popular mandate. Southern-rights Democrats, not Whigs, had dominated Virginia politics for twenty-five years. Only four times in seventy opportunities had the Whigs elected even a congressman in the 1850s—and two of those victories had occurred in the area which became West Virginia by 1865. Most Whigs had assimilated themselves to the prevailing sectionalist consensus, and such dissenters as former Congressman John Minor Botts had lost influence in the party. The Whigs had managed to win a tiny plurality for the Constitutional Union presidential ticket in 1860 and to give "conditional Unionists" control of the Virginia secession convention, but they owed those victories to fortuitous circumstances as much as to popular moderation. After the clash at Fort Sumter the conditional Unionists had led Virginia into the Confederacy, while the unconditional Unionist Botts accused them of treachery. Combining their credentials as "Union men" and as Confederates, Baldwin's associates swept the Pierpont government's 1865 election.

They achieved that triumph without building a formidable base of mass support. About 1,200,000 people lived in Virginia, and in 1860 almost 120,000 had voted within its postbellum borders. Nevertheless, only 40,000 voted in the 1865 election which chose the Baldwin legislature. Only the most moderate one-third of the antebellum electorate complied with Johnson's amnesty program to participate—far fewer than the intransigents who boycotted the Unionist election or the blacks whose race excluded them from it. Those who did vote chose mostly "Union Whigs," but the circumstances of the election offered them few alternatives.

After its election the Baldwin legislature provided little constructive leadership. It ignored Pierpont's proposals for economic relief and civil rights measures. It passed an appren-

ticeship law which military authorities suspended as an effort
to reinstitute black bondage. It rescinded recognition of West
Virginia and asked President Johnson to free Jefferson Davis
and appoint Robert E. Lee provisional governor in place of
Pierpont. The Baldwin "moderates" desired conciliatory reunion with the North, but showed that they misunderstood
northern opinion as thoroughly as did other former Confederates. Only one legislator voted to ratify the Fourteenth Amendment in 1866. Most of his colleagues complacently assumed
that their regime was secure until almost the day Congress
superseded it. As minority rulers, they did little to extend their
popular support.

While the Whig moderates forfeited their advantage, other
constituencies did little to organize and recruit allies. Traditionalists who believed in the slaveholding Confederacy could
find no place in the Unionist political spectrum. Many refused
to take the amnesty oath and ignored Reconstruction politics,
living in the past or hoping that the Union would again divide
and slavery be restored. The journalist Edward A. Pollard urged
southerners to retain their Confederate identity and wage a "war
of ideas" against the North.[4] His brother H. Rives Pollard, in the
revived Richmond *Examiner*, impartially denounced Republi
cans, northern Democrats, Pierpont, and the Baldwin legislature. He insisted that most southerners still found Union and
emancipation objectionable, and that that majority, not moderate "submissionists," should speak for the South.[5] Some, apparently hoping for that objective, proposed General Jubal Early in
1867 for governor. "If I were made Governor," Early wrote from
Canadian exile, "I would have the whole State in another war
in less than a week."[6] Nothing less, probably, could again rally
traditionalists as a viable political force.

4. Edward A. Pollard, *The Lost Cause: A New Southern History of the War
of the Confederates* (New York, 1867), 749–52.
5. Richmond *Examiner*, January 27, February 8, March 24, 1866.
6. Jubal A. Early to John W. Daniel, February 17, 1867, in John W. Daniel
Papers, Duke University.

To the left of the Baldwin grouping, wartime Unionists constituted a very small constituency. Pierpont's regime had originated in the northwestern counties, which in 1863 became the
state of West Virginia. In the Union-occupied counties of Virginia, Pierpont Unionists during the war had mustered barely
enough adherents to fill essential offices. Only a dozen counties
had sent members to the Alexandria government's legislature.
Very few people voted in its elections and, even so, Confederate sympathizers outvoted Unionists in some of them. Its officials could collect little revenue. The Alexandria circuit court
did not meet for two years, and the Fairfax county sheriff did
not dare step outside his home. Senator Charles Sumner described the Unionist legislature as "little more than the common council of Alexandria." Recognizing its lack of a significant
constituency, Union generals often ignored it, and neither Congress nor the 1864 Republican National Convention seated its
representatives.[7]

In their 1864 state constitution, the embattled Unionists acknowledged their numerical weakness by disfranchising and
disqualifying for offices everyone who had voluntarily supported the Confederacy after the beginning of 1864. When the
Pierpont legislature dropped that proscriptive requirement in
1865, the wartime Unionists scarcely tried to contest elections
with former Confederates. Only three won seats in the Baldwin
legislature. Most organized as Republicans, but instead of elec-
tioneering, they asked Congress to replace Pierpont's government with a territorial one, disfranchising former Confederates
and enfranchising freedmen. Like other factions, Republicans
did little during presidential Reconstruction to organize a statewide constituency. Their activity consisted mostly of local
meetings in Alexandria and Norfolk. Not until 1867 did Repub-

7. Richard G. Lowe, "Republicans, Rebellion, and Reconstruction: The
Republican Party in Virginia, 1856–1870" (Ph.D. dissertation, University of
Virginia, 1968), 137–39, 141–43, 148–49, 152, 158–59, 173–81, 183–84, 189–
90. Lowe quotes Sumner on p. 183.

licans begin to hold meetings in southwest Virginia, the stronghold of mountaineer opposition to the Confederacy.[8]

The Republicans took their time even in organizing the obvious black constituency. Until late 1866, black suffrage remained controversial within Unionist ranks. Blacks themselves
sought civil rights and held a statewide political convention to that
end in 1865, but they did not figure significantly in white Republican councils. While other Unionists neglected the task, the
Fredericksburg clergyman James W. Hunnicutt, a militant
Unionist, pursued it, addressing blacks in public meetings and
in his Richmond newspaper, the *New Nation*. Except for his
following, the spring of 1867 found the Republican party still
small, fragmented, and rudimentary in organization. Federal
Judge John H. Underwood, a Virginia Republican since 1856,
was its most widely recognized leader. Botts, one of the very
few antebellum Whig leaders in its ranks, assumed too conservative a stance for most other Republicans.

In Virginia, presidential Reconstruction was a time of wasted
opportunities for political organizing. No Confederate counterrevolution emerged to give form to traditionalist convictions.
Baldwin's former Whigs depended on their privileged position
and ignored other groups. Republicans, relying on congressional intervention and proscription of former Confederates to
put them in power, did little organizing. None showed any interest when two former southern-rights Democrats—Robert W.
Hughes and Robert F. Walker—launched a newspaper, the
Richmond *Republic*, to announce their conversion to Unionism
and urge former Confederates to accept whatever reunion terms
the federal government might offer.[9] Former Democrats shunned
the two as renegades, Republicans and former Whigs avoided
them as former Democrats, and the experiment died stillborn.

8. *Ibid.*, 200–4, 208–12, 219–20, 228–30, 236, 245.
9. See editorials reprinted in *Papers Showing the Political Course of R. W.
Hughes, the Republican Candidate for Governor, before and since the Fall of
the Southern Confederacy in 1865; prefixed by a Biographical Sketch* (Richmond, 1873), 16–19.

Governor Pierpont found vocal factions uniting only in a common desire to be rid of him. He finally embraced a moderate Republican position, but was as unprepared as any to forge a new majority for the Reconstruction era.

II

By passing the Reconstruction Acts in 1867, Congress provided the framework in which a new southern politics could take shape. Between Congress' action in March and the consequent election in October, six political groupings emerged in Virginia. They fell into three general categories: a "left" which embraced the Reconstruction Acts as deliverance from the Confederate past, a "right" which rejected their progressive objectives, and a "center" which sought a *via media* in the Virginia Whig tradition.

The champions of the Reconstruction program set out to organize a new government that would enfranchise freedmen and proscribe many former Confederates, create free schools and promote economic development along northern lines. Judge Underwood even hoped that it would institute woman suffrage. Underwood and his Alexandria associates had originally counted on the migration of northern Unionists and disfranchisement of former Confederates to give them control of the government. They found instead that the Virginia population had not greatly changed and that the Reconstruction Acts disfranchised only limited categories of Confederate leaders. A convention of former Union officers, under the leadership of Underwood's friend General Henry H. Wells, put forward a temperate platform intended to attract former Confederates; but Confederate veterans were taking advice from their own officers, not Yankee officers.[10]

The greatest accession to Republican ranks came from the rapid organization of black Virginians—and that accession challenged white Unionist domination of the party. Days after Con-

10. *Appleton's Annual Cyclopaedia, 1867*, 761–62.

gress passed the first Reconstruction Act, hundreds of Alexandria blacks tried to vote in a city election. A month later, freedmen in Richmond integrated the city streetcars by direct action.[11] Blacks registered to vote in higher proportions than whites. Their activity elevated Hunnicutt and the black leaders Lewis Lindsay and Thomas Bayne to prominence as spokesmen for a formidable Republicanism more "Radical" than the Alexandria Unionists'. According to a black moderate, Hunnicutt taught blacks "to have no confidence in the white man of the South."[12] He and many of his followers advocated land redistribution. His faction gained the upper hand in April when a state Republican convention drew 160 black and 50 white delegates, almost all from heavily black eastern counties, to assemble at the African Church in Richmond.

The April Republican convention demanded equal civil and political rights for blacks, free public schools, and a progressive tax structure based on the property tax. It also endorsed such Whiggish measures as a more lenient usury law and state aid to transportation lines and immigration. However, the majority gave a Radical cast to the state committee and platform, and appealed to white voters mainly in terms of lower-class solidarity. The platform dedicated the party to "the interests of the laboring classes" of both races, and to "the lifting up of the poor and degraded without humiliation or degradation to any."[13] The Republican party of Virginia appeared to be one of the most radical in the South, and such northern newspapers as the New York *Tribune* expressed moderates' alarm that it would alienate middle-class whites. Hunnicutt's movement attracted some white city laborers, but it did not effectively reach poor rural white people, who remained isolated from political controversy. Social solidarity remained unbroken in the middle-class

11. *Ibid.*, 759; John Preston McConnell, *Negroes and Their Treatment in Virginia from 1865 to 1867* (Pulaski, Va., 1910), 110.
12. Fields Cook, quoted in Lowe, "Republicans," 260n.
13. Text reprinted in James S. Allen, *Reconstruction: The Battle for Democracy, 1865–1877* (New York, 1937), 230–32.

farming counties of the northern piedmont and the Valley—a large part of the state in which neither wing of the Republican party made significant headway.

The solidarity of that region gave Conservatives an important asset; but the political right was not as well prepared as the left for the election of 1867. Conservative former Confederates, controlling the press, almost uniformly opposed black suffrage. They urged white Virginians to vote against calling a constitutional convention, and for Conservative convention delegates. Initially, they hoped to register 45,000 more white voters than black. In fact, whites outregistered blacks by only 14,000, and blacks outvoted whites by 17,000. Since almost a fifth of the whites voted for calling the convention, the Conservatives who had hoped for 150,000 actually won only 62,000 votes in the October election.

To its embarrassment, the right found itself obviously divided. The 15,000 whites who voted the Republican ticket were few in comparison with the multitude of diehard traditionalists who declined to vote at all in a biracial Reconstruction election. Some traditionalists thought no good could come from such elections; others hoped that white solidarity in "inaction" would force Congress to give up its coercive experiments. Unable to deliver the traditionalists' votes, the politically organized Conservatives found themselves at a disadvantage in 1867. In the first round, the right proved less effective than the left in building a majority coalition for the new Virginia.

In the center of the political spectrum, the former "Union Whigs" were as divided as the left and right. Occupying the borderline between the Republican and Conservative parties, they emphasized business development and social stability and deemphasized race and the sectional conflict. Most of them opposed black suffrage, and therefore joined the Conservative campaign. Although they were less rigid on suffrage than other Conservatives, and in some cities directed electoral appeals to blacks, they nevertheless sided with other former Confederates against the Republicans. Differentiating themselves by their emphases, they sometimes expressed hope of negotiating more favorable readmission terms with the northern leadership.

A smaller number of Whig centrists—notably John Minor Botts, Joseph Segar, and Alexander Rives—had been wartime Unionists, and now strove to realize Whig principles as conservative Republicans. Some former Confederates agreed to join them, accepting civil and political equality for blacks and recognizing that "cooperation" with Republicans was the way to obtain readmission for the state. A "cooperation" movement held meetings in at least nine counties, and three hundred leaders of at least local prominence signed its manifesto, but the conservative Republicanism they professed was sure to clash with Hunnicutt's plebeian radicalism. Cooperationists received encouragement when northern Republicans, disliking the April convention's militance, intervened in Virginia Republican politics. The Union Leagues of New York, Philadelphia, and Boston arranged a conference of Virginia Republican leaders to harmonize the factions and secure inclusion of the cooperationists. The participants agreed to hold a convention in August to consider adding planks to the April platform and members to the state committee. Packing the African Church before the meeting began, the Hunnicutt forces took control of the August conclave and allowed Botts and Pierpont to speak only after the official adjournment. Some cooperationists nevertheless became conservative Republicans, while others became moderate Conservatives.

Ostensibly, Virginia in 1867 was sharply polarized. Radicals and traditionalists greatly outnumbered centrists. The centrists nevertheless enjoyed tangible advantages. In their anachronistic attempt to perpetuate a Whig entente, the former Whigs had not yet joined forces with others who would welcome a moderate alternative. Centrists enjoyed disproportionate influence in business and the press, and credibility with northern newspapermen who harbored a naive affection for Virginia "Union

Whigs." They could also count on help from federal military commanders. Commanding General John McAllister Schofield, a conservative Republican, struggled with Virginia judges to secure fair trials for blacks, but he took an elitist view of qualifications to govern. He did not welcome universal suffrage. Disliking loyalty tests, he preferred to appoint "qualified" former Confederates rather than "unqualified" blacks and plebeian whites to offices. Schofield's successors, General George Stoneman and General E. R. S. Canby, continued his policies. The generals particularly respected businessmen, and Stoneman offered to use his dictatorial powers to help the former Confederate General William Mahone combine the three railroad lines that spanned southern Virginia. Freedmen's Bureau officers helped blacks to organize politically, but most of them exerted their influence to support moderate Republicans against Hunnicutt's faction.[14]

Moderate politicians did not entirely fail in electing candidates to the constitutional convention of 1867–1868. General Schofield was pleased to identify 22 delegates as "Republicans" (distinguishing them from 51 "Radicals") and 13 as "Conservatives" (distinguishing them from 19 "unreconstructed").[15] Despite the Hunnicutt influence, the convention's Underwood constitution was not more radical than most Reconstruction state constitutions. Its principal innovations were biracial equal rights, public schools, and a township system of local government. In addition to disfranchising the Confederate leaders barred from offices by the Fourteenth Amendment, it sweepingly banned from officeholding everyone who had voluntarily supported the Confederacy. However, proscription was a policy of Virginia Republicans generally, not a Radical peculiarity. The majority

14. Jack P. Maddex, Jr., *The Virginia Conservatives, 1867–1879: A Study in Reconstruction Politics* (Chapel Hill, 1970), 47–48; Lowe, "Republicans," 281–82, 306–7, 330–31.
15. Manuscript on members of Virginia Constitutional Convention 1868, in John McAllister Schofield Papers, Library of Congress.

of delegates rejected black demands for school integration. To undercut Hunnicutt's influence, most of the Republican convention delegates persuaded Schofield to remove Pierpont and appoint General Wells as provisional governor. The moderates then manipulated the Republican convention in May 1868, to nominate Wells over Hunnicutt for governor and exclude Hunnicutt's followers from the state ticket.[16]

In the Conservative leadership, moderates also asserted themselves. In December 1867, a state convention chose Stuart as its president and adopted the name "Conservative party" in deference to its large ex-Whig element. Hoping for a conservative turn in national politics, it put forth a platform accepting emancipation and looking to national reunification, but adamantly opposing black suffrage. Conservative delegates would play obstructive roles in the constitutional convention, but in their final manifesto they relaxed their rigid stance on the suffrage issue. In May the party nominated a predominantly Whig state ticket led by a former Confederate colonel, Robert E. Withers of Lynchburg.

Centrists were exerting influence in both parties, but they had cause to deplore the choice the 1868 election offered them. The Conservative party was committed to oppose black suffrage, defeat the constitution, and support candidates disqualified under the Fourteenth Amendment. On the other hand, the Republican party combined a plebeian social base with a long-standing commitment to the proscription of former Confederates. It mattered little that Republicans, as a palliative, talked about removing the disabilities of those former Confederates who supported the Republican election campaign. Fortunately for the centrists, General Schofield shared their dislike of the election choices and decided that the state treasury could not afford to finance the impending election. Congress appropriated no funds for the election, so Schofield's military interven-

16. Lowe, "Republicans," 302–6, 312–13.

tion delayed the Reconstruction process in Virginia for a year. That gave centrists time to fashion alternatives more to their taste.

III

The beginning of 1869 marked the turning point of Reconstruction politics in Virginia. The election of General Ulysses S. Grant on the Republican presidential ticket dispelled Conservative hopes that a Democratic backlash would change the federal requirements for readmission. Centrist Conservatives began to confer about accepting biracial suffrage, and centrist Republicans began to reconsider the test-oath requirement for officeholding. Outnumbered in Virginia by intransigent Conservatives and Radical Republicans, both centrist groups initially addressed themselves to federal leaders, who proved receptive to their proposals. Republican congressmen were now concerned with consolidating their reforms instead of extending them, and many of them doubted that a Virginia regime dependent on the test oath would be a stable one. Virginia centrists enjoyed a favorable national press, and General Schofield, as interim secretary of war, was in Washington to second their representations.

Two centrist groups visited Washington to lobby, and other individuals and cliques worked behind the scenes. The moderate Unionist Franklin Stearns led a centrist Republican delegation that opposed the test oath and asked Congress to submit it to the voters for ratification separately from the rest of the constitution. State Treasurer George Rye, an antebellum antislavery dissident, came to Washington with Wells' official Republican delegation, but deserted to Stearns'. Among the Conservatives, Stuart touched off controversy by proposing a new constitution that would combine "universal suffrage and universal amnesty," and he organized a Committee of Nine to lobby in Washington for his plan. The Nine (all former Whigs except one) soon learned that they would have to accept the Underwood constitution, but they urged separate submission of the test oath, disfranchisement, and the local government, church property, and debtor relief provisions. In providing for ratification elections in the three still unreconstructed states— Virginia, Mississippi, and Texas—Congress authorized President Grant to submit any sections he chose for ratification independently of the constitutions themselves.

In Virginia, both parties altered their 1868 tickets and policies. Governor Wells had not won the popularity his original supporters had anticipated. His allies excluded Hunnicutt from party councils, reduced the role of black leaders, and brought the Alexandria *State Journal* to Richmond to replace the *New Nation* as the party paper. Besides angering radicals, they also alienated centrists by insisting on the proscriptive test oath. Wells offended General Stoneman by pardoning many black convicts. He disturbed many Virginians by acting, while governor, as attorney for business interests in their litigation with the state and by attempting to sell the state stock in the Virginia and Tennessee Railroad to the Baltimore-controlled Orange and Alexandria.

The last of those actions particularly incurred General Mahone's wrath. Mahone, a railroad executive, was trying to consolidate three railroads in southern Virginia into a line he would call the Atlantic, Mississippi, and Ohio Railroad, to direct trade from the Tennessee and Ohio valleys to the port of Norfolk. Mahone would need to win control of the Virginia and Tennessee as the crucial link through southwestern Virginia to the transappalachian West. Mahone's principal rival, for the moment, was John W. Garrett's Baltimore and Ohio railroad, with which the Orange and Alexandria was connected. In Mahone's hands, the Virginia and Tennessee would link southwestern Virginia, and points beyond, to Norfolk; in the Orange and Alexandria's hands, it would link the region with Baltimore and augment Garrett's interests, completely thwarting Mahone's ambitions. The state-owned stock would probably decide the eventual control of the Virginia and Tennessee. Mahone, a centrist Conservative, could work with any political group that would cooperate with his railroad plans. He had already found an opponent in Withers and now discovered that Wells was assisting his enemies as well. Mahone rallied Virginians against the intruding Baltimore interests, and Robert H. Walker, an official in the Wells administration, served as his Richmond agent and spy. Many centrists would welcome a third gubernatorial ticket to the field, and Mahone had tangible reasons to sponsor one.

With Hunnicutt out of the way, centrist Republicans tried to replace Wells on the party ticket with James H. Clements, who in 1868 had been the Republican candidate for lieutenant governor. At a tumultuous party convention at Petersburg on March 9, the Wells forces won an insecure ascendancy. They failed, however, in an attempt to nominate W. W. Douglass, who had been a Confederate army surgeon, for lieutenant governor. A discontented black delegate nominated Dr. J. B. Harris, a black West Indian physician. Edgar "Yankee" Allan, a centrist leader who enjoyed personal popularity among blacks, supported Harris to subvert Wells' election prospects, and the convention chose Harris instead of Douglass. Having rendered the Wells ticket unpalatable to wavering whites, centrist Republicans took steps to field a third ticket endorsing black suffrage without proscription. A few of them, meeting with Mahone, nominated a "True Republican" ticket: Gilbert C. Walker, a northern businessman who had moved to Virginia in 1864, for governor; John F. Lewis, a wartime Unionist, for lieutenant governor; and James H. Taylor, a former Confederate, for attorney general. Mahone threw his support to Walker, who was one of his business associates, and Republican centrists rallied to the new ticket.

Conservative centrists also began agitating for their party to withdraw its 1868 ticket and change its policy. Withers' support eroded; his running mates resigned from the ticket and he reluctantly agreed to follow suit. On April 28, against spirited traditionalist opposition, a Conservative state convention voted to withdraw the party ticket and oppose only those clauses of the constitution which President Grant would submit for a separate vote. The dismay of traditionalists increased two weeks later, when Grant decided to submit only the test oath and disfranchisement clauses separately. Nevertheless, the Walker ticket became the rallying point of an imposing center-right coalition. Whiggish Republicans supported it, as did Hunnicutt and a few other disenchanted Radicals. Conservatives united in voting for it, although the more extreme Conservatives deplored the withdrawal of Withers. Conservatives eagerly solicited black support for Walker and stood aside for True Republican congressional candidates. Wells found himself on the defensive. Stoneman tried to remove him in March, and Allan accused him of political tampering with the mails. In May Wells belatedly declared himself opposed to the proscriptive clauses of the constitution, thus confirming the centrist trend.

More than 220,000 Virginians voted on July 6. They ratified the constitution overwhelmingly and defeated the proscriptive clauses by about 40,000 votes. Walker defeated Wells by 18,000, winning 54 percent of the votes. Conservatives and True Republicans elected 30 members of the state senate and 138 of the house; Republicans, 13 of the senate and 42 of the house. The new legislature included 27 black members, 3 of whom were adherents of the Walker coalition. The coalition elected 5 congressmen; the regular Republicans, 3. News of the "new departure" in Virginia attracted national attention and inspired predictions of a dawning era of national consensus.[17]

The centrist advocates of "universal suffrage and universal amnesty" had prevailed, but not by their numbers. Having the election redesigned according to their specifications, they had won it. The course of events led many partisans to moderate their opinions; but even so, it appears that most of Wells' supporters desired the test oath, most of Walker's would have preferred Withers and the 1868 Conservative policy, and some traditionalists still refused to vote. The unrepresentative center—promising moderation on Reconstruction issues and a stable climate for economic development—had won the inside

17. A fuller account of the events of 1869 appears in Maddex, *Virginia Conservatives*, 67–85.

track and kept it in the following years. The centrist stance, after its precarious triumph in 1869, became the model for political rhetoric in both parties in the subsequent years.

The victory of the Conservative party over the Republican was as problematical as the victory of moderate consensus over partisan polarization. The Conservatives exploited their control of most of the land, businesses, and newspapers. The Confederate experience had given their constituency a strong sense of camaraderie, and they played on racial fears and hostilities to unite the great majority of white voters for "the white man's ticket." The Conservatives' timely change of policy may have decided the 1869 election. Anticipating the Republicans in the drive to centrist policies, they were able to attract more centrist voters who might have gone for Wells under other circumstances. As events actually occurred, the Republicans won 46 percent of the voters, including more whites than Conservatives liked to admit. In 1870, Republicans outvoted Conservatives in predominantly white Richmond. James A. Seddon, who had been Confederate secretary of war, interpreted the election returns as showing that many "'mean [poor] whites' . . . will affiliate even with negroes from Lust of office[,] schools and endeavors towards probity & property."[18] With those voters, Hunnicutt's policy of class solidarity prevailed over the racial appeal for white solidarity. In Virginia, however, that happened principally in cities. The Republican party came close to achieving an electoral majority, but it did not achieve the goal.

Could the Republicans, in any circumstances, have become the majority in Virginia as they did in other southern states? The key to the answer lay in western Virginia. In other states of the Upper South, Republicans won control of the overwhelmingly white mountain counties, but in Virginia those counties became Conservative strongholds. If Virginia mountaineers had voted in 1869 as those in North Carolina and Tennessee did, the Republicans would have carried the Old Dominion. Ethnically, western Virginia was similar to Republican areas in

18. James A. Seddon to R. M. T. Hunter, June 9, 1870, in Hunter-Garnett Papers, University of Virginia.

the Appalachians, and it did not seem more sensitive to racist appeals. However, most of it did not share the Appalachian region's economic deprivation or cultural isolation. The Shenandoah Valley was a prosperous region of middle-class farms in which nonslaveholders had rarely quarreled with slaveholders. Southwest Virginia was truly an Appalachian area, however. It had displayed much Unionist resistance to the Confederacy.[19] It elected Republicans as well as Conservatives to the 1867–1868 constitutional convention, and it was later to become a center of Republican insurgency. General Mahone's railroad interests probably advanced Conservatism in southwest Virginia in the 1870s, but it is hard to suppress a suspicion that Repubicans also neglected an organizing opportunity there. Republican conventions, committees, propagandists, and campaign managers oriented toward the biracial eastern part of the state, and often behaved as though it were the entire state. Neither Underwood nor Hunnicutt nor Botts propounded a strategy for western Virginia. Their experience had not prompted them to do so, and the really promising part of western Virginia was separated from them by a wide expanse of hostile territory.

Virginia Republicans were characteristically pessimistic about their ability to win over a majority of Virginians. Wartime experience prompted the Unionists to seek security by disfranchising former Confederates and disqualifying them from office, rather than by trying to convert a minority of them to the progressive cause. Until 1869, most Republican leaders expected that proscriptive provisions would define political participation in the state during the coming years. Perhaps they neglected some possible sources of support. J. W. D. Bland, a black Republican critic of proscription, felt that the party leadership suffered from "the weakest *minds* and *nerves* the world have ever seen in party leaders."[20] Demographically, the Republican party's problems were much greater in Texas than in Virginia, and Texas

---

19. Henry T. Shanks, "Disloyalty to the Confederacy in Southwestern Virginia, 1861–1865," *North Carolina Historical Review*, XXI (April 1944), 118–35.

20. Quoted in Lowe, "Republicans," 295n.

Republicans initially concentrated on lobbying in Congress to control the conditions of their state election for 1869. When their effort failed, they nevertheless reorganized and directed new appeals to Texas voters and won a surprise victory over a center-right coalition similar to the Walker coalition in Virginia. Virginia Republicans built a powerful base of support in the face of great difficulties, but the example of Texas and the conundrum of southwest Virginia raise the possibility that a Republican electoral majority might have been attainable in Virginia as in the other "reconstructed" states.

IV

During Reconstruction the Republicans who governed most of the southern states warned that the Conservative-Democratic opposition, if it came to power, would overturn the postbellum social changes and aggravate the oppression of blacks and poor whites. In response, Conservatives assured blacks that they would recognize their rights, traditionalists that they would sweep away Republican innovations, and businessmen and farmers that they would advance their interests and bring prosperity to the South. They particularly promised to fulfill state financial obligations and provide necessary state services without the alleged extravagance, mismanagement, and heavy taxation of Republican rule. In Virginia, where Conservatives were in power, they had the opportunity to show how they would address contemporary southern problems, but their record did not validate the glowing predictions of party orators. The centrist hegemony survived, with its promise of orderly development, but the order which emerged remained very regressive by northern standards.

Some hoped in 1869 to create a centrist "Walker party," but the two-party alignment endured and the True Republican grouping broke up. Many True Republicans, such as Governor Walker, became Conservatives; others, such as Lieutenant Governor Lewis (who had become a United States senator) became regular Republicans. The centrist influence, no longer characterizing a distinctive Whig circle, predominated in both parties. All politicians took for granted the formula of universal suffrage and universal amnesty. The Conservatives increased their control, electing as governors the Confederate military heroes James Lawson Kemper in 1873 and F. W. M. Holliday in 1877, and giving their centrist posture a pronounced rightward slant. Nevertheless, many antebellum statesmen never found places in the new leadership. Former Governor Henry A. Wise denounced the Conservative party for "out-carpetbagging the Carpetbaggers & out-scallawagging the Scallawaggers."[21] Many other traditionalists shared Wise's chagrin that the Conservative leadership was embracing the new order instead of restoring the old.

Under Conservative rule the Underwood constitution continued to guide the state government, although Governor Kemper shared the traditionalists' hostility to the Republican document. The Conservatives removed its limit on interest rates in 1872. In 1874 they revised its system of local government to reduce the role of grass-roots democracy. In 1876, additional amendments reduced the number of legislators and frequency of sessions, and disfranchised persons who had been convicted of petty larceny or had not paid the poll tax for the election year. The poll tax disqualification operated only six years before being repealed, and with no additional amendment the constitution remained in force until 1902. Conservatives accepted many of its innovations which they had decried in 1868. Traditionalists, particularly the Presbyterian theologian Robert L. Dabney, continued to oppose public education. The great majority of Virginians nevertheless embraced that Reconstruction reform, and Conservatives and Republicans cooperated to construct a school system that won national commendation. State superintendent William Henry Ruffner, an antebellum skeptic about slavery, emphasized the centrist argument that universal education would stabilize society and promote economic growth.

The Conservative leaders of "the white man's party" championed white supremacy but observed the niceties of biracial Reconstruction politics. They carried out the Reconstruction amendments (narrowly interpreted) but kept the sources of power in white hands. The state provided segregated schools, land-grant colleges, and mental institutions for both races, and recruited both into segregated militia units. It recognized equal judicial rights, but took no action to guarantee them. Blacks therefore suffered in courts in which they very rarely served on juries and in a penal system that hired convicts out to private companies and occasionally still used the whipping post. Blacks continued to vote and (in predominantly black districts) to hold office without endangering statewide Conservative rule. Kemper refused to reschedule a local election to reduce black turnout, and in 1874 he vetoed a bill to transfer to an appointed board many of the powers of the elected (Republican) city council of Petersburg. Nevertheless, he approved a subtler partisan modification of the Petersburg charter, and the 1876 constitutional amendments reduced the black vote without eliminating it.

Content to defend white predominance and limited government within the Reconstruction order, Conservative leaders accepted the national political patterns which traditionalists despised. "The strict construction that we thought right & proper 20 or 30 years ago," one reminded a friend, "is not accepted now by one person in ten in America, & is not going to be acted upon by any party or govt. in your day or mine."[22] Antebellum Virginia had rejected federal aid, but the new leaders requested federal funds to educate freedmen, complete the James River and Kanawha Canal, and even assume the debts of the states. The Conservative congressmen from Virginia were among the small minority who in 1875 voted not to end federal subsidies to corporations.[23]

22. L. Q. Washington to R. M. T. Hunter, June 8, 1873, in Hunter-Garnett Papers.
23. Roll call vote in Edward McPherson (ed.), *A Hand-book of Politics for 1876; Being a Record of Important Political Action, National and State, from July 15, 1874, to July 15, 1876* (Washington, 1876), 142–43.

Although working with the national Democratic party, the Conservative state leaders kept their separate party name and claimed independence of national partisanship. They desired a national centrist party that would deemphasize Reconstruction issues and therefore welcomed Horace Greeley's Liberal Republican presidential candidacy in 1872. In state campaigns they attacked Virginia Republicans but denied being hostile to the Grant administration or to propertied northern Republicans. Some Conservatives wished to ally with the administration. In 1874 Kemper hinted that the Conservatives might support Grant for a third term if Grant would use his influence to deter the pending Sumner civil rights bill. In the late 1870s Virginia Conservatives rejoiced that the centrist tendency was prevailing in both national parties.

The pattern of class rule in Conservative Virginia differed from that in Republican states in degree rather than in nature. Business lobbies were as active in Virginia as anywhere else, and northern companies found many legislators of both parties willing to assist their projects politically. "Virginia interests" such as Mahone's railroad and the James River Canal also commanded assistance, and landowners probably enjoyed more governmental sympathy than in Republican states in the South. However, the state could do little to help them. Embracing the doctrine of laissez-faire, the state government was reducing its role in the economy. Many landowners and promoters urged the state to promote immigration, but it did almost nothing in response. The state sold its railroad stock in 1871 and its stock in the canal in 1880 at a loss of about twenty million dollars on its investments. After state ownership ended, regulation also atrophied. Some railroads even stopped filing legally required annual reports. The system of state tobacco inspection came effectively under the control of warehouse proprietors, and growers complained that biased grading enriched the warehouses at their expense. Governor Kemper tried to make the inspection impartial, but in 1877 the legislature abolished it altogether. Taxation hindered business interests no more than regulation did. Taxes on public-service corporations did not aggregate

$50,000 in an average year, and the ones on banks and insurance companies yielded about the same amount.

The state government therefore played mainly a negative role in the economic struggle between General Mahone's railroad—the Atlantic, Mississippi, and Ohio—and its northern rivals, particularly Thomas A. Scott's Pennsylvania Central Railroad. Posing as the champion of "Virginia interests" against foreign "bucktails," Mahone accomplished much, but his antagonists checked him with superior resources. Mahone obtained a favorable state charter in 1870 and consolidated his rail lines, but Scott blocked his western ambitions by acquiring the connecting lines in Kentucky and Tennessee. Mahone acquired the state stock in his roads cheaply in 1870, but in 1871 the Pennsylvania Central acquired control of competing Virginia lines by buying state stock. Contributing heavily to election campaigns, Mahone won a sympathetic ear in Richmond. In 1875, he sneaked through the legislature a measure which rewrote the state railroad laws to the disadvantage of his adversaries, but state regulation was becoming ineffective, and it had little impact. The depression that followed 1873 set back Scott's southern railroad ambitions, but it destroyed Mahone's entirely. He lost control of his line in 1876, and it came under northern ownership in 1881. Dependent on the depressed economy of rural Virginia, Mahone could not match the "bucktails'" advantage, and his friends in the Conservative leadership could not change that.

Republican state governments in the South sometimes proved ineffective in their concern for the propertyless, but the Conservative regime in Virginia showed practically no concern in the first place. The first Reconstruction legislature ended the stay on debt collection that had continued since 1865, and the courts effectively nullified the Underwood constitution's exemption of homesteads from seizure for debt. Constitutional amendments weakened the township system, which gave poor blacks a voice in local government. Capitation taxes reached many of the poor, but hardly any state services except schools did. The poor suffered disproportionately from the harsh penal system, and the state borrowed federal troops to evict freedmen who were occupying former Freedmen's Bureau lands. The federal commissioner of labor estimated in 1875 that farm laborers were more poorly paid in Virginia than in any other state.

Southern conservatives, accusing Republicans of extravagance and corruption, often claimed to be uniquely qualified to govern cheaply and honestly. In the brief Wells administration, Virginia Republicans had shown some tendencies to irregularity but not to extravagance. Virginia accrued no Reconstruction debt, and the Republican constitutional convention ended state investment in transportation works and forbade the incurring of additional state indebtedness. In Virginia, it was the first Conservative administration that gave rise to charges of extravagance and corruption. Critics accused Governor Walker of spending ostentatiously and supporting a "corps of flunkies" at state expense. The first Conservative legislature contrived to collect both per diem pay and mileage for the recesses between its initial sessions to "reconstruct" the state. Insinuations of bribery touched both parties, but some Conservatives admitted that their associates appeared even more venal than the carpetbaggers had been.[24]

Few objected when the legislature, in 1871, funded two-thirds of the state debt in 6 percent bonds with tax-receivable coupons. Since the debt was an "honest" antebellum debt, not a Republican one, some even felt dishonored by the legislature's expecting West Virginia to assume the remaining third of the obligation. Conservatives expected that their regime would usher in economic growth and sound finance, rendering payment of the debt easy. Actually, the property tax yielded half as much and ordinary government expenses ran to twice as much as Governor Walker initially estimated. After the panic of 1873, while other southern conservatives were blaming carpetbag rule for fiscal difficulties, the Conservatives in Virginia regularly ran deficits of several hundred thousand dollars a year. Superintendent Ruffner calculated that the administration annually with-

24. William Mahone to Thomas S. Flournoy (copy), August 15, 1869, in William Mahone Letter Books, Duke University. Cf. quotations in Maddex, *Virginia Conservatives*, 92–94, 291–92.

held from the school system about $100,000 legally earmarked for schools. The state paid only two-thirds of the interest it had pledged in the Funding Act—and "paid" most of that negatively by receiving coupons for taxes. Little actual money came into the treasury. Conservative Virginia's bonds did not compare favorably with Republican Louisiana's on the securities markets.[25] Virginians came to regret the Funding Act, and a "readjuster" faction sought to scale down the debt, arguing that the postbellum economy could not bear the antebellum obligation. The opposing "funder" faction regarded the agitation as a blot on the fiscal integrity of the state. Conservatives, and Republicans, differed among themselves about the meaning of sound finance.

Conservative officials tried unsuccessfully to balance state budgets. Proposals to increase revenue touched off vehement protests. Virginia, like Republican states, had already greatly increased the antebellum property tax—from .3 percent to .5 percent. Landed property provided 60.9 percent of the revenue in 1870, in contrast to 48.0 percent in 1860. Landowners contrived to evade current rates by securing decreases of assessed valuations and would stand for no increase. The legislature experimented with changes in business taxes, but large businesses enjoyed even more political influence and avenues for evasion than landowners. The capitation tax was already a dollar a year, and even the poor on whom it fell found ways to evade it. In 1875 an eighth of the liable whites and a fourth of the liable blacks did not pay it. Unable to increase revenue substantially, state leaders enunciated the common fallacy of southern conservatives: that the large increase of state spending since 1860 represented extravagance. Officials and legislators slashed expenditures, including their own compensation. State institutions suffered severely, and by 1878–1879 half the schools were closing for lack of funds. Nevertheless, in 1877–1878 the deficit came to $855,000—higher than ever.

25. Chart in George H. Thompson, *Arkansas and Reconstruction: The Influence of Geography, Economics, and Personality* (Port Washington, N. Y.,

The Virginia Conservatives' performance did not confirm their claim of managerial competence. State agencies placed too little value on specialized talents and formalized procedures. An independent auditor found the treasury's procedures slipshod, especially in regard to the state debt, but neither the officials nor the legislature instituted improvements. The system extended an invitation to the dishonest. Kemper discovered in 1874 that Joseph Mayo, Jr., the state treasurer, and William D. Coleman, the secretary of the Commissioners for the Sinking Fund, had embezzled large amounts in state assets. Both culprits were among the ten members of the Conservative party's central committee. Coleman went to prison and Mayo to a mental institution, but the treasury's inefficiency continued and scandals recurred from time to time.

The Conservative leadership neither restored the old order which many of its adherents fondly remembered, nor inaugurated the prosperous and progressive new order for which many fondly hoped, but it helped to define the limited "New South" which was emerging. It provided no miraculous solutions to the dilemmas that were confronting other southern state governments and no deliverance from the pervasive realities of the region and the era. The same forces came into play as in other states, but in different proportions and combinations. The Conservative leadership managed to mute the political extremes, silence the inarticulate, and placate rural landowners somewhat more than did their Republican counterparts farther south. Their rule, enjoying the support of propertied former Confederates, appeared more stable than most southern Republican regimes—but that appearance reflected only another difference of degree. The Conservative predominance in Virginia encountered important political challenges and outlived its Republican counterparts by only a few years.[26]

1976), 246.

26. For more extended discussion of the topics treated in section IV see Maddex, *Virginia Conservatives*, 86–248.

V

Southern politics during Reconstruction were exceptional in American political history in that neither party fully recognized the other as a legitimate, permanent force. In partisan conflicts the embattled Republicans regarded themselves as the representatives of loyalty and freedom, and the Conservatives as "the rebels" who derived their identity from the Confederacy. Republicans felt that to become fully reconstructed, the former Confederates must cease to constitute a party organized against Republican reform. Similarly, the Conservatives regarded their party as representing the true "people of Virginia" in their established social structure. They depicted the Republican party as an abnormal importation, led by aliens and dependent on alien influence. Conservatives might recognize black political activity as beneficial under the auspices of the white power structure, but never as a countervailing force opposing that structure. Although the parties routinely shared power in the parliamentary system, their party philosophies pointed to a one-party system as a desideratum.

In Virginia the most effective Conservative strategy was to exploit and reinforce the social solidarity of white former Confederates. The Petersburg *Index* insisted that "The normal condition [attitude] of every Virginian towards every Radical is one of antipathy."[27] Conservatives enforced "the color line" by ostracizing and intimidating white men who voted the Republican ticket. Putting the Republicans on the defensive after 1869, they aspired to a one-party monopoly. In the 1873 election they again called for what Kemper called a "union of all Virginians" against intruders.[28] "[S]uccess is not all we want," a Conservative businessman wrote. "We want to roll up such a big majority in Nov. that the Radicals will never dare to make another nomination

27. Petersburg *Index and Appeal*, June 20, 1877.
28. Quoted in Robert R. Jones, "Conservative Virginian: The Post-War Career of Governor James Lawson Kemper" (Ph.D. dissertation, University of Virginia, 1964), 191.

in Va."[29] By the middle of the decade, Conservatives felt that they were finally reducing the opposition to the impotence it deserved.

The Conservative one-party ideal discouraged the articulation of controversial issues in party councils. In election campaigns the party usually reduced its program to "Virginians Ruling Virginia" in opposition to "the scalawags and carpetbaggers." Many Conservative leaders did not think that the party as a whole should adopt positions on state issues. The party was theoretically all-inclusive—"designed," the Richmond *Whig* editorialized, "to be commensurate with the limits of the Commonwealth—to cover every inch of ground, and to embrace every citizen within its borders."[30] Introducing issues appeared to threaten the party's inclusiveness. Individual candidates and local meetings spoke out on issues, but state Conservative conventions rarely did so. An observer concluded that the Conservatives "seem to have no policy at all."[31] A Conservative might be a Negrophobe or a racial moderate, a funder or a readjuster, a traditionalist or a "New South" enthusiast, a self-conscious aristocrat or a precursor of Populism.

Having lost the 1869 election, the Republican leadership began the era of civil government divided. The more implacable wing held the majority at a state party convention in November 1869, but it offered little that was positive. Having previously rejected plebeian insurgency, it now relied only on proscription and federal power. The convention deplored the recent election as "a Confederate triumph, which . . . was achieved by artifice, intimidation, and fraud." It blamed defeat primarily on President Grant's decision to submit the proscriptive clauses for separate ratification. The convention asked Congress either to set aside the election and hold a new one to ratify the unexpurgated constitution, or to exclude from office those elected

29. Quoted in *ibid.*, 187.
30. Richmond *Daily Whig*, July 9, 1872.
31. I. D. Osborne to William Cabell Rives, Jr., November 29, 1873, in William Cabell Rives Papers, Library of Congress.

candidates who could not take the oath of wartime loyalty and seat their Republican opponents. The centrist minority of the convention walked out and held a meeting to express its conciliatory policy. It asked Congress to accept the election results, but to add stipulations to the act of readmission to keep the Conservatives from abusing their power.[32]

Congress, in readmitting Virginia, followed the centrist recommendations, and the centrist element steadily gained influence in the Virginia Republican party. The organizer of the convention walkout, Robert W. Hughes, was a very recent convert to Republicanism, but he quickly became its foremost Virginia leader. Hughes had been a southern-rights Democrat and a writer for the extremist Richmond *Examiner* until 1865. Then he had become a progressive centrist, trying without reference to party to reconcile former Confederates to the new order. In 1868 he had served as a delegate to the Democratic National Convention, supporting Chief Justice Salmon P. Chase for the presidential nomination. He had joined the Republican party only in May 1869, after Wells disavowed the proscriptive clauses of the constitution. Writing in the Richmond *State Journal*, Hughes gained control of its policy and won the confidence of centrist Republicans in Virginia and of federal leaders.[33]

Hughes' associates cooperated with True Republicans and centrist Conservatives, and some pondered the possibility of a united organization. The two-party alignment nevertheless persisted, and returning True Republicans strengthened the centrist hand in the Republican leadership. The *State Journal* endorsed many measures of the Walker administration. When some Conservative legislators balked at reelecting the True Republican George Rye as state treasurer, Hughes personally lectured every Republican legislator to assure Rye's election.[34] On

32. *Appleton's Annual Cyclopaedia, 1869*, 714–15.

33. *Papers Showing the Political Course of R. W. Hughes*, 3–32; Robert F. Walker to William Mahone, December 4, 1869, Mahone Papers.

34. Robert F. Walker to William Mahone, February 12, 1870, Mahone Papers.

that issue and on others, most of the minority caucus followed his direction. Early in 1870 he called in the *State Journal* for a new state Republican convention to reorganize the party under leaders who had not been prominent in military Reconstruction. The Republican convention of September 1870 did reorganize the state committee. Former Governor Wells became state chairman, centrists greatly increased their influence, and the western counties won significant representation. In its platform the convention identified Republicanism with the Grant administration and the Underwood constitution, and spoke out for the public school system, equitable taxation, and economic development. It pointed out that the Conservative party's rightward leaning distorted its centrist professions. The way to secure the full benefits of the Underwood constitution, the convention argued, was to elect Republicans. Hoping to attract centrist white voters, it spoke for nominating candidates "in the spirit of a conciliatory policy" and with "regard to the public service," and black Republicans soon observed that the implementation of that policy gave them few nominations.[35]

In the early 1870s Virginia Republicans still hoped to win over enough white voters to carry the state, but they no longer looked mainly to propertyless plebeians. Pursuing the centrist strategy, they continued to appeal to moderate Whigs and proponents of capitalist development. In their 1871 state platform they praised national Republican economic policies and identified the Conservatives with the Tammany Hall Democrats of the North. They blamed the economic sluggishness of Virginia on the Conservatives' financial mismanagement and their partisan, class, and racial favoritism. To the Whig orientation Hughes added an appeal to financially pressed landowners. The 1871 Republican convention aligned itself with the popular reaction against the Funding Act, even though most Republican legislators had voted for the measure. The convention insisted that under Conservative rule "Taxation has been increased almost

35. Text in *Appleton's Annual Cyclopaedia, 1870,* 745–46.

beyond the limits of human endurance." Hughes worked for federal and state relief for debtors, and he expressed concern for the insecure landowners of the tidewater and of his own southwestern part of the state.[36] He combined rural and economic development appeals by championing the James River Canal and Mahone's Atlantic, Mississippi, and Ohio Railroad.

Erosion of Republican numbers in the legislature suggested that most of the voters Hughes sought to conciliate preferred to pursue their objectives by supporting the most acceptable of the available Conservative candidates. Hughes was apparently correct, however, in concluding that centrist Virginians responded favorably to the Grant administration. In the 1872 national election Republicans scored their greatest victory in Virginia since 1867. Traditionalists who supported Conservative state tickets declined to vote for the antislavery crusader Horace Greeley for president, and a few prominent Virginians declared themselves "Grant Conservatives." The Republicans not only carried Virginia for Grant, but elected five of the nine Virginia members of the House of Representatives (including one whom the House seated in a contested election). The Republican success challenged Conservative pretensions to one-party control. Looking ahead to 1873, Withers admitted that "the prospects for beating even an avowed Radical are not as bright as they might be."[37] To keep control of the state would not be easy.

In the 1873 campaign both parties held more securely than ever to the centrist standard. The Republican convention endorsed the Grant administration, proposed federal completion of the James River and Kanawha Canal and repeal of the federal tobacco tax, and adopted a pronouncement on the state debt and finances carefully worded to please all factions. It promised to advance economic development and protect civil rights, as the Conservatives had not, and promised tax relief to the hard-

36. Text in *ibid.*, *1871*, 766.
37. Robert E. Withers to James Lawson Kemper, December 7, 1872, in James Lawson Kemper Papers, University of Virginia.

pressed tidewater region. The Conservative convention disclaimed any "captious hostility" to the Grant administration, agreed with the Republicans on the Canal and the tobacco tax, and ignored the state debt issue. It boasted that Conservatives had governed much better in Virginia than Republicans had in other southern states, promised to improve public education, spoke vaguely about impartial justice to both races, and promised tax relief to the tidewater.[38] In the absence of overt radicalism and traditionalism, the two platforms showed a centrist family resemblance. Taking the Republican challenge seriously, the Conservatives threw all their resources into the campaign, and some of their leaders again used racist demagogy to keep white voters in the party fold. Hughes, the Republican nominee, won only 43.6 percent of the votes against Kemper for governor. His leadership had kept the Republican party competitive, but had not enlarged its base of support.

After Hughes became a federal judge in 1874, Republican fortunes continued to decline, but the party leadership retained its centrist stance. "The *State Journal* talks very much like a Conservative paper in these days," the Richmond *Enquirer* remarked in 1875.[39] Black Republicans, who had enjoyed a large share of the leadership in Hunnicutt's day, found moderate white men controlling the party machinery and federal patronage. In 1875, a statewide convention of blacks condemned both the white Republican usurpation of patronage and the proposed Conservative constitutional amendments to restrict suffrage.[40] Similar leaders and policies held sway in both parties. Republicans in the legislature capitalized on the majority party's mistakes and unpopular measures, but did not present clearly differentiated alternative policies. "The Radical members," the Conservative Staunton *Vindicator* commented, "are ever boasting of what they would do for the State if they had the power, being in a bomb-proof minority as far as responsibility is con-

38. Platforms in *Appleton's Annual Cyclopaedia, 1873*, 766–67.
39. Richmond *Enquirer,* September 4, 1875.
40. *Appleton's Annual Cyclopaedia, 1875*, 751–52.

cerned."[41] The state debt issue divided the Republican leaders as well as the Conservatives, so both straddled the question. Politicians carried on debate from the centrist premises they shared, and on many issues they did not divide along party lines.

VI

By the late 1870s the Conservative party appeared to have achieved its objective of one-party control. In 1876 it carried Virginia for the Democratic national ticket by 59.1 percent. It also secured ratification of the constitutional amendments that it hoped would reduce voting by blacks. In 1877 the Republican party ran no state ticket against Conservative gubernatorial candidate F. W. M. Holliday. Considering the intensity of the state debt controversy, Hughes advised that course "so that there may be no jar in our State policy."[42] Ostensibly, the Conservatives had cause to rejoice. Actually, the year that marked "the end of Reconstruction" found their party in serious difficulty.

Monoply status proved a mixed blessing for the Conservative party, which in elections strove to function as a monolithic, disciplined organization of white voters. As the Republican menace became more remote, some questioned the need for continuing white unanimity at the polls. Conservatives who lost convention nominations or opposed nominees' policies increasingly ran for office as independents. Most of the rebellious independents were rural critics of the state financial structure, and where Republicanism was weak, they could usually count on Republican support. Conservative leaders, alert to the menace to party discipline, equated scratching the party ticket to desertion in battle. In 1873 the Conservative state convention warned that voting for an independent was as bad as supporting a Republican. Nevertheless, the Conservative caucuses in the legislature admitted successful independent candidates to their membership.

41. Staunton *Vindicator*, March 9, 1877.
42. Robert W. Hughes to F. W. M. Holliday, August 10, 1877, in F. W. M. Holliday Papers, Duke University.

By 1877 the issues of the state debt and finances elevated the independent phenomenon to more than an occasional curiosity. Virginia, like other southern states, encountered difficulties in state finance during the depressed years after 1873. In many southern states, conservatives used those difficulties to embarrass the incumbent Republican administrations, defeat them at the polls, and repudiate Reconstruction state debts to alleviate the fiscal problem. In Virginia, the embarrassed incumbents were Conservatives, and the movement for change and repudiation therefore emerged under a different party label.

The Funding Act had long been unpopular. Most political leaders considered it regrettable but inescapable; some rural insurgents denied its validity altogether. Bondholders would not accept a refunding program less advantageous to them, and although economy measures slashed public services they never enabled the state to pay the stipulated interest. In 1877 General Mahone, seeking the Conservative nomination for governor, allied his large following with the readjuster cause. He distinguished himself from the other Conservative candidates by insisting on school support as an obligation prior to debt service, and hinting at "forcible" readjustment—scaling down—of the state debt. Mahone lost the nomination, but his campaign touched off a fiery debate within the Conservative party about the debt. Voters marveled as the unopposed Conservative candidates for lieutenant governor and attorney general stumped the state, each apparently campaigning against the other's fiscal program.

In 1878 and 1879 Governor Holliday confronted a controversy that was manifestly splitting his party. Mahone and the readjusters moved steadily toward organizing as a separate party, and both factions unashamedly called on sympathetic Republicans for help. The legislature passed the "Barbour Bill" to give school finance priority over debt service, but Holliday vetoed it with comments belittling public schools. Appreciating the need to settle the question quickly, the funder leadership adopted a refunding proposal which former secretary of the treasury Hugh McCulloch presented in behalf of a consortium of bondholders' representatives. Funders claimed the plan would render the fiscal problem manageable, but readjusters objected that it irrevocably surrendered future revenue to the bondholders and financiers. The conflict dissolved the supposedly impregnable Reconstruction division between the parties (and their constituencies). Republican blacks and Conservative farmers deserted more cautious party leaders, and in the 1879 election they gave the new Readjuster party a majority in the legislature.[43]

Once again, Virginia was out of step. While conservative Democrats elsewhere were securing their hammerlock on "the solid South," Virginia for awhile became a two-party state. At last, the white voters of the Valley and the southwest made common cause with the black voters of the southeast to scale down a state debt that had no connection with Reconstruction. Since 1874 the Conservatives had carried all but one of the nine congressional districts in Virginia, but in 1880 Republicans and Readjusters each elected two congressmen. In 1881 the two organizations combined when Mahone, elected to the United States Senate, joined the Republican caucus. The united party elected William E. Cameron, the former Conservative mayor of Petersburg, as governor, and went on to enact its debt settlement. In 1882 it elected five of the ten Virginia members of the House of Representatives (not counting one whom the Democratic majority unseated in a contested election).

Union with the Readjusters revived the reformism that had been waning in the Republican party, and joining with the Republicans enabled many Readjusters to discard prejudices they had held as Conservatives. The Readjuster-Republican coalition instituted a host of permanent reforms before the reorganized Democrats, attracting disaffected Readjusters, recovered control in 1883. In addition to readjusting the debt, the coalition rationalized state administration and finance, increased

43. On the events that brought about party realignment in 1877–79, see Maddex, *Virginia Conservatives*, 248–75, and the works on the Readjuster movement suggested by the bibliographical essay for this essay.

support of schools and state institutions, abolished the whipping post and the poll-tax suffrage requirement, and improved fertilizer quality by regulation. It also created a black state college, appointed many blacks to low-level offices, and staffed black schools with black teachers at equal pay. The coalition permanently changed the voting habits of many whites, especially in southwest Virginia. In Wythe County, the Republican share of the presidential votes increased from 29.7 percent in 1872 to 52.6 percent in 1888; in Tazewell County, it increased from 22.9 percent to 62.4 percent. Even in the Valley county of Rockingham, the Republican percentage rose from 34.6 in 1872 to 51.3 in 1888. The Republican upsurge in western Virginia made its mark on statewide election returns. In the 1880 presidential election, the separate Republican and Readjuster tickets won 54.3 percent of the votes in Virginia. In 1884 the Republicans polled 48.9 percent, and in 1888 they polled 49.5 percent against the Democrats' 50.0 percent.[44] In its Readjuster incarnation Virginia Republicanism became an imposing force.

The Readjuster upheaval called into question the stability of the party alignment of the 1870s. Centrist leaders such as Walker, Kemper, and Hughes dominated Virginia politics in that decade because of the turn events had taken in the late 1860s. If insurgent Radicals like Hunnicutt had reached more poor whites with their message, or if traditionalists like Jubal Early had received an opportunity to register their numbers for some restorationist program, they might have drastically changed the image Virginia presented in the 1870s. On the other hand, more flexible centrist Conservatives might have prolonged their dominance at the bondholders' expense by embracing a modified readjustment program.

The Readjuster movement attracted to progressive Republicanism a constituency which had shown little taste for it during Reconstruction. In several southern states the relation between "Negro Republicans" and "mountain Republicans" was com-

44. Walter Dean Burnham, *Presidential Ballots, 1836–1892* (Baltimore, 1955), 817, 837, 839.

plex, but in Virginia the "mountain Republicans" did not make their entry until the end of the 1870s, as part of a farmers' revolt. That fact suggests the possibility that economic grievances may have contributed more than geography or Unionism did to mountain Republicanism in the South. The plebeian black quest for equality and land reached its crest in Virginia a decade before the mountain white attack on the antebellum debt and the Conservative fiscal policies. The first manifested Radical Republicanism; the second foreshadowed the Populist revolt of the 1890s. The discontinuity between their histories was the most important reason for the political exceptionalism of Virginia, where Republicanism failed in its time of southern success and succeeded in its time of southern failure.

Bibliographical Essay

STUDIES OF RECONSTRUCTION IN VIRGINIA HAVE SUF-
fered from a rule historians have unfortunately used to define
the period. The rule appears to be that Reconstruction ended
nationally in 1877, but that in each southern state it ended
precisely when Democrats displaced Republicans as the majority party. The rule creates difficulties in studying Alabama,
where a Republican administration succeeded a Democratic one
in 1872, and North Carolina, where Republican governors co-
existed for years with Democratic legislatures. In Virginia, its
application has meant that studies end or begin in 1870, but
very rarely span it. That chronological division has encouraged
a truncated view of Reconstruction in Virginia.

The best history of Virginia politics in the era preceding
secession is Henry T. Shanks, *The Secession Movement in Virginia, 1847–1861* (Richmond: Garrett and Massie, 1934). Charles
H. Ambler's *Sectionalism in Virginia from 1776 to 1861* (Chicago: University of Chicago Press, 1910) retains value, but leaves
some erroneous impressions that Richard O. Curry, *A House Divided: A Study of Statehood Politics and the Copperhead
Movement in West Virginia* (Pittsburgh: University of Pittsburgh Press, 1964) corrects. On the Unionist government at Alexandria, readers should consult Charles H. Ambler's *Francis H.
Pierpont: Union War Governor of Virginia and Father of West
Virginia* (Chapel Hill: University of North Carolina Press, 1937),
and Richard G. Lowe, "Republicans, Rebellion, and Reconstruction: The Republican Party in Virginia, 1856–1870" (Ph.D.
dissertation, University of Virginia, 1968). Henry T. Shanks'

"Disloyalty to the Confederacy in Southwestern Virginia, 1861–1865," *North Carolina Historical Review*, XXI (1944), 118–35, documents disaffection in an area that became politically important.

On presidential and military Reconstruction, Lowe's dissertation and Ambler's biography of Pierpont provide important information. The classic early-twentieth-century academic study of the period is Hamilton J. Eckenrode, *The Political History of Virginia during the Reconstruction* (Baltimore: Johns Hopkins Press, 1904). It resembles contemporary studies of other southern states in its conservative bias and attention to detail, but is the most narrowly political of the group. A more popular and impassioned conservative account is W. H. T. Squires, *Unleashed at Long Last: Reconstruction in Virginia, April 9, 1865–January 26, 1870* (Portsmouth: Printcraft Press, 1939), the only work that applies to Virginia the melodramatic legend of "the horrors of Reconstruction." James Douglas Smith has restudied the era comprehensively in "Virginia during Reconstruction, 1865–1870: A Political, Economic, and Social Study" (Ph.D. dissertation, University of Virginia, 1955). Alrutheus A. Taylor's *The Negro in the Reconstruction of Virginia* (Washington: Association for the Study of Negro Life and History, 1926) provides much information about freedmen, and incidentally constructs a pro-black and pro-Radical account almost entirely from Conservative sources. Jack P. Maddex, Jr.'s *The Virginia Conservatives, 1867–1879: A Study in Reconstruction Politics* (Chapel Hill: University of North Carolina Press, 1970) explores the development of the Conservative party, as Lowe's dissertation does that of the Republican party. James L. McDonough's *Schofield: Union General in the Civil War and Reconstruction* (Tallahassee: University Presses of Florida, 1972) contains material on military administration. Fuller treatments of the topic appear in William T. Alderson, "Military Rule and the Freedmen's Bureau in Virginia" (Ph.D. dissertation, Vanderbilt University, 1952), and John R. Kirkland, "Federal Troops in the South Atlantic States during Reconstruction, 1865–1877" (Ph.D. dissertation, University of North Carolina at Chapel Hill, 1968).

The civil administrations that began in 1870 have received much less attention from historians than the military and Readjuster periods. The studies of the Readjuster movement discuss them to explore the origins of the fiscal revolt. The principal studies that concentrate on the 1870s are Maddex's *Virginia Conservatives* and Robert R. Jones' "Conservative Virginian: The Post-War Career of Governor James Lawson Kemper" (Ph.D. dissertation, University of Virginia, 1964). Allen W. Moger considers the transportation developments of the time in "Railroad Practices and Policies in Virginia after the Civil War," *Virginia Magazine of History and Biography*, LIX (1951), 423–57. Two articles on Ruffner and the school system are Charles C. Pearson, "William Henry Ruffner: Reconstruction Statesman of Virginia," *South Atlantic Quarterly*, XX (1921), 25–32, 137–51, and Walter J. Fraser, Jr., "William Henry Ruffner and the Establishment of Virginia's Public School System, 1870–1874," *Virginia Magazine of History and Biography*, LXXIX (1971), 259–79. Several studies of longer periods begin with 1870: Charles E. Wynes, *Race Relations in Virginia, 1870–1902* (Charlottesville: University of Virginia Press, 1961); Allen W. Moger, *Virginia: Bourbonism to Byrd, 1870–1925* (Charlottesville: University Press of Virginia, 1968); and Raymond H. Pulley, *Old Virginia Restored: An Interpretation of the Progressive Impulse, 1870–1930* (Charlottesville: University Press of Virginia, 1968). They concentrate on later periods, but include interpretive chapters on the 1870s. William D. Henderson's *The Unredeemed City: Reconstruction in Petersburg, Virginia, 1865–1874* (Washington, D.C.: University Press of America, 1977) provides political and social detail on the early 1870s as well as on the military period, which is its primary focus.

The standard older studies of the Readjuster movement are Charles C. Pearson, *The Readjuster Movement in Virginia* (New Haven: Yale University Press, 1917), and Nelson Morehouse Blake, *William Mahone of Virginia: Soldier and Political Insurgent* (Richmond: Garrett and Massie, 1935). Recently, interest in the movement has been increasing. Valuable new interpretations appear in James Tice Moore, *Two Paths to the New*

South: The Virginia Debt Controversy, 1870–1883 (Lexington: University Press of Kentucky, 1974) and in Carl N. Degler, *The Other South: Southern Dissenters in the Nineteenth Century* (New York: Harper and Row, 1974), 264–315. The authors share a sympathetic view of the movement, but differ about aspects of its history. James H. Johnston's "The Participation of Negroes in the Government of Virginia from 1877 to 1888," *Journal of Negro History,* XIV (1929), 251–71, deals with blacks' roles in the movement.

Of the biographical works concerning Reconstruction in Virginia, this essay has already mentioned Ambler's book on Pierpont, McDonough's on Schofield, Blake's on Mahone, Jones' dissertation on Kemper, and Pearson's and Fraser's articles on Ruffner. Most of the other biographies are early and filiopietistic. Three particularly interesting ones are Alexander F. Robertson, *Alexander Hugh Holmes Stuart, 1807–1891: A Biography* (Richmond: William Byrd Press, 1925); Thomas Cary Johnson, *The Life and Letters of Robert Lewis Dabney* (Richmond: Presbyterian Committee of Publication, 1903); and Lily Logan Morrill, *A Builder of the New South: Notes on the Career of Thomas M. Logan* (Boston: Christopher Publishing House, 1940). The principal political autobiographies for the period are Robert E. Withers, *The Autobiography of an Octogenarian* (Roanoke: Stone Printing & Manufacturing Company, 1907) and John E. Massey, *Autobiography of John E. Massey* (New York: Neale Publishing Company, 1909). John S. Wise's *The Lion's Skin: A Historical Novel and a Novel History* (New York: Doubleday, Page and Company, 1905) outshines most of those works, but it is a very partisan autobiographical novel in which it becomes hard to distinguish fact from fiction. The biographical material deals overwhelmingly with Conservatives. Mahone, Massey, and Wise became Readjusters, but only Pierpont was a Republican during Reconstruction. Luther Porter Jackson's *Negro Office-Holders in Virginia, 1865–1895* (Norfolk: *Guide* Quality Press, 1945), a slim but painstaking compilation, hardly begins to even the score.

Behind the books on the subject stand innumerable primary sources. The standard series of official state documents are particularly important, and William Henry Ruffner's annual reports as superintendent of public instruction deserve special attention as expressions of the more progressive side of Conservative social philosophy. The Richmond dailies are the most important newspapers. The *New Nation* and later the *State Journal* spoke for Republicans. H. Rives Pollard's Richmond *Examiner* and later his weekly *Southern Opinion* voiced intransigent traditionalism in the late 1860s. The *Whig* spoke initially for antebellum Whigs and later for the Mahone interests; the *Enquirer*, initially for former southern-rights Democrats and later for Walker and his closest associates. The *Dispatch* perhaps represented Richmond business interests more thoroughly than did its rivals. Only fragmentary files of black newspapers are extant; the Alexandria *People's Advocate* is the best represented.

The William Mahone Papers at Duke University constitute the most voluminous and valuable single collection of personal manuscripts of the period. Other important collections are the papers of James Lawson Kemper at the University of Virginia, Virginia Historical Society, and Virginia State Archives; John W. Daniel at Duke University and the University of Virginia; J. Randolph Tucker at the University of North Carolina; F. W. M. Holliday at Duke University; R. M. T. Hunter at the University of Virginia; and William Henry Ruffner at the Historical Foundation of the Presbyterian and Reformed Churches, Montreat, N.C. Collections of papers of Virginia Republicans are almost nonexistent; the Robert W. Hughes Papers at the College of William and Mary are very disappointing. For the late 1860s, papers of Congressional leaders include letters from Virginia Republican leaders, and Robert F. Walker's letters in the Mahone Papers afford a view of the workings of the Wells administration.

V

North Carolina
An Incongruous Presence

OTTO H. OLSEN

The great issue involved in the controversy between the Radicals and Conservatives is not a simple difference of opinion arising from prejudice or partizan ambition, but is one of principle lying at the foundation of free government in the country, . . . i.e. the inherent right of the people in the several States to manage and control their internal affairs without restraint from any external source.

Raleigh *Daily Sentinel*, February 20, 1868

The Republican party was never indigenous to Southern soil. In truth, it has never become acclimated there, but has remained from the first an exotic.

Albion W. Tourgee, Carpetbagger, 1878[1]

EXCEPT for some ephemeral wartime experiments on the federally occupied coast, the story of North Carolina Reconstruction began with President Andrew Johnson's appointment of William W. Holden as provisional governor of the state on May 29, 1865. To understand the significance of this appointment and of the subsequent emergence of Holden as the state's leading Republican demands, however, a glance further back in the state's past.

---

1. *The "C" Letters as Published in the North State* (Greensboro, 1878), 24.

During the early 1850s, William W. Holden, editor of his party's leading newspaper, the Raleigh *Standard*, was probably the state's most influential Democrat as well as an ardent defender of southern rights, including that of secession. Holden broke with much of that party's leadership, however, when he sought to move beyond his role as editor in pursuit of high public office. To the party's controlling and largely slaveholding gentry, Holden's faults were many. He was of illegitimate and humble birth, neither a college graduate nor to the manor born, and too much an advocate of Jacksonian democratic reform. As a result, he was successively denied anticipated nominations for governor and United States senator in 1858. Shortly thereafter his alienation was intensified by his support of ad valorem taxation, which would increase the tax on slaves, and his affiliation with the Raleigh Workingmen's Association.[2]

These various developments reflected basic class, political, and sectional divisions in the state, and Holden was identified with the common man and the western, urban, nonslaveholding portion of the party. With the approaching sectional crisis, some affinity between these forces and Unionism was revealed when Holden and his allies denounced the secessionists and supported Stephen A. Douglas for the Democratic presidential nomination. Following Lincoln's election, many Holden Democrats joined a greater number of former Whigs in a Union movement that successfully resisted secession until the firing on Fort Sumter and Lincoln's call for troops. Thereupon the white population displayed a remarkable degree of unity in accepting the necessity for secession and war.

This new unity did not eradicate existing antagonisms, however, and the former opponents of secession, including Holden, soon launched a new Conservative party that opposed the incumbent Democratic-Secessionist state government. In 1862 the Conservative candidate, Zebulon B. Vance, a Confederate officer and former western Whig, was elected governor, and

2. R. D. W. Connor, *North Carolina: Rebuilding an Ancient Commonwealth, 1584–1925* (Chicago, 1929), 79–82; Samuel A. Ashe, *History of North Carolina* (2 vols., Raleigh, 1925), II, 516, 533–35, 539–40.

Conservatives thereafter largely dominated Confederate North Carolina.

Despite their earlier Unionism, almost all Conservative leaders were ardent defenders of slavery and southern independence. It is true that they depicted the war as having needlessly originated in the foolish extremism of northern and southern radicals, but they now vigorously defended that war as having become an unavoidable struggle against a rapacious, foreign invader. Primary allegiance in their eyes lay with the state, and the state had seceded and joined the Confederacy. Subsequent bitter differences between North Carolina Conservatives and the Confederate central government were differences of policy not cause, although it was somewhat strange to find longtime nationalist Whigs vigorously denouncing Confederate centralization in the name of states rights and freedom. What they succeeded in doing by this was to mobilize remarkable support for themselves and the struggle for independence by diverting much of the hostility against a burdensome war into a denunciation of both the original secessionists and the Confederate administration at Richmond.[3]

Despite his prominent role in the launching of the Conservative party, William W. Holden's relationship to that party proved tenuous. He never succeeded in endearing himself to his new Whig allies, who were often more aristocratic in attitude than his former friends, and it soon became clear that he

3. The preceding paragraph and the subsequent analysis of Holden's relationship with the Conservatives is based primarily upon correspondence in J. G. de Roulhac Hamilton (ed.), *The Correspondence of Jonathan Worth* (2 vols.; Raleigh, 1909) and *The Papers of Thomas Ruffin* (4 vols.; Raleigh, 1920); William A. Graham Papers and Battle Family Papers, Southern Historical Collection, University of North Carolina; and Zebulon B. Vance Papers, David L. Swain Papers, William A. Graham Papers, and Walter Clark Papers, State Archives, Raleigh. See also Ashe, *History of North Carolina*; Horace W. Raper, "William Woods Holden: A Political Biography" (Ph.D. dissertation, University of North Carolina, 1951); and Mary Shannon Smith, "Union Sentiment in North Carolina During the Civil War," *Proceedings of the Sixteenth Annual Session of the State Literary and Historical Association of North Carolina* (Raleigh, 1915).

lacked their dedication to the southern cause. A growing conviction of ultimate Confederate failure led Holden to split from the Vance administration in 1863 and lead a movement calling for separate state action in behalf of peace. A major attraction of this states-rights' movement was the promise that it might yet preserve slavery by surrendering independence, but in the gubernatorial election of 1864, Holden was decisively defeated as a peace candidate by Governor Vance, who remained a last ditch supporter of the war. Holden had been supported by only three men of major prominence in the state—Robert P. Dick, Thomas Settle, and Alfred Dockery—all of whom would join Holden as Republican Reconstruction leaders.

Although the state's support of the war effort remained a strong and lasting one, not all North Carolinians were so dedicated. Blacks certainly were not, and among whites, lasting unionism, reinforced by the burdens of war and older class antagonisms, steadily generated overt and covert resistance to the Confederacy. Unionists defied state authority and joined and guided Union armies invading the state. Confederates hounded, persecuted, and murdered Unionists, and Confederate deserters captured in Union uniform were summarily executed.[4] Impressment and conscription activities left an angry heritage, and bitter guerilla war raged, particularly in the West. The lasting hatreds that resulted were crucial to Reconstruction history.

Efforts by Holden and his followers to distinguish between their own legitimate peace activities and the unlawful resistance of outright Unionists were not very successful, and there is no doubt that the actions of the Holdenites did undermine the war effort. Members of the peace movement thus alienated themselves from a white majority which supported the southern cause and believed that those who opposed or weakened that cause were ipso facto traitors to the state and the South. Holden and his followers were widely viewed in that light.

4. John C. Barrett, *The Civil War in North Carolina* (Chapel Hill, 1964), 174–201; Confederate Diary, typescript, 174, Henry A. Chambers Papers, State Archives.

To the North, on the other hand, Holden's war record was a recommendation that led to his appointment as provisional governor by President Johnson. In the immediate aftermath of the war, the North continued to fear and resent Confederates, and Holden appeared just the type of leader to mobilize a force of reliable southern Unionists. But as the provisional governor built a new Union party that was clearly anti-Confederate in attitude and which advocated a full acquiescence to all federal demands, together with democratic reform within the state, most former Confederates denounced that party as representative of a treacherous minority that had undermined the state's war effort and was now serving the interests of an alien foe.

The indigenous leaders of North Carolina, whether of Whig or Democratic antecedents, usually accepted but lamented the defeat of the South. "The people who felt most bitterly at the end of the war," said one of them, "were not the majority *in numbers* but they were the majority so to speak in social rank and influence, refinement, intelligence and wealth."[5] While initially somewhat cowed by defeat, these leaders were neither inactive nor silent in behalf of their own interests. Having already suffered humiliation and great losses and exasperated by northern self-righteousness and by new challenges from within, they were quick to resist any further erosion of their power from either internal or external forces.

North Carolina leaders soon appeared to be resuming the same struggle against the North that they had so recently waged against both the North and the Confederacy—a struggle against external domination. The goal of independence was exchanged for that of internal self determination or "home rule," and the further the North moved in making demands, the more pervasive and rigid resistance became. The federal structure of the United States provided a hallowed states-rights tradition for this stance, which was also endorsed by the Democratic party of the North. But there was something additional and stronger, some-

5. "A Sketch of the University of North Carolina," Cornelia Phillips Spencer Papers, Southern Historical Collection.

thing quasi-national in the position and viewpoint of southern whites, something that stemmed from a long history of cultural difference and conflict between the slave states and the free, and something that had a popular as well as an elitist source. Despite defeat, the Confederacy and the war had hardened this quasi-national commitment. White North Carolinians who accepted defeat and reunion, and even emancipation, as the legitimate results of war continued to maintain a strong, even primary, allegiance to their section and their lost cause. They spoke repeatedly of "our country," by which they meant "the injured, the unjustly treated and yet proud and noble late southern Confederacy." They resented "the wanton desolation" of their "beloved South," their "beautiful country," their "Southland," and they were wont to compare their fate with that of the Irish or the Poles. The war destroyed my former allegiance, said one former Unionist, and it would now be "perfectly idle and would be hypocricy in me to talk of having brotherly feeling for a Yankee. *I hate them*—and always will."[6]

The surrender terms initially obtained from General William T. Sherman, which perpetuated the authority of the Confederate state government, were indicative of the hopes of the state's wartime leaders. Disappointed but not deterred by the disallowance of those terms at Washington, objections were next registered against even the mild Reconstruction demands being made by President Johnson and particularly against Provisional Governor Holden's controversial implementation of those demands.[7]

In 1865 it was the Conservative-Confederate leadership of

6. Unsigned to My Dear Friend, March 22, 1869, Murdock-Wright Papers, Southern Historical Collection; A. M. McPheeters to Rufus L. Patterson, June 10, 1865, Patterson Family Papers; R. L. Beall to Cornelia P. Spencer, August 29, 1866, David L. Swain Papers; Daniel H. Hill to Dear Friend, December 28, 1866, D. H. Hill Papers; Laura Mordecai to Marcus L. Ward, February 4, 1866, Pattie Mordecai Collection, all in State Archives.

7. E.g. William A. Graham to ?, May 13, 1865, William A. Graham Papers, typescript, State Archives; Thomas Ruffin to David L. Swain, September 11, 1865, Walter Clark Papers.

North Carolina that dominated the opposition to Holden because Democrats remained so discredited by their identification with secession and the Confederate central government. With good reason, Conservative-Confederates claimed that it was they who truly represented the will of the state's white population, the only group that mattered to all major political factions at that time. They insisted that they were in no way responsible for the war, but had stood by their section when no alternative was left, and had done so honorably and well. Their success in thus disassociating themselves from any responsibility for the commencement of the war minimized the Union party's opportunity to build a following out of widespread postwar disillusionment with that war. Conservatives now sincerely accepted defeat and pledged their loyalty to the Union. The catch was, of course, that they had their own definition of precisely what this meant. It meant reunion and emancipation and nothing more. They would continue to honor the Lost Cause and do all they could to maintain their society, their principles, and their leadership. All of these intentions were in obvious conflict with certain postwar expectations of the North.

Provisional Governor Holden could hardly endorse such a rationale. Already catering to his peace followers and consistent Union men, as well as to the desires of the North, he was also being forced by the hostility of former opponents to discriminate against them far more than he had hoped. His resultant preferences were resented, and in November 1865 Conservatives again succeeded in denying Holden high elective office when they supported the gubernatorial candidacy of Jonathan Worth, a former Whig Unionist who had been a follower of Governor Vance and a member of his Confederate state administration. Worth obtained a majority over Holden of 5,937 in a total vote of almost 60,000. In the same election emancipation and anti-secession ordinances were passed respectively by seemingly large majorities of 19,039 to 3,970, and 20,870 to 1,983. Perhaps a more significant fact was that the great majority of the state's sixty thousand active voters had failed to vote on these ordinances at all. "The results of the recent election in North Carolina," telegraphed President Johnson, "have greatly damaged the prospects of the State in the restoration of its governmental relations. Should the action and spirit of the legislature be in the same direction, it will greatly increase the mischief already done and might be fatal."[8]

State political rivalry continued on similar lines during 1866, although as the breach widened between Congress and the President, the consistent readiness of the Union party to accept any federal demands finally aligned it with Congress. It was thus ironically the Holdenites, who had been earliest and most thorough in their acceptance of Johnsonian Reconstruction, who finally found themselves allied with the increasingly radical demands of the Republican Congress. At the same time, the strength of the Union party was dwindling. In August 1866, certain democratic amendments to the state constitution that it supported were narrowly defeated by the East in a marked sectional vote. Two months later Governor Worth was reelected by a three to one majority over the Union party candidate, Alfred Dockery. Now a weak minority, the Holdenites made their last fight of that year in support of the proposed Fourteenth Amendment, warning that if it were not endorsed more severe measures would be imposed upon the South. "May a kind Providence avert these evils from our unhappy country! But if they should come, remember that our skirts are clear. We have done our duty. We have done it in the face of opposition and excitement. *When negro suffrage comes, as it will, if these warnings are not regarded,* let no man say that we are to blame for it."[9]

True to Holden's prediction, the South's rejection of the Fourteenth Amendment was a final provocation, and Congress responded in March 1867 by enfranchising the freedmen of the South and temporarily disfranchising some former Confeder-

8. J. G. de Roulhac Hamilton, *Reconstruction in North Carolina* (New York, 1914), 141.
9. Raleigh *Standard*, September 29, 1866.

ates. At this time blacks constituted about one-third of the population of North Carolina, and they had been carefully active since the surrender in pursuit of further rights. Blacks numbered more than a third of the new electorate because of the state's forty thousand war dead and an estimated eleven thousand whites disfranchised by the Reconstruction Acts. In the first Reconstruction registration 106,721 whites and 72,932 blacks were enrolled to vote. The new black voter offered an opportunity for the success of the dying Union party and its reform program, provided that this white minority would cooperate with the enfranchised blacks. The bulk of the Union party proved willing to do just that as it joined with blacks and other white factions to establish a state Republican party early in 1867.

This new Republican coalition was a diverse group indeed, and its precise composition remains obscure. Most white Republicans probably came out of the ranks of the Union party, although other members of that party were impelled by black suffrage into the arms of the Conservatives. While the leading Republican, Holden, was a former Democrat, most Republican leaders had been former Whigs. A correlation of voting support along those same lines also has been suggested but never decisively proven, and obviously the war and its aftermath had extensively disrupted traditional party allegiances and encouraged all manner of new alignments. What is clear is that the majority of both former Whig and Democratic leaders joined the Conservative rather than the Republican party, and the same is probably true of their followers. What is also clear is that prominent white Republicans were likely to have been Whigs or Douglas Democrats, opponents of secession, outspoken critics of the Confederacy, leaders in the peace movement, and/or advocates of democratic reform. The strongest centers of white Republicanism were among urban artisans and in the mountainous West among a yeomanry noted for its hostility to the slaveowning aristocracy, its long struggle for more democracy, and its opposition to the Confederacy. Correspondingly, the state campaign of the Republican party in 1867 was based heavily on a condemnation of the Confederate aristocracy and its disastrous war together with a stirring cry for democratic reform and economic progress. There is no question but that this entire combination of developments, particularly the freeing and enfranchisement of the blacks, created an unusually intense spirit of progressive hope among many members of both races. This is perhaps best evidenced in the multiplicity and programs of mass meetings, the activities of the Union Leagues, and the sudden rise of local leaders, black and white, throughout the state during the early years of radical Reconstruction.[10]

The commitment of white Republicans to racial equality was limited, however, and was seldom as intense as their hatred of Confederates or their interest in reform. Contrasting conservative currents were also in evidence. Some white Republicans were doing little more than supporting concessions to the North as a means of effecting the rapid restoration of the state. Others were willing to accept the civil and political equality of the blacks but had little interest in reform or simply hoped to control the impact of the black vote. Other white Republicans were primarily attracted by the nationalism or the economic principles of the party, and there were those who sought nothing more than office for themselves. A party of such diverse origins and attitudes could expect to be plagued by future factionalism and obviously much of this support was temporary or very conditional. "When the storm is over," predicted the state's most prestigious Republican voter of 1868, "the Conservative party, representing as it does, the property and intelligence of the State, will take the guidance of affairs, and all will be well."[11]

Since the congressional program envisioned the restoration of full sovereignty to the southern states after the requirements of Reconstruction were fulfilled, the ultimate test would be the

10. James L. Lancaster, "The Scalawags of North Carolina, 1850–1868" (Ph.D. dissertation, Princeton University, 1974): Otto H. Olsen, *Carpetbagger's Crusade: The Life of Albion W. Tourgee* (Baltimore, 1965), 38–48, 68–92; Allen W. Trelease, "Who Were the Scalawags," *Journal of Southern History*, XXIX (1963), 445–68.

11. Richmond M. Pearson letter, Raleigh, *Standard*, August 11, 1868.

ability of North Carolina Republicans to maintain themselves. Unfortunately, the North's approach to Reconstruction totally misjudged political realities in the South. The Reconstruction Acts were but the last of a series of northern impositions that intensified resentment at the very moment that the North believed it had found a satisfactory means of restoring home rule. Consequently, North Carolina Republicans found themselves identified with almost everything that the bulk of the white population had opposed over the past decade, and they were ill prepared for the challenges they faced. Black Republican voters were abysmally illiterate, impoverished, and inexperienced; reliable and competent allies were scarce; and every variety of social power seemed dominated by the opposition.

Despite their many handicaps, North Carolina Republicans did enjoy a great deal of initial success. Their opponents were disunited in their immediate response and made no convincing appeal to the new black voters. The self-interest of the blacks thus clearly suggested that they support that party that had freed them, extended them rights, and now allowed them an opportunity for meaningful political participation. In the fall elections of 1867, the Republicans swept almost every county of the state to elect 107 of the 120 delegates to the constitutional convention of 1868. Not only had black voters overwhelmingly supported the new party, but Republicans also commanded a majority of whites in the western regions of the state. Republicans then prepared an admirable new state constitution, and in the spring elections of 1868 they ratified that constitution and captured full control of the restored state government. It appears that over thirty thousand whites had cooperated with about twice that many blacks to elect William W. Holden the first Republican governor of the state. Republicans effectively organized voting support, they established state reforms that were to prove of enduring value and popularity, and they reasonably challenged racist traditions within the state through biracial cooperation and the election of a significant number of blacks to party, local, and state office. To this point black suffrage was obviously an encouraging success. But with the restoration of statehood and the withdrawal of military support, Republicans would be beset by insurmountable difficulties.

Insofar as it was black voters who were primarily responsible for ousting the Conservatives and establishing Republican power and reform, radical Reconstruction in North Carolina truly was black. Few blacks achieved high office or much power, however, and the antagonisms that Reconstruction inspired were more than racial ones. Not only was the black vote totally lost to the opponents of Republicanism, but in their eyes it had elevated to power treasonous Unionists and Holdenites, foreign Yankees, degraded whites, and inferior blacks. Furthermore, these supposedly base and alien elements were enacting radical reforms that seemed to threaten sacred beliefs and property rights and even social stability itself. Conservative Governor Worth expressed an indicative abhorrence: "The tendency is to ignore virtue and property and intelligence—and to put the powers of government into the hands of mere *numbers*. . . . The majority in all times and in all countries are improvident and without property. Agrarianism and anarchy must be the result of this ultra democracy."[12] Confirmed in their racism and distrust of democracy by the voting behavior of blacks, Conservatives soon found it convenient to direct their vengeance primarily against the troublesome Negro.

Out of the intense opposition to Republicanism emerged a pervasive new political unity among the state's ruling elite that was expressed in the state convention of February 6, 1868. Called by the Conservative party, this convention was attended by both old Whig and Democratic leaders. Waiving "all former party feeling and prejudice," the delegates endorsed cooperation with the national Democratic party and denounced the Reconstruction Acts of 1867. While the delegates also pledged to protect blacks "in their civil rights and to allow such privileges as were not inconsistent with the welfare of both races," more

12. Jonathan Worth to William Clark, February 16, 1868, Hamilton (ed.), *The Correspondence of Jonathan Worth*, II, 1156.

pertinent was their formulation of a lasting racist stance that was about equal parts conviction and tactical demagoguery: "The great and all absorbing issue, now soon to be presented to the people of the States, is negro suffrage and negro equality, if not supremacy, and whether hereafter in North Carolina and the South, the white man is to be placed politically, and as a consequence socially, upon a footing of equality with the negro."[13]

The same leaders who had united North Carolina whites in support of slavery and independence would now do so again, and more successfully, in behalf of white supremacy and home rule. It was Conservatives who chose to draw the color line in politics. Republicans were not only open to white influence and support but needed and welcomed it. Few of the able and educated white men of the state responded to that opportunity.

In a manner hardly befitting their chosen party name, Conservatives also soon made it apparent that they sought to destroy rather than compete with Republicanism, and that they were willing to utilize any means necessary to do so. They would neither sufficiently endorse black aspirations to attract black voting support, nor would they accept what one might call ordinary political rivalry. Instead Conservatives would oppose Republicanism in a manner that made it impossible for either party politics or the Republican state government to function properly.

Despite their intrinsic strength, the opponents of Republicanism in North Carolina were too disorganized and extreme in their stand to succeed during 1868. They vehemently opposed the rather admirable new state constitution before it had even been completed, and they flatly denied the legality of the entire Reconstruction process. Only when forced to do so by federal military directive did Governor Worth surrender his office to the newly elected Republican governor. In the fall presidential campaign Conservatives supported a national Democratic party

13. Hamilton, *Reconstruction in North Carolina*, 278–79; Olsen, *Carpetbagger's Crusade*, 119.

that promised to forcefully disperse the southern Reconstruction governments, and one North Carolina newspaper proclaimed "the election of SEYMOUR AND BLAIR as the only hope of averting ANOTHER WAR."[14]

But North Carolinians were not attracted by the thought of more war, and Conservative rashness induced additional men of prominence to endorse the constitution of 1868, the legitimacy of Reconstruction, and the candidacy of Grant. The sweeping state Republican victory in April 1868 and Grant's election to the presidency in November culminated, however, in a typically skillful adjustment on the part of Conservatives. To regain the support of moderates and lessen the danger of renewed federal interference, they now professed their full acceptance of all federal Reconstruction laws together with their continuing determination to oust the Republicans and restore white rule. This remained the basic posture of the Conservative, and soon renamed Democratic, party as it catered with remarkable success to both moderate and extremist opponents of Republicanism. To attract the support of moderates, Conservative-Democrats promised to fully honor the rights of blacks while they also labored to prove that Republican rule was so corrupt, unreliable, and alien that it deserved defeat. At the same time most Conservative-Democrats showed little respect for the rights of either blacks or white Republicans and little restraint in their methods.

Particularly crucial to the fate of Reconstruction was the extent to which Conservatives dominated the power structure of the state. Conservatives controlled the overwhelming proportion of the wealth, land, experience, and press. They dominated all the business and professional classes, as well as the churches, social life, and power structure at the community, county, and state levels. In areas of substantial black population they constituted almost the entire white population, while in the West Republicans were identified with the poorer whites of

14. Greensboro *Patriot and Times*, August to November 1868.

the mountains and valleys. Perhaps most important of all, the Conservatives represented an ideological heritage, including a commitment to white supremacy, that overwhelmingly dominated the state.

Not only did the Conservative coalition possess preponderant power and skill, but its passions knew little restraint. Intensifying those passions was the popularity of various Republican reforms including a constitution that Conservatives vehemently opposed. The constitution of 1868 remained the state issue of greatest substance between the two parties, although the popularity of that constitution eventually served to intensify the reliance of Conservatives on political extremism and the issue of race. Conservatives took advantage of practically every opportunity and weapon, including slander, falsehood, and violence. Their appeal to racism was constant and intense, and Republicans were socially ostracized, legally harassed, economically discriminated against, and even expelled from church. Also, Conservatives were far more skillful than Republicans in maintaining voting unity and minimizing interparty discord by such tactics as not holding state nominating conventions.

Hardly a mistake was made by Republicans that Conservatives did not capitalize on with remarkable effectiveness. When mistakes were not forthcoming, the Conservative press assiduously circulated lies and half truths to build a web of distortion and slander that abused and confounded Republicans and ultimately made them scapegoats for all the ills of the state, including those left by the war. It was in this fashion that the false but lasting Reconstruction legend was built, and it was no coincidence that the man considered most responsible for that accomplishment, the editor Josiah Turner, Jr., would win renown as a strictly negative genius. "Perhaps no man of equal importance in the history of North Carolina," said one of his admirers, "has combined greater capacity for destruction with less capacity for construction."[15]

15. Connor, *North Carolina*, 320.

Conservatives would, in truth, "rule or ruin," and their convictions were summarized well by an historian who shared them:

During these two years of Radical misrule, when the ideals of the community were shattered, when an ignorant, inferior, and lately enslaved race, controlled by selfish and corrupt aliens, held the balance of power and, by combination with a small minority of native whites, administered the government, then the practical necessities of the case overcame scrupulous notions of political morality, and a determination to rule by any methods possessed the mass of the white people and held them during the three following decades."[16]

While this statement perfectly reveals the character of the Redemption process, its lasting stereotype of Republicanism was untrue. In general, Republican leaders were reasonable men who endorsed a free enterprise system according equal civil and political rights to blacks and who supported moderate reforms that already had been achieved in most of the United States. Although black voters were inexperienced, the men they helped elect were on the whole neither vicious nor incompetent, as the results of the convention of 1868 suggested. Conservatives would neither make that admission nor allow a continuing fair test. Instead they united in defense of racism, reaction, and political extremism, and their ability and power promised their ultimate success.

North Carolina Republicanism was also far less alien than Conservatives insisted and appeared to believe. Although it is true that external interference had momentarily tipped the scales, the goals, the leadership, and the voting base of the Republican party were overwhelmingly native to the state, and the fundamental issue had become one of who would rule at home. Continuing patronage and campaign assistance from the North was well within the traditional pattern of national poli-

16. Hamilton, *Reconstruction in North Carolina*, 422.

tics, and both parties remained eager to accept it. As for the military, it intervened in southern affairs with extreme reluctance and with little, if any, lasting political effect. In retrospect, it appears that federal patronage and aid to southern Republicans was indeed insultingly limited.

If there was ever a party that needed unusual succor, it was the Republican party of the South. Instead, largely because the North retained its view of an enemy South, these new Republicans were denied political and economic rewards commensurate with their contributions, needs, and sacrifices. The federal government, for example, catered to one group of racist and reactionary officeholders in North Carolina simply because its members had been Republicans prior to 1867, although their efforts were to be consistently directed toward sabotaging the state Republican party. To the extent that the North continued to blame and punish, rather than sympathize with or aid the South, the cause of southern Republicanism also suffered. North Carolinians resented the special cotton tax and the collection of old land taxes; and they objected to the discriminatory new system of national banking. Staunch Unionists had been as arbitrarily deprived of their slave property as rebels and had suffered other material losses at the hands of the national government. Throughout the Reconstruction period there was too little in the way of federal appropriations for state development or of the appointment of North Carolinians to prestigious office. It was indicative that when one of the state's most able Republicans, Thomas Settle, aspired for a place on the national Republican ticket in 1880, special efforts were considered necessary to establish his loyalty to the nation.[17]

Above all, however, it was the uneven distribution of ability and power and the destructive Conservative approach that lay at the heart of the Republican dilemma. A revolutionary situation of sorts existed that lacked an adequate indigenous base and had never really developed its own organization, leader-

17. Edward P. Brooks to Thomas Settle, October 7, 1879, Thomas Settle Papers, Southern Historical Collection.

ship, or goals. Most Republican leaders had stepped in to assist and control a situation that they had played little or no part in creating and never fully represented or understood. Reflective of this state of affairs, Republicans were soon plagued internally by the very same issues that lay at the heart of the Conservative opposition—the issues of class, race, and alien domination. Native Republicans often resented carpetbaggers, and the vast majority of white Republicans in the state had not endorsed Negro rights at all prior to 1867. Their opposition to black aspirations was a reflection not only of tactical considerations but also of a comparatively milder racism that sapped Republican strength. While Republicanism in most of the state rested on the black vote, that in the West depended primarily on a white one. Intrastate rivalry not only would soon disrupt the statewide alliance itself, but would also intensify the impact of the race question on western white voters. Indicative of the paradoxes involved, Holden would resign from the Republican party in 1883 complaining of its favoritism to the North and warning that "Negro equality is a great and threatening evil."[18]

The phenomenal accomplishments of the Union Leagues and the Republican party during 1867 and 1868 did not remedy these weaknesses. In fact, the successes of those years created another significant Republican division that culminated in a repudiation of the mass based Union Leagues themselves. This division involved defensive as opposed to offensive strategies and appeared to reflect different class orientations or needs. On the one side stood leaders closely associated with the white and black masses whose basic problem was that of survival, especially after the emergence of the Ku Klux Klan. On the other side stood liberal and enlightened members of the state's gentry who appeared more concerned with such matters as efficiency, propriety, and wealth.

Often local leaders were shunned because they were poor, inept, or black, or because they were whites too closely affili-

18. William W. Holden to Raleigh *News and Observer*, August 31, 1883, copy, William W. Holden Papers, Duke University.

ated with blacks.[19] The Republican party seemed torn between the needs and aspirations of the mass of its supporters, most of whom were black, and the cautious pragmatism of its top leadership. Men like John W. Stephens (scalawag), O. R. Colgrove (carpetbagger), and Wyatt Outlaw (black), all of whom were murdered by the Klan, never even received the kind of sympathy and support from the top levels of party leadership that might at least have saved them if not the Republican party.

Instead the Republican state leadership appeased its critics in a futile effort to win acceptability. Republicans pleaded for an acceptance of their principles and their very existence as reasonable, or as something demanded by the federal government, rather than fighting to impose them through the kind of power struggle typical of historical change. North Carolina Republicans were very much men of reasonableness and persuasion rather than of power, a fact reflective of both the kind of moderate attitude that had accepted federal demands in the first place and the limited affinity between the leadership and the voting base. Relying on the federal government and the ideology of political democracy, these Republicans lacked the power and the inclination for effective mass struggle.

Indicative of their faith in the political process, Republicans imposed no proscriptions against former Confederates in the constitution of 1868. They expected the resumption of normal political rivalries under new conditions. Conservatives, on the other hand, even after their tacit acceptance of Reconstruction law, continued what can be described as a form of counterrevolution designed to destroy an alien, inferior, and treasonous foe. In contrast to Conservative confidence, certainty, and unrestraint, Republicans were characterized by timidity, blundering, and uncertainty, as well as an astonishing preoccupation with establishing their own propriety. Frustrated in their inabil-

19. W. McKee Evans, *Ballots and Fence Rails: Reconstruction on the Lower Cape Fear* (Chapel Hill, 1966), 254–55; Olsen, *Carpetbagger's Crusade*, 123–25; Robert W. Lassiter to Thomas Settle, February 27, 1872, and W. McLaurin to Thomas Settle, March 15, 1873, Thomas Settle Papers.

ity to cope with the opposition, Republicans eventually turned on one another. Carpetbaggers, blacks, and lower-class leaders were vilified and betrayed, and a variety of factions compounded the party's problems.[20]

There was, of course, sincerity, if not always legitimacy, in Conservative discontent. Emancipation, black enfranchisement, and challenges from blacks and poor whites did rankle, and in many counties racist whites could not adjust to black majority control. Government expenses and taxes did increase, and taxes were levied more heavily on the wealthy, although new expenditures often were beneficial and generally would have increased with or without Republican control. To a great extent blacks and Republicans were simply becoming scapegoats for losses incurred because of the war and the postwar economic decline of the South. Taxes had increased while state income had declined, and one recent study suggests that blacks gained an increased share of the diminished total wealth, while the share of landowning classes declined.[21] Obviously this could have intensified political and economic conflict between the races. There was also waste, fraud, and incompetence, but such was not unique to Republicans or Reconstruction, and the Republican record cannot even begin to justify the stereotype that would prevail nor the erosion of two-party politics in the state.

Perhaps the most disastrous burden of the Radical Republican regime originated in a hopeful program of state aid to railroads. It was generally agreed in postwar North Carolina that further railroad development was the key to renewed prosperity. Because of the lack of private capital, state aid was the only means of achieving that end, and political and economic pressures for such aid were irresistible.[22] A variety of bills passed by

20. Abundant evidence of Republican factionalism during the 1870s exists in the Thomas Settle Papers, Southern Historical Collection, and the Governor Tod R. Caldwell Papers and Governor Curtis H. Brogden Papers, State Archives.

21. Roger Ransom and Richard Sutch, "The Economic Reorganization of the Post Reconstruction South" (typed manuscript in the author's possession).

22. The following account of railroad projects is based primarily upon

the Republican dominated convention and state legislature of 1868 provided railroads with state bonds in exchange for a mortgage or railroad bonds or stocks. The capital obtained from the sale of the state bonds was designated for railroad construction. But following a pattern common to the nation, certain of the promoters involved began using this capital carelessly as a means of building personal railroad and banking empires. Republicans also established a degree of state control of railroads commensurate with the extent of state investment. This control was intended not only as a means of protecting state investments but also as a means of creating a patronage machine of crucial importance to a party so devoid of an economic base. There is no doubt, however, that the plans were designed to create a system of profitable and beneficial railroad lines to be primarily owned by the state or by private investors within the state. The program was intelligently conceived, it was of political promise to the Republicans and of economic promise to the state, and had it succeeded would have been a worthy accomplishment.

Instead the returns were disappointingly slow, and a number of grounds for criticism soon emerged which Conservatives chose to exploit without restraint. Liquor had been freely dispensed, loans made available to friendly legislators, and suspicions raised, and later confirmed, of profiteering and bribery. The entire program also became overly ambitious, and a number of bills appeared to violate certain constitutional restraints. Private investors also resented the extent of state control.

It was in response to the Conservative onslaught and a rising fiscal crisis, rather than in the railroad appropriations themselves, that Republicans fully displayed their weaknesses. During 1868 the railroads failed to meet interest payments that were due to the state. The state thus lacked expected funds, and Governor Holden and the state treasurer urged an increase in taxa-

Charles L. Price, "Railroads and Reconstruction in North Carolina, 1865–1871" (Ph.D. dissertation, University of North Carolina, 1959). See also Price, "The Railroad Schemes of George W. Swepson," *Essays in American History, East Carolina College Publications in History*, I (Greenville, 1964), 32–50.

tion to meet the deficit. Already smarting under Conservative fiscal criticism, Republican legislators defied these recommendations and refused to act. The state thus defaulted on its own interest payment on state bonds in January 1869, which together with the dumping of a large quantity of bonds on the market initiated a marked decline in the price of North Carolina bonds. This decline was accelerated by vociferous Conservative denunciations of the entire program and threats of ultimate repudiation. The Republican party now divided within itself, many Republicans joining Conservatives in discrediting and undermining the Republican sponsored program. A final effort to save the venture was destroyed by the fiscal panic of September 1869. Although the state retained promising railroad investments, for the moment it was left with a substantial debt and little to show in the way of actual construction.

Republican railroad efforts had been characterized by elements of incompetence and dishonesty, and Republicans must bear the major responsibility for those weaknesses. Conservatives had originated most of the railroad bills, however, guided them through the legislature, and received almost all of the money involved. Charles L. Price, the authoritative student of this subject, has concluded that "Conservatives were as deeply involved in the corruption as the Republicans. But the Republicans were in power, and the Conservative press under the dynamic leadership of Turner succeeded in persuading the public (and even many Republicans) that full blame lay with the Republican Party."[23]

True to form, Conservatives had been successful but destructive. The railroad program had opened an opportunity for profiteering, and it had confirmed many southerners in their suspicions of the immorality of a capitalist-oriented Republicanism and the dangers of democracy and black suffrage. As in the case of racism, emotional conviction and political calculation worked together with a vengeance. The consequences con-

23. Price, "Railroads and Reconstruction in North Carolina," 606.

tributed to the popularity of racism and of archaic economic concepts rather than to the welfare of the state, and the element of irresponsibility in Conservative party behavior drove one of the state's most brilliant men, Samuel F. Phillips, to join the Republicans after his participation in a legislative investigation of the entire railroad affair.

Ultimately some disputed railroad bonds were repudiated (some North Carolinians delighting in thus depriving Yankee bondholders of their wealth), and the remainder of the debt was compromised on terms favorable to the state. Consequently the venture never was a financial burden, and the most detrimental fiscal effect may have been the extent to which the state's credit and ability to borrow was undermined by the repudiationist stance of the Conservatives.[24] In the long run this also discredited state-supported railroad programs and opened the way for external ownership and control. The supposed restoration of state self-rule under the auspices of Conservative-Democrats thus actually paved the way for freer economic domination by the North.

Additional extremism in the ranks of the Conservative party was revealed in a common pattern of electoral coercion, intimidation, and violence, all of which was epitomized by the terrorism of a variety of organizations generally designated as the Ku Klux Klan.[25] The atrocities of the Klan were, of course, motivated by a wide range of racial, economic, political and even personal considerations, but in essence they were all part of the total struggle against Republicanism. Klan crime was not a product of a base element but was led by respected men. Perhaps it can best be described as a unique guerrilla movement

24. Samuel F. Phillips to Kemp P. Battle, January 14, 1873, Battle Family Papers, and R. W. Donnell to David F. Caldwell, August 20, 1877, David F. Caldwell Papers, Southern Historical Collection.

25. The following account of the Klan is based primarily upon Allen W. Trelease, *White Terror: The Ku Klux Klan Conspiracy and Southern Reconstruction,* (New York, 1971), and Otto H. Olsen, "The Ku Klux Klan in North Carolina: A Study in Reconstruction Politics and Propaganda," *North Carolina Historical Review,* XXXIX (July 1962), 340–62.

dedicated to the destruction of an alien regime and the restoration of white supremacy and home rule. The origin, leadership, and discipline of the Klan all suggested Confederate military antecedents and thus a continuation of the war against the North. Characteristic of guerrilla movements, the Klan was locally autonomous and its members found refuge and support among the white populace wherever it was most active. A connection between the Klan and the Conservative party was obvious. The membership and leadership of both organizations merged, and almost the entire Conservative press joined in obscuring, justifying, and encouraging Klan atrocities.

Without a doubt, klansmen were abysmally cowardly, cruel, and racist; but in their defiance of the North and the law, there was also a warped idealism and courage. Again Conservatives were successful in their destructiveness. By decimating Republican leadership and exposing the inability of the Republican regime to protect person and property in the state, they contributed immensely to the declining strength of southern Republicanism and its ultimate abandonment by the North.

Reports of threats and depredations by the Klan were received by Governor Holden as early as October 1868. By the spring of 1870, hundreds of severe beatings and other outrages, including at least twenty-five murders, had been attributed to the Klan in twenty-two counties scattered throughout the state. Most of these counties were controlled by Democrats, but the Klan was most rampant in narrowly contested counties of unusual biracial Republican success. Invariably the outrages were directed against politically active blacks and their closest white allies or against other challenges to white supremacy.

North Carolina Republicans failed to protect their own electorate against such violence. Prominent Republicans repeatedly restrained their followers from counter violence, and the state government, with all its power and law, was ineffective in preventing or prosecuting anti-Republican terrorism. While Northern missionaries and Union Leagues did an impressive job of teaching blacks the responsibilities of freedom and the sanctity of voting, legal, and property rights, they did next to nothing to help protect those rights against the Ku Klux Klan. Republicans were overly dependent on the federal government and content with a naive faith in law and reason. They literally begged ruthless opponents to be cooperative; they undermined their own political existence by dissolving the perfectly legitimate Union Leagues; they even prosecuted and punished Negroes more vigorously in the courts to prove their own decorum.

For a year and a half, Governor Holden, handicapped by inadequate legal power, fought the Klan primarily with verbal denunciations and appeals, appeasement, and requests for federal aid. Federal power proved ineffective because, in accordance with the principles of civil supremacy and federalism, military authorities were unwilling to do more than provide a temporary presence. At such moments, klansmen adroitly backed off only to reactivate themselves after the military withdrew. This guerrilla-like tactic thoroughly confounded state and federal authorities and was central to Klan success. It nullified the significance of the military and discredited Republican cries of a breakdown of law and order.

Perhaps Governor Holden's most questionable policy was his persistent refusal to utilize a black militia on the grounds that such action would inflame race hatreds and threaten race war. But victory in the Civil War had been dependent on a willingness to join armed blacks in fighting whites, and the very survival of southern Republicanism may have turned on this refusal to take a similar stand. Instead, when a white state militia was sent by the governor to Jones County following the murder of that county's Republican sheriff, O. R. Colgrove, its only accomplishment was the disbanding of the local black militia as a means of restoring harmony. When the state militia subsequently departed, the white Republican who had organized the local black force, Colonel M. L. Shepard, was promptly assassinated. Similarly, State Senator John W. Stephens pleaded in vain for two hundred stand of arms with which to organize a local black force in Caswell County just days prior to his murder in May 1870. With such proceedings how could Republicanism survive?

Detectives employed by the state did uncover enough evidence to secure the indictment of thirty-one men for Klan crimes in 1869, ten of them for murder. But early the following year, these men were all released in accordance with a policy of appeasement, and none ever came to trial. In justice to Governor Holden, it must be said that his policy of conciliation did claim a disputed success in two counties. The limits of this success meanwhile were revealed elsewhere, particularly in Alamance and Caswell counties, the only counties in the state that Republicans had gained between the spring and fall elections of 1868 while losing thirteen others. Republicanism in these two counties was marked by unusually effective racial cooperation in the local party leadership, and it was here that Klan activity became most intense.

Near midnight on February 26, 1870, a large body of mounted and robed klansmen took over the county seat of Alamance, dragged the county's leading black Republican, Wyatt Outlaw, from his home, and hanged him in the courthouse square. The governor responded by proclaiming a state of insurrection in that county and seeking federal military aid. The Grant administration, which was embarrassed by the need for continuing federal interference in the South, doubted its authority to intervene and advised a more vigorous response by the state.

Terrorism reached a new climax three months later with the brutal murder of the state senator from Caswell, John W. Stephens. A meeting of state Republican leaders now determined to resort to state military action in imitation of Governor Powell Clayton of Arkansas, whose policy of military arrests, trials, and executions constituted the only successful resistance to the Klan that occurred anywhere in the Reconstruction South. President Grant promised to back this policy with full federal power in the event of resistance.

Typical of Republican ineffectuality, it took two months to implement this military response. Shunning the use of local blacks, white troops were recruited in the western part of the state under the command of a former Union officer, Colonel George W. Kirk, and sent into Caswell and Alamance in mid-July. About one hundred suspects were arrested and by order of the governor were refused release on writs of habeas corpus. Many other suspects fled the state. Momentarily the Klan appeared crushed, and a number of confessions and repudiations were soon obtained.

Conservatives responded with indignant denunciations of military rule, and many were the tales of outrage, atrocity, and indignity committed by the state militia. There was, indeed, some misbehavior, one of the most infamous instances seems to have been nude bathing at the village pump, but not one shot was fired, drop of blood shed, or serious injury recorded. Had Holden remained free to continue with the planned military trials, and chosen to do so, the consequences could have been far more severe. Legal action instituted by the Conservatives prevented that possibility. When state Chief Justice Richmond M. Pearson was applied to, he promptly issued habeas corpus writs, which the governor just as promptly refused to honor on the grounds that civil law had been suspended. While this was in accord with legal precedent, Governor Holden was embarrassed by a specific prohibition against suspending the writ of habeas corpus that had been placed in the Republican constitution of 1868 in a reaction against Confederate use of that power during the Civil War. The chief justice gracefully acquiesced in the governor's refusal, however, by ruling that the power of the court was exhausted. Conservatives, who had demanded that a civil posse be summoned to enforce the writs, were furious and anxious for just the kind of forceful encounter that Republicans were always so anxious to avoid.

Conservatives then ironically turned to the federal courts and sought writs for the imprisoned men under the Fourteenth Amendment and the habeas corpus act of 1867. After unusual private pleading, the federal district judge, George W. Brooks, who had been appointed to that post on Holden's recommendation in 1865, endorsed Conservative appeals and issued the writs. Although Holden was then advised by President Grant to yield to the federal judiciary, Grant and his attorney general seem to have anticipated that Judge Brooks would remand the prisoners to the state when the case came before him in court. The state then again botched affairs by not offering evidence against the prisoners in court, and in an act of questionable interference in state affairs, Judge Brooks ordered the prisoners released and thus completely discredited Governor Holden's course.[26]

Meanwhile a more severe blow had fallen on Republicans when Conservatives captured control of the state legislature in the elections of August 4, 1870. Both Klan terrorism and a popular reaction against the militia movement contributed to that result. Klan activity was reported in at least ten of the fifteen counties gained by the Conservatives, and the Conservatives' victory was due less to an increase in their vote than to a decline in that of the Republicans. If anything, the entire episode illustrated why Republicans were always running so scared. In a crucial confrontation, even at a time when they controlled all branches of the state government, they simply could not match the power, influence, and resourcefulness of the opposition. Nor could they rely on the federal government for the additional sustenance needed.

Conservatives were elated by their legal and electoral victories, and showing none of the concern for propriety that so characterized Republicans, they ruthlessly consolidated their power. Colonel Kirk and one of his subordinates fled the state to avoid armed mobs and further legal harassment. The issuance of a bench warrant by Judge Brooks in this matter was subsequently overruled by Judge Hugh L. Bond of the federal circuit court in a clearly stated rebuke of Brooks that upheld Governor Holden's entire course.[27] This was now of little use to the governor, who

26. Amos T. Akerman to Ulysses S. Grant, August 8, 1870, copy, in Governor William W. Holden Papers, State Archives; Cortez A. M. Ewing, "Two Reconstruction Impeachments," *North Carolina Historical Review*, XV (1938), 210.

27. William H. Battle, *A Report of the Proceedings in the Habeas Corpus Cases....* (Raleigh, 1870), 141.

was himself indicted and obliged to leave the state to avoid arrest.

Klan activity, though lessened, did continue in several areas, particularly in a group of western counties, while the power of the governor to deal with this problem was curtailed by the Conservative legislature. Meanwhile Congress responded to the problem with stronger legislation that led to federal arrests, indictments, and convictions that ended Klan activity by 1872. A significant postscript was provided when subsequent revelations culminated in local indictments against sixty-three klansmen for felony and eighteen for the murder of Wyatt Outlaw. The Conservative legislature at once repealed the law under which the felony indictments had been obtained, and over the next two years legislated full pardons for all crimes that had been committed in behalf of any secret organization, including the Union Leagues.

The gesture of amnesty for Republicans was a false and cynical one. Not only was there not a single crime involved that was attributable to the Union Leagues, but no mercy was extended to a number of blacks who had been convicted and imprisoned by Republican courts for illegal retaliation against the Klan. All matters connected with Republican railroad projects were specifically excluded from the amnesty, while Conservatives mocked the idea of a pardon for Governor Holden who had been successfully impeached for his role in the militia movement and removed from office early in 1871.

In further pursuit of Conservative aims, congressional and state senatorial districts were gerrymandered with such effectiveness that when Republicans succeeded in carrying the gubernatorial election of 1872, Conservatives were left in firm control of all legislative power.[28] Towns and cities were also gerrymandered, while voting procedures and requirements were altered in a manner hostile to black and lower-class voters. Residence requirements were lengthened, voters were disfran-

28. Hamilton, *Reconstruction in North Carolina*, 560, 570; Governor Tod R. Caldwell's Annual Messages of November 20, 1871, and November 18, 1872, *North Carolina Executive and Legislative Documents* 1871–1872, 1872–1873.

chised for petty crimes, and laws forbidding identifiable party tickets and requiring a confusing multiplicity of ballot boxes were utilized to confuse less literate voters. In addition, election procedures were often administered in a partisan manner—blacks were refused registration; Republicans of both races were kept from the polls by threats of violence, economic reprisal, and social ostracism; and returns from Republican dominated precincts were thrown out on patent pretext.[29] Steps also had been taken to impeach Chief Justice Pearson but were abandoned, and since a Republican lieutenant governor, Tod R. Caldwell, succeeded Holden in the governor's chair, the legislature stripped the governor of his powers of appointment. This incited a lengthy legal struggle that culminated in a judicial victory for Governor Caldwell.[30]

As this particular victory indicated, the Republican party remained very much in contention. It still controlled the state executive and judiciary as well as numerous local governments and the federal patronage. Conservatives, in turn, were soon plagued by factionalism of their own and embarrassed by their inability to remedy existing economic hardships. Their failure to settle the debt question, their neglect of the common schools, and their favoritism for, but slowness in reviving, the state university, were all sources of difficulty.

The political program of the Republicans remained essentially defensive as it centered on rebutting racist appeals, Reconstructionist stereotypes, and Conservative attempts to alter the constitution of 1868. The democratic and welfare provisions of that constitution retained widespread support among both races, while the wisdom of its legal and political features had steadily gained approval. Conservatives thus found it expedient

29. James M. Justice to Tod R. Caldwell, June 12, 1871, and Edward Ancrum to Tod R. Caldwell, September 15, 1872, Governor Tod R. Caldwell Papers; Daniel L. Russell to Thomas Settle, September 16, 1874, and William A. Smith to Thomas Settle, November 13, 1876, Thomas Settle Papers. Nevertheless one prominent Republican later wrote: "I will frankly say that I think our party has suffered more in the past from the factional strife of its leaders, than from the frauds of Democracy." Robert M. Douglas to S. S. Olds, April 27, 1884, Thomas Settle Papers.

30. Hamilton, *Reconstruction in North Carolina*, 561.

to promise not to tamper with such specific constitutional provisions as the homestead, the laborers' lien, the school system,
and equal rights, while focusing their demands for revision on
the judiciary and local self-government. The latter was vital to
continuing Republican strength everywhere and for that very
reason considered obnoxious, especially in the black dominated counties of the East. Nevertheless in 1871 Conservative
legislators could not sufficiently rally their own members to obtain the necessary two-thirds vote in each house to call a constitutional convention. They then defied that constitutional barrier
by passing an act for a state referendum on the question. Governor Caldwell, supported by four justices of the state Supreme
Court, responded by proclaiming the referendum bill unconstitutional and refusing to implement it, whereupon the legislature censured the governor and the four justices and directed
the county sheriffs to institute the measure.

In the campaign that ensued, Conservatives were handicapped by the popularity of the constitution, their own arrogant
proceedings, and renewed fears of federal interference. In August the proposed convention was soundly defeated by a vote of
95,252 to 86,007. The Republican victory was a limited one,
however, since in the vote for convention delegates Conservatives had garnered a majority of two delegates and over 10,000
votes.

Nevertheless the Conservatives had suffered a defeat, and
that setback together with other state and national developments encouraged a decline in extremism. Nationally, Democrats had already moved toward their New Departure policy,
and by 1872 federal action against the Klan and a split among
Republicans encouraged Conservatives and Democrats to mol-
lify the North and seek an alliance with the Liberal Republican movement. Although federal firmness had encouraged this
southern drift, Republicans responded to the Liberal Republican movement with a new moderation of their own. This was
apparent in Grant's lenient policies and in North Carolina Republicanism during the administrations of Governors Tod R.
Caldwell and Curtis H. Brogden.

Unlike Holden, Caldwell was a graduate of the state university, a distinguished attorney, and a former Whig from the West who had some standing with the gentry. Although he had remained a Unionist during the war, he was not identified with either blacks or white radicals. Caldwell was dignified, honest and firm, and during his administration the party appeared determined to combat demagoguery by upholding the law and proving its own sensibility and moderation.[31] Caldwell was also quick to defend his authority as governor and to expose and combat all questionable actions on the part of the Conservative dominated legislature.

To a great extent Republicans did win a new respectability, although that fact seldom achieved much recognition from the opposition at election time, and it was achieved at some cost to Republican unity and morale, particularly after Brogden succeeded to the governorship following Caldwell's death in 1874. For example, Republican hesitancy to nominate candidates of less than impeccable character often denied the aspirations of able or ambitious blacks, carpetbaggers, and lower-class whites. Also a growing utilization of independent candidates invariably meant that Republicans were being asked to step aside for moderates from the Conservative party.[32] Such developments obviously represented some weakening of the party's equalitarian commitment and stimulated factionalism and discontent. The development of a new leadership among the rank and file was being curtailed, and blacks, carpetbaggers, and radical whites must have questioned the wisdom of risking their lives and livelihood for a party that offered so little while making such extensive concessions to racism and other Conservative demands.

The negative impact of the moderate trend cannot be fixed, however, and should not be exaggerated. Local Republicans did continue to maintain themselves, and blacks remained prominent in various instances. The basic issues of reform and equal

31. See Governor Caldwell's Annual Messages of November 20, 1871, and November 18, 1872, *North Carolina Executive and Legislative Documents*, 1871–1872, 1872–1873.
32. Olsen, *Carpetbagger's Crusade*, 117, 124–25, 192.

rights retained importance, and some election results were encouraging. Governor Caldwell's firm but moderate stance, his strong support of public education, and his sensible railroad and fiscal policies won support at the very moment that many voters were being alienated from the Conservative party by revelations about the Ku Klux Klan and other Conservative excesses.

Following its defeat on the convention question in 1871, the Conservative dominated legislature had turned to slower legislative procedures for constitutional change. A number of proposed revisions obtained initial passage but had yet to obtain a necessary second passage in the succeeding legislature of 1872. In that year, however, despite Liberal Republican defection, the Republicans reelected Governor Caldwell and sufficiently increased their legislative strength to block major constitutional change. Conservatives suffered another defeat in the presidential election where they faced the distasteful task of supporting the long-hated, and soon-defeated, Horace Greeley. Obviously moderate but firm Republican policies in North Carolina had brought unusual success. But that success was dependent on the unusually calm climate of 1872. To the opposition that climate had meant failure.

It was hardly surprising then that Conservative extremism soon reappeared, and it did so at the very time that the Republican stance appeared to weaken under Governor Curtis H. Brogden. Although a man of humble origins and little education, Brogden proved less objectionable than his predecessor, partly because he had been a loyal state official during the war but especially because he lacked Caldwell's firmness and readily cooperated with the legislature.[33] Republicans may also have weakened moderates among the opposition by helping elect Augustus S. Merriman, the defeated gubernatorial candidate, to the United States Senate over Zebulon B. Vance. Most of Merriman's Democratic supporters in the legislature were not returned in 1874.

33. Samuel A. Ashe (ed.), *Biographical History of North Carolina from Colonial Times to the Present* (8 vols.; Greensboro, 1905–1917), VI, 106–12.

By 1874 emotionalism was additionally provoked by the proposed federal Civil Rights bill, which included provisions against school segregation, truly a volatile issue in the South. Conservatives now set aside the difficult constitutional issue and relied heavily on demagoguery and racist appeals. Republicans, still handicapped by a lack of newspapers and funds, again focused on establishing their respectability. They repudiated the proposals of a state Negro convention, denounced the proposed Civil Rights bill, and criticized all efforts to promote racial mixing or agitate for racial equality.[34] Such clarification did little to restore calm or honesty to Reconstruction politics. One Republican in the eastern portion of the state equated his party's position with that of free soilers in the antebellum period, while another complained of absolutely no enforcement of the election laws in the face of thousands of instances of abuse. "The time has come when the Republican party must protect itself or cease to exist," he concluded, but he looked to federal legislation for relief.[35]

In a contest where Republicans remained exceedingly moderate but their opponents did not, Conservatives again swept the state. The race issue had been crucial, although illustrative of the Republican dilemma, the only elected Republican congressman was a black. Conservatives joyfully proclaimed their victory with an illustration of Miss Liberty captioned "Sic Semper! White Supremacy," and predicted the future in a prominently displayed letter from a "Democratic Conservative." We assure the Negro equality before the law, the letter stated, but we also assure that we will strike down the Republican party forever "and proclaim to the world that the race of men, God saw fit to enslave for a time never were, and never can be our equals."[36]

Although Conservatives had avoided constitutional revision

34. Olsen, *Carpetbagger's Crusade*, 192–94.
35. W. D. Pearsall to Daniel L. Russell, August 11 and October 7, 1874, Daniel L. Russell Papers, Southern Historical Collection, and Daniel L. Russell to Thomas Settle, September 16, 1874, Thomas Settle Papers.
36. Greensboro *Patriot*, August 12, 1874.

as an issue in that election, that matter quickly surfaced and a convention bill was soon passed. Conservatives were still intimidated by the issue, however, and their leading strategist conveniently suggested that "a constitution with such an origin and such features" required justification rather than criticism, while the state executive committee apologized that "limited space" did not permit it "to catalogue the numerous defects and imperfections of our present constitution or to enumerate the remedies to be offered."[37] One specific reform that was urged was the ending of local self-government.

That the race issue was still not necessarily overpowering was illustrated in August 1875 when it appeared that Republicans had elected a bare majority of delegates to the proposed constitutional convention. But Democrats were not to be foiled, and on election day, the state chairman of the Democratic party, William R. Cox, dispatched two successive telegrams to the four Democratic commissioners of Robeson County: "As you love your state hold Robeson" and "Robeson must give certificates to your candidates. State depends on it."[38]

The five county commissioners of Robeson, four of whom were Democrats, already had appointed all the county's registrars and election judges, thus assuring Democrats a fair count. After the election it was the duty of the commissioners "to add the number of votes returned" from the polls. Instead, responding to Cox's telegrams, they reversed a Republican victory by throwing out the returns from four Republican townships and presenting the two Democratic candidates with election certificates. When the matter was then brought before Republican Supreme Court Justice Thomas Settle, he refused to intercede stating that he had no more power to interfere with the action of the commissioners than they had had to interfere with the votes returned. The two Robeson delegates then improperly voted on

37. William A. Graham to Conservative Senators, December 15, 1874, William A. Graham Papers, Southern Historical Collection; Democratic Party Address, Greensboro *Patriot*, June 9, 1875.
38. Reconstruction Papers, State Archives.

the question of their own eligibility, and the Democrats captured control of the convention by one vote.

Because of their narrow majority, Democrats were forced to minimize their intentions, but major constitutional changes were adopted that reflected a unified hostility against blacks and Republicans and when ratified by a popular vote would seal the fate of Republicanism in the state. These included the extension of legislative control over local government and an increase in the residence requirement for voting; a curtailment of the power of the governor; and various alterations in the judicial system, still largely occupied by Republicans. Constitutional barriers against interracial marriage and integrated schools were also adopted.

Corresponding to the racist and anti-democratic posture of the entire movement for redemption, most of these changes were of no benefit to the state. The constitutional sanctification of racism corrupted whites while further hindering and degrading blacks. A new system of rotating superior court judges led to confusion, increased cost, and inefficiency and was later modified, while a reduction in the number of superior and supreme court judges was unrealistic and subsequently reversed. As for the alteration in the power of the executive, a study concluded in 1950 that North Carolina "cannot have effective management in state administration today because the constitutional convention of 1875 wrote into the state's constitution amendments expressing some of its current indignation against Governor W. W. Holden."[39] Finally, the extension of legislative control over local government, which did end black control in certain counties, constituted a step that stifled local self-government, the political development of the black population, and the continuation of meaningful two-party politics in the state.

The Reconstruction conflict culminated in the election of 1876. Within the state not only the governorship and the legislature but also the constitutional reforms of 1875 were at stake,

39. Roma Sawyer Cheek, *A Preliminary Study of Government Management in North Carolina* (Raleigh, 1950), 50.

while the presidential contest between Rutherford B. Hayes and Samuel J. Tilden would end in abandonment by the North. Both state and national elections were now scheduled simultaneously in November, and Republicans bore the burden of Grant's discredited regime, unpopular federal taxes, and a depression that had been underway since 1873. Primary state interest focused, however, upon the gubernatorial contest between Thomas Settle and Zebulon B. Vance.

The Republican nomination of Thomas Settle, a prewar Democrat and associate of Holden, represented a shift toward the more radical past. At the head of the party's campaign committee was another relatively radical reformer, the carpetbagger Albion W. Tourgee. In an apparent renewed commitment to the interests of the black and white masses, Republicans enunciated a free labor and equal rights position and attacked the state's new Landlord and Tenant Act. A continuing limitation to this equalitarianism was indicated by Republican resistance to a proposed revival of the Union Leagues and the forced withdrawal of the one black on the state ticket, James E. O'Hara, a nominee for presidential elector.

Democrats devoted their primary attention to denouncing Republicanism and championing white supremacy and the war record of their gubernatorial candidate, the former Confederate governor, Zebulon B. Vance. In a bid for western support they also promised to complete existing railroad projects, and they defended the proposed constitutional amendments as measures of economy and good government. Alien domination also remained a primary concern: "Shall the people of the states or the corrupt Federal officers rule in this and all the other states?"[40]

Republicans countered by denouncing both the proposed constitutional amendments and Vance's ardent support of the Confederacy. They defended civil and political equality and their own record and attributed the state's economic difficulties to the recent foolish war. Years of Democratic legislative and

40. Speech manuscript, n.d. [1876], David F. Caldwell Papers.

county control also provided a variety of opportunities to de-
nounce Democratic corruption and fraud. The most prominent
instance involved the misappropriation of money by the state
superintendent of education. Republicans also promised to cite
two instances of Democratic thievery for every one attributed to
a Republican, and their one time *bête noire*, Josiah Turner, Jr.,
provided welcome assistance. According to Turner while "there
were colored men in the penitentiary for stealing Dominique
chickens and speckled pigs," he could point to hundreds of
Democrats "riding around in fine carriages and rolling in wealth
who ought by rights to be there." The moral seemed to be, suggested Thomas Settle, that "the Republicans just did not understand the stealing business, while they steal chickens, the
Democrats steal millions of dollars."[41]

Highlighting the campaign of 1876 were fifty-seven public
debates between Settle and Vance. The two candidates were
men of prepossessing appearance, strong intellect, and debat-
ing skill. Vance was a man of majestic appearance, whose
photograph had been selected after an international search to
appear in Matthew Fontaine Maury's elementary geography as
the perfect representative of the Caucasian race. The former
governor and war hero epitomized the ability and glory, and
perhaps the limited logic as well, of white supremacy and the
Lost Cause. As a stump speaker and dispenser of humorous an-
ecdote he had no equal, but his manner and presence have
been judged superior to his intellect and accomplishments.[42]

Thomas Settle was also a handsome man of magnetic personality though more serious and reserved than his opponent. Gifted
with a "quick and acute" mind, he was a well-informed and per-
suasive debater. Settle challenged whites "to stand up and be
men" and mocked the proposition that "forty million people of
the Anglo-Saxon race should not be willing to give four million

41. Raleigh *Era*, September 28, 1876, quoted in Sandra Porter Babb, "The
Battle of the Giants: The Gubernatorial Election of 1876 in North Carolina"
(M.A. thesis, University of North Carolina, 1970), 45.
42. *Ibid.*, 29.

poor, ignorant and slave-ridden Africans an equal and fair race in the contest of life."[43] Apparently such pleas had too little appeal, and while the reasoning element among Vance's supporters "were disappointed in his speeches," that consideration also failed to determine the day.[44] Vance and Tilden carried the state, and the constitutional amendments were approved.

"Righteousness, by righteous methods, had at last prevailed and Reconstruction in North Carolina was ended," so at least concluded the standard historical glorification of that accomplishment. Actually there were signs of fraud and intimidation. The voting totals in Democratic-controlled counties had increased far beyond that in those controlled by Republicans, and it is no secret that dishonest returns were thereafter common in the state. Democrats were jubilant nonetheless. "Gloria in Excelsis," the Raleigh *News* exclaimed: "North Carolina is redeemed. The nation is saved." The meaning of that redemption was expressed more frankly by the Charlotte *Democrat*: "In short, North Carolina is now a white man's state and white men intend to govern it hereafter."[45]

Democrats now proceeded to guarantee the permanence of white supremacy and Democratic rule and to perpetuate concepts of Reconstruction justifying their total triumph. Political rivalry was thus undermined and the state increasingly solidified despite the strong showing that Republicans had made in the election of 1876. In that election, six years after the short Republican reign, in a state where blacks numbered only one-third of the total population, Settle had received 104,330 votes to Vance's 118,248. Here was certainly the substance for a continuing significant political rivalry. That promise was undermined by racism and persisting convictions of the totally alien

43. Winston-Salem *Union Republican*, August 17, 1876, quoted in Babb, "The Battle of the Giants," 53.
44. Hamilton, *Reconstruction in North Carolina*, 649.
45. Raleigh *News*, November 8, 1876, and Charlotte *Democrat*, November 13, 1876, quoted in Babb, "Battle of the Giants," 68.

and evil nature of the Republican opposition, and North Carolina chose to travel the road of white supremacy and one-party rule.

Northern developments aided that transition. With the passage of time the fear and idealism engendered by the war had declined, and the North became increasingly weary of the southern problem and preoccupied with its own affairs. Business-oriented Republicans in the North were little concerned with the aspirations of lower-class blacks or whites or sympathetic to reform of any sort. At the same time, the changing stance of southern Democrats, best illustrated perhaps by the emerging concept of the "New South," catered with great effectiveness to dominant northern concerns. The Democratic senator from North Carolina, Matt Ransom, typified the nationalism and economic philosophy the North desired, while Democrats continued profuse in their promises to protect the constitutional rights of socially inferior and thoroughly dominated blacks. The stage was thus set for an expedient new consensus—the "reunion and reaction" of 1877. Northern Republicans obtained the presidency and the promise of stability and a more acceptable attitude in the South. Southern Democrats in turn were granted federal patronage and "home rule" at the slightly concealed expense of scalawags, carpetbaggers, and blacks. Time had proven that the white South's commitment to states rights and a high degree of self-determination, not to mention white supremacy, were not so much in conflict with northern beliefs after all. North Carolina Republicans were left to lament the policies of "John-Tyler-Millard-Fillmore-Andrew-Johnson-Benedict-Arnold-Judas-Iscariot" Hayes.[46]

Although the North Carolina Republican party continued to function with some effectiveness, meaningful two-party politics and equal rights had ended. The tragic sources of that failure did not rest in either the incapacity of blacks as voters or the evils of Republican rule. They rested rather in the reactionary

46. Edward P. Brooks to Thomas Settle, March 9, 1879, Thomas Settle Papers.

power and ruthlessness of indigenous white leaders who opposed a reasonable accommodation to emancipation and equal rights. The so-called Redeemers had helped provoke an unacceptable Reconstruction settlement, and they then committed the state to racism, reaction, and political immorality in an ironic triumph for home rule that deserves little of its traditional identification with purity and progress.

In response to the powerful opposition it encountered, North Carolina Republicanism, rather than being radical, had been characterized by a timidity that hesitated to venture beyond federal demands and that reflected economic, political, and racial orthodoxy. After their initial impressive success, Republicans were unable to retain mass white and black enthusiasm. Not only were they undermined by their own mistakes and weaknesses, but they seemed to have nowhere to go and were constantly on the defensive. Conservative-Democrats eventually did endorse many of the constitutional reforms of 1868 and since Republicans had nothing new to offer, it became easier for whites to accept the white supremacy call without feeling that they were abandoning their own interests.

Admitting these Republican weaknesses, however, it is not clear that a promising alternative existed. Whether the fact is attributable to elitist demagoguery or intrinisic racism, North Carolina white society was not prepared to tolerate Republicanism or equal rights, and blacks and their allies were not equipped to force them to do so. The voting base of the Republican party was abysmally weak, while its leadership was too often isolated, restrained, and inept. On the whole Republicans probably did as well as could be expected. They retained the support of thousands of white voters, came close to permanent success, and made lasting and positive contributions to the state. In the long run the odds against them were just too great.

At the heart of those unfavorable odds was both the impact and the alien origins of black suffrage. The Reconstruction program had been originated by northerners and it conflicted with the federalist system, the indigenous conditions of the state, and the general principles of self-determination. In the eyes of dominant North Carolinians not only was black suffrage detestable for a variety of racial, political, and economic reasons, but also because it was one of a long series of aggressions against the South. This enfranchisement of the blacks was thus a final indignity that intensified resistance at the very moment the North assumed it had found a means of safely restoring home rule.

While it is true that there was strong, even majority, voting support for Republicanism in North Carolina at various times, it is also true that the forces of origin and self-maintenance usually associated with such a remarkable political development had not yet naturally emerged within the state. Instead, under the crisis created by a sectional war, southern Republicanism was created and pushed into power by the external force of the North. Thereafter, North Carolina Republicans faced insurmountable internal obstacles and were dependent for continued success on an unreliable and severely handicapped external force. That the state might have been better off if it had accepted and worked with the principles of Reconstruction and equal rights may seem obvious to the modern mind, but that does not mean that it was sensible for the North to force on the state a settlement that the North would not enforce or that North Carolina could not or would not willingly accept.

Bibliographical Essay

THE STANDARD SCHOLARLY ACCOUNT OF NORTH CARO-
lina Reconstruction remains J. G. de Roulhac Hamilton's *Re-
construction in North Carolina* (New York: Columbia University
Press, 1914), which is an informative account marred by racism
and an anti-Republican bias. The major challenges to Hamil-
ton's account are Otto H. Olsen, *Carpetbagger's Crusade: The
Life of Albion Winegar Tourgee* (Baltimore: Johns Hopkins
Press, 1965), and two volumes by W. McKee Evans: *Ballots and
Fence Rails: Reconstruction on the Lower Cape Fear* (Chapel
Hill: University of North Carolina Press, 1966), and *To Die
Game: The Story of the Lowry Band, Indian Guerrillas of Re-
construction* (Baton Rouge: Louisiana State University Press,
1971). More restrained revision is provided in Richard L. Zuber,
Jonathan Worth: A Biography of a Southern Unionist (Chapel
Hill: University of North Carolina Press, 1965); Jonathan Daniels'
biography of an unattractive Carpetbagger, *Prince of Carpetbaggers* (Philadelphia: J. B. Lippincott, 1958); and a brief, elementary account by Richard L. Zuber, *Reconstruction in North
Carolina* (Raleigh: North Carolina Office of Archives and History, 1969). An annotated, detailed bibliography is available in
the work by Olsen, and the works of Evans and Zuber also contain useful bibliographies.

General works that deal significantly with North Carolina include Allen W. Trelease, *White Terror: The Ku Klux Klan Conspiracy and Southern Reconstruction* (New York: Harper and
Row, 1971); Michael Perman, *Reunion Without Compromise:
The South and Reconstruction, 1865–1868* (London: Cam-

bridge University Press, 1973), which focuses on Conservative thought; Carl N. Degler, *The Other South: Southern Dissenters in the Nineteenth Century* (New York: Harper and Row, 1974), which considers Republicans; and Jonathan Truman Dorris, *Pardon and Amnesty under Lincoln and Johnson: The Restoration of the Confederates to Their Rights and Privileges, 1861–1898* (Chapel Hill: University of North Carolina Press, 1953). William K. Boyd (ed.), *The Memoirs of W. W. Holden* (Durham: Seeman Printery, 1911), is a defense of Republicanism, and an excellent introduction to anti-Republicanism is found in two collections edited by J. G. de Roulhac Hamilton: *The Correspondence of Jonathan Worth* (2 vols.; Raleigh: North Carolina Historical Commission, 1909), and *The Papers of Thomas Ruffin* (4 vols.; Raleigh: North Carolina Historical Commission, 1920). A variety of viewpoints may be found in James A. Padgett (ed.), "Reconstruction Letters from North Carolina," *North Carolina Historical Review*, XVIII–XXI (1941–1944), and Elizabeth G. McPherson (ed.), "Letters from North Carolina to Andrew Johnson," *North Carolina Historical Review*, XXVII–XXIX (1951–1952).

Extensive collections of newspapers are available at the North Carolina State Archives in Raleigh, the Duke University Library, and the University of North Carolina Library, and almost all of the pertinent newspapers are available on microfilm from the state archives. Important Republican newspapers include the Raleigh *North Carolina Standard* (1865–1870), Asheville *Weekly Pioneer* (1867–1874), Greensboro *New North State* (1872–1877), Wilmington *Herald* (1865–1866), Wilmington *Post* (1867–1876), and Winston-Salem *Union Republican* (1875–1877). The Raleigh *Daily Progress* (1865–1867) was a strong Holden supporter. Major Conservative-Democratic papers include the Charlotte *Western Democrat* (1865–1877), Greensboro *Patriot* (1867–1877), Raleigh *Sentinel* (1866–1876), Wilmington *Star* (1867–1877), and the Wilmington *Journal* (1864–1877). Most of the above newspapers varied in name and frequency of publication during the cited periods.

Also available are full collections of North Carolina legislative journals, legislative documents, convention journals, and special reports, as well as pertinent federal reports by the Senate and the House that are especially valuable for the period 1865 to 1872.

James L. Lancaster, "The Scalawags of North Carolina, 1850–1868" (Ph.D. dissertation, Princeton University, 1974) is a superb study. Other particularly significant doctoral dissertations include Kenneth Edson St. Clair, "The Administration of Justice in North Carolina" (Ohio State University, 1939); Catherine S. Silverman, "Of Wealth, Virtue and Intelligence: The Redeemers and Their Triumph in Virginia and North Carolina, 1865–1877" (City University of New York, 1972); Jesse Parker Bogue, Jr., "Violence and Oppression in North Carolina During Reconstruction 1865–1873" (University of Maryland, 1973); and the following completed at the University of North Carolina: Horace W. Raper, "William Woods Holden: A Political Biography" (1951); Jack B. Scroggs, "Carpetbagger Influence in the Political Reconstruction of the South Atlantic States" (1952); William D. Cotton, "Appalachian North Carolina: A Political Study, 1860–1889" (1956); Charles L. Price, "Railroads and Reconstruction in North Carolina, 1865–1871" (1959); and Edward H. McGee, "North Carolina Conservatives and Reconstruction" (1972). Significant M.A. theses include Barbara B. Garrison, "A Crusading Abolitionist in Reconstruction North Carolina: Daniel Reaves Goodloe" (Wake Forest University, 1967); and the following completed at the University of North Carolina: John B. McCloud, "The Development of North Carolina Election Laws, 1865–1894" (1947); William D. Harris, "The Movement for Constitutional Change in North Carolina, 1863–1876" (1932); John R. Kirkland, "Federal Troops in North Carolina During Reconstruction" (1964); and Sandra P. Babb, "The Battle of the Giants: The Gubernatorial Election of 1876 in North Carolina," (1970).

Pertinent unpublished material is far too voluminous to list here but is mainly to be found in the Manuscript Division, Duke

University Library, Durham; North Carolina State Archives, Raleigh; and the Southern Historical Collection, University of North Carolina, Chapel Hill. Also significant are the records of Army Commands, the Freedmen's Bureau, and the Department of Justice, National Archives, Washington, D.C.

Listings of periodical literature may be found in the bibliographies recommended at the beginning of this essay.

VI

Louisiana
An Impossible Task

JOE GRAY TAYLOR

RADICAL Reconstruction probably had no chance of success anywhere in the South after the American Civil War, but this was not so evident in the 1860s as it is in the 1970s. On the contrary, for a number of reasons Louisiana might in the 1860s have seemed to be a spot where Radical Republicans had the best chance of achieving their objectives. At least one recent writer believes that a unique opportunity for successfully establishing complete citizenship for the black people of Louisiana had been lost before the end of the war itself.[1]

Reconstruction began in Louisiana before it began elsewhere. New Orleans was occupied in April 1862, and before the onset of winter Union control had been established along both banks of the Mississippi from Baton Rouge southward and to the west across the sugar parishes from New Orleans to the Atchafalaya River. The Union could not permanently control the territory west of the Atchafalaya and south of the Red River from present-day Lafayette to Opelousas and on to Alexandria, but permanent control of this region was also denied to the

1. C. Peter Ripley, *Slaves and Freedmen in Civil War Louisiana* (Baton Rouge, 1976), 2–3, 181–98.

Confederacy.[2] Thus from late 1862 on a population large enough for meaningful political action was to be found in the Union-occupied parts of Louisiana. Fruitless congressional elections were held before the end of 1863, and in 1864 a full-fledged state government was established and a new state constitution was drawn up and ratified.

Another advantage of Louisiana, from the Radical Republican point of view, was the presence in the state of potential black leaders. The upper class of Louisiana's pre-war "free people of color" included many prosperous and well-educated men. Most of them were to be found in New Orleans, but there were enclaves of free blacks elsewhere.[3] No doubt their largely French culture and the fact that most of them were Catholic in religion handicapped these people in gaining acceptance by the largely Anglo-Saxon and Protestant North, but they were nonetheless possible political leaders. In addition, some Louisiana slaves, especially those who had lived in New Orleans, had gained a degree of education and also of sophistication that could qualify them as leaders. Finally, scattered here and there through Louisiana, were black men naturally gifted with the qualities of leadership, many of them preachers, others veterans of the Union army; they were often illiterate, but if an opportunity came, they could lead. In fact, leaders from all these groups did appear during the course of Radical Reconstruction in Louisiana.[4] Louisiana was much better supplied with potential black leadership than any other southern state. South Carolina, which boasted a small but talented free black community in Charleston, ranked far behind Louisiana in this respect.

2. Corinne Marek, "The Civil War in Southwestern Louisiana" (M.A. Thesis, McNeese State University, 1977).

3. H. E. Sterkx, *The Free Negro in Antebellum Louisiana* (Rutherford, N.J., 1972); Rodolphe Lucien Desdunes, *Our People and Our History*, trans. Sister Dorothea Olga McCants (Baton Rouge, 1973), ix–xiv, 109–39; Gary B. Mills, *The Forgotten People: Cane River's Creoles of Color* (Baton Rouge, 1977), 77–217.

4. Charles Vincent, *Black Legislators in Louisiana During Reconstruction* (Baton Rouge, 1976).

Not only did Louisiana have black leadership, but the state also had a total black population large enough, if united, to dominate politics in fair elections. In 1860 Louisiana had 357,000 whites and 350,000 blacks, but a voluntary migration of black workers from the southeastern United States to the Southwest, a migration that probably exceeded in volume the pre-Civil War slave trade, created by 1870 a slight black majority, 364,000 to 362,000.[5] The proportion of black to white was not so great as in South Carolina or Mississippi, but the two races were so evenly matched in numbers that the disfranchisement of a relatively few ex-Confederates, or the adherence of a very few whites to the Republican party, could assure Radical victories in state-wide elections.

One other characteristic of Louisiana possibly made it a state where Radical Reconstruction had a better chance to succeed. A substantial minority of the white people of Louisiana had a Latin background and were Roman Catholic in religion. It has been suggested that Catholic Latin Americans were more willing than Anglo-Saxons to look upon Negroes as fellow human beings,[6] and if this was true, perhaps the white people of Louisiana might have been somewhat more willing than the whites of other southern states to accept a government in which blacks shared political rights. Furthermore, Louisiana had a metropolis, New Orleans, in which business rather than agriculture was dominant. It was conceivable that the businessmen of the city would prefer an orderly government in which blacks participated to an all white government of lasting disorder and uncertainty. As a matter of fact, something very much like such an attitude was displayed by businessmen in the "Second Reconstruction" of the 1960s.[7]

5. Bureau of the Census, *Historical Statistics of the United States: Colonial Times to 1970* (Washington, 1975), Part 1, p. 28.

6. Stanley M. Elkins, *Slavery: A Problem in American Institutional and Intellectual Life* (Chicago, 1968), 63–80.

7. Charles P. Roland, *The Improbable Era: The South Since World War II* (Lexington, Ky., 1975), 11–20, 90–91; Earl Black, *Southern Governors and Civil Rights: Racial Segregation as a Campaign Issue in the Second Reconstruction* (Cambridge, Mass., 1976), 334–36.

On the other hand, pre-Civil War politics in Louisiana had been normally characterized by fraud and violence,[8] and there was no reason to expect that such practices would not be resumed once occupation troops had ceased to keep order. Indeed, the New Orleans Riot of 1866 took place when federal troops were in the city, though they were away from the scene because of a misunderstanding.[9] Furthermore, whatever may have been the racial attitudes of Catholic Latin Americans in the Caribbean and south of the Rio Grande, the Catholics of South Louisiana were very little, if any, less Negrophobic than their Protestant fellow Christians in north Louisiana, and the Democrats of New Orleans were at least as uncompromising on Reconstruction issues as were those of Shreveport or Monroe.

Whatever expectations the sponsors of Radical Reconstruction measures may have had, and whether they based their expectations on the factors discussed above or others, Radical Reconstruction in Louisiana was not a success. On the contrary, it was an abject failure. This was true from almost any point of view. The black people of Louisiana were granted political and civil rights by the Civil Rights Acts of 1866 and 1875, by the congressional Reconstruction Acts of 1867 and 1868, by the Fourteenth and Fifteenth Amendments to the United States Constitution, and by the Enforcement Acts. Also the Louisiana constitution of 1868 attempted to guarantee political and some civil rights. But to whatever extent these rights had actually existed, they disappeared as if they had never been. No special economic rights were ever granted to Louisiana blacks, unless emancipation can be so described, nor were guarantees of economic rights ever seriously considered. It is quite possible that the average black family in Louisiana was worse off insofar as food, clothing, and shelter were concerned after the Civil War than it had been before the struggle.

The Civil Rights Act of 1866 was an attempt to reverse the

8. John S. Kendall, *History of New Orleans* (Chicago, 1922), I, 182–88, 196–98.
9. Donald C. Reynolds, "The New Orleans Riot of 1866, Reconsidered," *Louisiana History*, VII (Fall 1965), 379–92; John Rose Ficklen, *History of*

Supreme Court's Dred Scott decision by statute.[10] The bill was passed over President Andrew Johnson's veto by both houses of Congress, but even so there was considerable doubt as to whether the courts would rule the act constitutional. For this reason the congressional supporters of black rights turned to a constitutional amendment. The extreme reaction of the southern states to this proposed Fourteenth Amendment, and Louisiana was certainly no exception, has too often led to its being considered a Radical measure. Although it is extremely difficult to say just what was Radical and what was not at the time the amendment was being considered by Congress, it can be positively stated that the final version was a compromise between Radical and moderate Republicans, and that in general the moderates had the best of it. There was good political reason for this moderation; the congressional elections of 1866 were approaching, and although a majority of northern voters favored basic human rights for ex-slaves, they did not favor guaranteed Negro suffrage or other more Radical measures.

Thus the Fourteenth Amendment did what the act of 1866 was intended to do. It put citizenship for black people into the constitution, put the states under the same compulsion as to due process of law that already bound the federal government, and attempted to protect the rights of blacks as citizens against state governments and to guarantee them equality before the law insofar as state governments were concerned. On these provisions all the North except die-hard Copperheads could agree. Guaranteed black suffrage, however, whether immediately or in the indefinite future, was believed to be more than the voters would stomach, and at the time it probably was. Instead the amendment contained a provision that those states that denied suffrage to adult male citizens should have their representation

---

Reconstruction in Louisiana (Through 1868) (Reprint; Gloucester, Mass., 1966), 146–79; Joe Gray Taylor, *Louisiana Reconstructed, 1863–1877* (Baton Rouge, 1975), 107–13.

10. Albert P. Blaustein and Robert L. Zangrando (eds.), *Civil Rights and the Black American* (New York, 1970), 229–33.

in Congress reduced proportionately. The imperative "shall" in this part of the amendment would prove to be a shilly-shallying "may," and the clause would never be invoked. The disfranchisement clause was perhaps more to the liking of the Radicals, but after a few years it too became meaningless as Congress freely granted pardons to almost all who applied. The repudiation of the Confederate debt was already an accomplished fact, and the guarantee of the United States debt was not necessary.[11]

The privileges and immunities clause of the Fourteenth Amendment stood for only half a decade. In a Louisiana case, the United States Supreme Court held that under the doctrine of dual citizenship most privileges and immunities issued from the states and therefore could be withheld by a state.[12] Only in the twentieth century has the Supreme Court ruled that most of the guarantees of the Bill of Rights against the federal government were extended to apply to the states by the Fourteenth Amendment. The clause requiring due process of state governments was used more to protect business from state regulation than to preserve individual liberties until well into the 1900s. The clause requiring states to give equal protection of the law to their own citizens became highly significant in the second half of the twentieth century, but in the nineteenth it was meaningless except as justifying segregation of the races on a fictitous "separate but equal" basis.[13] Thus the Fourteenth Amendment, however much it may have meant after 1950, effected no real reforms in the 1860s and 1870s.

The Fifteenth Amendment, which forbade discrimination in suffrage on grounds of race, color, or previous condition of servitude, was ratified in 1870. In the southern states adult black

11. Joseph B. James, *The Framing of the Fourteenth Amendment* (Urbana, Ill., 1965), 117–52; Eric L. McKitrick, *Andrew Johnson and Reconstruction* (Chicago, 1960), 326–63; Alfred Avins (ed.), *The Reconstruction Amendment Debates: The Legislative History and Contemporary Debates in Congress on the 13th, 14th, and 15th Amendments* (Richmond, 1967), 147, 149–61, 210–38, 248–49.

12. *Slaughter House Cases*, 16 Wallace 36 (1873).

13. *Plessy* v. *Ferguson*, 163 U.S. 537 (1896).

males had already been qualified to vote under the Military Reconstruction Acts, and in Louisiana the state constitution of 1868, drawn up by a convention in which the delegates were evenly black and white, had reiterated this right. In practice, during most of the nineteenth century the Fifteenth Amendment was ineffective. From 1870 through 1876 the black vote in Louisiana was counted as the Radical-dominated Returning Board wanted it counted. This board probably pretty closely expressed the views of black voters, but after 1876 the black vote of all north Louisiana and much of south Louisiana was counted as the dominant Bourbon Democrats wanted it counted, and this certainly was not in accord with the desires of either black voters or the originators of the Fifteenth Amendment. In Louisiana, as in other states, the black vote was used by the Bourbons to crush the Populist movement of the 1890s. And finally, of course, the poll tax, the literacy test, and the understanding clause set up under the Louisiana constitution of 1898 reduced the number of black voters in Louisiana from more than half the total registered in 1896 to only a few thousand. Any slight influence these few thousand might have had on the general election was negated in 1905 when the state legislature put into effect a primary election for nominating party candidates. The candidate nominated by the Democratic party primary was inevitably elected to office, and only whites voted in the Democratic primary.[14]

In 1871 and 1872 Congress was sufficiently disturbed by the terroristic activities of the Ku Klux Klan and, in Louisiana, the Knights of the White Camellia, to pass new statutes designed to protect civil and political rights. This Klan terrorism was basically intended to keep Republican voters in general, and black

14. Francis Newton Thorpe (ed.), *The Federal and State Constitutions: Colonial Charters and Other Organic Laws of the States, Territories, and Colonies Now or Heretofore Forming the United States of America* (Washington, D.C., 1909), III, 1441–1465; William Ivy Hair, *Bourbonism and Agrarian Protest: Louisiana Politics, 1877–1900* (Baton Rouge, 1969), 234–79.

voters in particular, from going to the polls. Called variously the Enforcement Acts, the Force Acts, and the Ku Klux Acts, these laws provided that any action taken to deprive people of their rights under the Reconstruction amendments should be considered an offense against the United States and that those accused of violating the acts should be tried in a federal court. They also provided, in certain circumstances, for the suspension of habeas corpus and the initiation of martial law to protect rights under the amendments, but these provisions were never invoked in Louisiana.[15] These acts were in force five years or less before they were struck down by the Supreme Court. In *United States v. Reese* (1876) penalties against persons interfering with the right of others to vote were negated on the ground that the Fifteenth Amendment did not grant suffrage to anyone but merely forbade exclusion on the basis of race, color, or previous condition of servitude.[16] Of more significance, however, was another case that arose in Louisiana.

The Louisiana state election of 1872, like all Louisiana elections from November 1868 until 1900, was so characterized by fraud, trickery, and intimidation that to this day no one can say who won or who would have won if the election had been honest. Republican William Pitt Kellogg and Democrat John McEnery (who had some Republican support in the contest) each claimed to have been elected governor, and each boasted a group of loyal legislators. This conflict over the results of the election was not confined to New Orleans, then the state capital, but extended into many rural parishes. In Grant Parish, created only two years earlier and named for the president, a Democrat and a Republican each claimed to have won the office of sheriff. Kellogg, who was recognized by the Grant ad-

15. *Acts and Resolutions*, 41st Cong., 2d Sess., May 31, 1871, p. 95; *Acts and Resolutions*, 41st Cong., 1st Sess., April 20, 1870, p. 294; Richard Bardolph (ed.), *The Civil Rights Record: Black Americans and the Law, 1848–1970* (New York, 1970), 50–63.

16. *U. S. v. Reese*, 92 U.S. 214 (1876).

ministration as the rightful governor, gave his support to the Republican claimant and sent him rifles with which to arm his almost entirely black followers. The supporters of the Democratic pretender, all white, launched an attack upon the courthouse at Colfax, the parish seat. The black Republican defenders were quickly routed. At least 69 of them, and probably more than 100, were killed, including more than 20 prisoners taken out and shot in cold blood the night after the battle.[17]

Nine white men accused of having taken part in the killing were arrested and put on trial in federal court in New Orleans. Specifically they were charged with having deprived the murdered men of their civil rights in contravention of the Enforcement Acts. After one mistrial, four of the accused, including one William B. Cruikshank, were convicted. The conviction was appealed, and the appeal was heard by the United States Circuit Court of Appeals, which consisted of the trial judge and Associate Justice Joseph P. Bradley of the Supreme Court. The trial judge naturally voted to uphold the conviction, but Justice Bradley concluded that the power of Congress to enforce the two Reconstruction amendments did not include the power to provide punishment if the crime committed was punishable under the law of the state where it took place. The disagreement between the two judges resulted in the case being certified to the Supreme Court, and in 1876 that august body expressed its agreement with Bradley. Indeed, the Supreme Court went even further and asserted that the Fourteenth Amendment did not add any new civil rights but merely prohibited the denial of existing rights by the states. Thus it was left up to the state of Louisiana to prevent the denial of civil rights by individuals.[18]

White Louisianians did not wait for the Supreme Court's decision; Justice Bradley's opinion was signal enough. They knew already that state authority could not prevent the intimidating and terrorizing of black voters or, for that matter, white Republican officeholders. Therefore, so long as they did not go so far

17. Taylor, *Louisiana Reconstructed*, 267–72.
18. *U. S.* v. *Cruikshank*, 92 U.S. 542 (1876).

as to bring on federal military intervention, they could do just about whatever they pleased to reduce the effectiveness of Republican suffrage in the state.[19]

If the right of black people to vote and to assemble peacefully fared poorly, other aspects of civil rights prospered no better. The state constitution of 1868 had a strong civil rights section, but in practice it amounted to little. Henry Clay Warmoth, the first Republican governor of Louisiana, was almost as much a white supremacist as any member of the Knights of the White Camellia, though he had great skill at pleasing black crowds. The better educated former free people of color of New Orleans despised him. Warmoth vetoed the first civil rights act passed by the Louisiana legislature. Later in his term he signed a much weaker act under pressure, but it was still meaningless because he made no effort to enforce it. It was not until 1873, after Kellogg had replaced Warmoth as governor, that a reasonably strong civil rights act, at least on paper, could be enacted. But Kellogg actually governed only New Orleans and a continually declining number of rural parishes with Republican officials. Thus however much he may have desired to enforce the civil rights statute (and it is not at all certain that he wanted to enforce it), he was hardly in a position to do so. Outside of New Orleans very few, if any, blacks had the courage, or foolishness, to attempt to assert their legal rights under state law; in New Orleans such efforts were too sporadic to be significant.[20]

The Louisiana constitution, alone among the Radical Republican constitutions in the southern states, declared that the public schools should be open to children of both races on an integrated basis, but from the time Warmoth became governor in 1868 until after Kellogg's inauguration in 1873 this provision of the constitution seems to have been completely ignored. Warmoth was himself opposed to integrated schools, and he certainly took no action to encourage obedience to the constitutional mandate for integration. An ambitious system of public

19. Taylor, *Louisiana Reconstructed*, 273.
20. *Ibid.*, 436.

school administration, one not particularly well adapted to the rural parishes of Louisiana, was enacted into law during Warmoth's regime, but public education as a whole, black or white, was no better than it had been before the passage of the Military Reconstruction Acts, and it may have been worse. The Catholic Church was opposed to public education because of its fear of secularization; planters were opposed because they were reluctant to pay the necessary taxes. Ordinary whites feared integration. The schools in New Orleans were weak, and outside of New Orleans they were weaker.[21]

Kellogg, for whatever reasons, was much more willing to enforce the integration of public schools. Probably this was so because he was utterly dependent on black votes in general, and black votes in the legislature in particular, but he may have been moved by a genuine belief in equal educational opportunity for all children. Outside of New Orleans his efforts did not lead to integrated schools. In the country parishes where there were few blacks, such public schools as existed were all white. In other parishes they were all black. White parents preferred to send their children to private schools, or to no school at all, rather than to let them share a classroom with black children. In New Orleans the schools seem to have remained all white or all black except in the Second District, which included the Vieux Carré. Some Second District schools were integrated from 1873 through the spring of 1877. Mob action not unlike that of the 1960s drove many black children away from these integrated schools, at least temporarily, but integration persisted until after redemption. Governor Francis T. Nicholls ordered segregation of schools in the Second District in 1877, and, despite protests from black leaders, the courts upheld the governor's decree.[22]

21. *Ibid.*, 460–65; Leon Odom Beasley, "A History of Education in Louisiana During the Reconstruction Period, 1862–1877" (Ph.D. Dissertation, Louisiana State University, 1957), 91–109; Betty Porter, "The History of Negro Education in Louisiana," *Louisiana Historical Quarterly*, XXV (July 1942), 761–77.
22. Louis R. Harlan, "Desegregation in New Orleans Public Schools During Reconstruction," *American Historical Review*, LXVII (April 1962), 663–

Whether a program of integrated schools from the end of the Civil War onward could have overcome the educational handicap that slavery had inflicted on black people is, to say the least, doubtful. However, failure to carry out the constitutional mandate to integrate the schools, and the discrimination against blacks in education that persisted for more than two generations after Reconstruction had ended, made it inevitable that most blacks would remain at an educational disadvantage in comparison with most whites. Yet the attitude of white Louisianians toward public education was hostile overall; opportunities for both white and black children were limited. Until after 1900 Louisiana remained abysmally backward educationally for both races when compared to most other states. Black people, the supposed beneficiaries of Radical Reconstruction, suffered the most, however, and this unpleasant fact is still evident in the state's schools in the last quarter of the of the twentieth century.[23]

In 1875 Congress passed a new national Civil Rights Act, a measure long advocated by Senator Charles Sumner of Massachusetts. The act probably never would have been enacted had it not been for Sumner's death; many members of Congress felt that the great Radical's passing should be marked by some sort of legislative monument. But the Congress did not want to go very far down the civil rights road. By the time the act became law, it had been watered down considerably. A clause requiring the integration of public schools was excised. As passed, the act did have a weak public accomodations section, but in Louisiana it was disregarded almost completely outside of New Orleans, and it was largely ignored in the Crescent City. After a few blacks brought lawsuits against bars and restaurants that refused to serve them, the operators of some of these establish-

---

75; George Washington Cable, *The Negro Question: A Selection of Writings on Civil Rights in the South*, ed. Arlin Turner (Garden City, N.Y., 1958), 9; New Orleans *Daily Picayune*, June 27, 29, July 11, September 27–29, October 15, 24, November 10, 1877.

23. See, for example, Baton Rouge *Morning Advocate*, February 26, 1978.

ments ostentatiously served blacks but just as ostentatiously refused to serve whites who accompanied them. In other places, the proprietor professed his willingness to serve black customers, but white patrons proceeded to forcibly eject them. The few blacks who attended the theater or opera possibly got good seats, but these seats were carefully separated from those occupied by whites.[24]

In only a few years those rights extended to Louisiana blacks, at least in theory, by the act of 1875 would be swept away by the United States Supreme Court. Taking to its logical conclusion the earlier stated doctrine that the Fourteenth Amendment applied only to states and not to individuals, the court ruled that insofar as civil rights acts prohibited discrimination by private businesses or individuals, they were in conflict with the constitution. Then in 1896, arising from an incident that took place in Louisiana, came the famous, or infamous, case of *Plessy* v. *Ferguson*, which held that the providing of separate but equal accomodations for blacks and whites did not violate the equal protection clauses of the Fourteenth Amendment.[25] In the long run, Reconstruction in Louisiana did nothing to prevent the slights, insults, and deprivation of rights that were an essential part of a caste system designed to "keep the Negro in his place" by daily humiliation.[26]

If emancipation and Reconstruction did little or nothing to bring lasting improvement to the political and social lot of Louisiana blacks, save for a fortunate few, Reconstruction did no more for their economic betterment. A small number of black families, through intelligence, hard work, and luck, had notably improved their economic position by the time Reconstruction was over. A few became small entrepreneurs, usually with a black clientele, in New Orleans or one of the lesser towns. A

24. *U.S. Statutes at Large*, XVIII, March 1, 1875, p. 335; Taylor, *Louisiana Reconstructed*, 436.

25. *Civil Rights Cases*, 109 U.S. 3 (1883); *Plessy* v. *Ferguson*, 163 U.S. 537 (1896).

26. Germaine A. Reed, "Race Legislation in Louisiana, 1877–1898," *Louisiana History*, VII (Fall 1965), 379–92.

few more managed to acquire land and to survive as yeoman farmers. No reliable figures are available as to the number of these fortunate families in late-nineteenth-century Louisiana, but for what it may be worth, this writer is convinced that they did not greatly outnumber the free black families of antebellum Louisiana.

There had, of course, been slaves in Louisiana towns before emancipation, but there was a sizable migration of blacks from country to town during the Civil War, and this continued during Reconstruction. Many of these migrants were more or less skilled artisans. In New Orleans many black workers approached real independence; longshoremen, for example, formed unions that were from time to time successful in bargaining with employers. Such independence was exceptional. Most black town workers, especially those outside of New Orleans, were almost compelled to seek the protection of a white sponsor or patron. Certainly sponsorship was an essential part of the life of the hired domestic servant, and domestic service was almost the only legitimate occupation open to black women who did not work in the fields.[27]

After some experimentation with sharecropping, wage labor became the prevailing practice on Louisiana sugar plantations. Sugar plantation labor was gang labor under close supervision, and until the concentration of refining toward the end of the nineteenth century, the difference in work routine from that which had existed under slavery was slight. Wages were rather good for a time after the war, but it must be remembered that a family that worked in the cane fields lived in a cabin owned by the planter, often an antebellum slave cabin, and made any purchases from a commissary operated by the planter. More often than not, the worker received rations for himself and his family on the same basis as in slavery days; often the rations were the same except that the pork was of lower quality than that issued before the Civil War. The field hand on a sugar plantation was

27. Taylor, *Louisiana Reconstructed*, 383–84; John W. Blassingame, *Black New Orleans, 1860–1880* (Chicago, 1973), 49–77.

unquestionably freer than he had been as a slave, but he was far from being as free as his white neighbors. The lash was seldom encountered, but the freedmen quickly learned the power of economic coercion. What was called a strike in 1886 would have been called an insurrection in 1860, but the strike was crushed just as violently and bloodily in 1886 as an insurrection would have been crushed in 1860.[28] In fairness, it must be added that the difference in economic status between the black worker in the cane fields and the white worker in George Pullman's Chicago plant was only a matter of degree.

The tenant on a cotton plantation remained in a condition more like slavery than that of the cane worker. This was true despite the fact that the cotton tenant usually managed to get his family out of the old slave quarters and into an isolated cabin on the acres he worked. Cotton planters, encouraged by the Freedmen's Bureau, experimented with wage labor, but for various reasons, especially crop failures in 1866 and 1867, the wage system was unsuccessful. In fact, more often than not it was the freedmen rather than the landlord who rejected the wage system and demanded a share of the crop. Those who have given serious attention to the matter are aware that share-cropping, the crop lien, and legislation carefully drawn to serve the interests of planters and merchants made the sharecropper into, at best, a serf. Some misconceptions still exist, however, as to the degree of independence in the sharecropper's farming operation. When a relatively small tract of land was worked by only one or a few families, a sharecropper might be more or less independent in deciding what he would do and when he would do it, and he might confine his labor entirely to his own fields. On plantations, however, sharecroppers more often plowed, hoed, and picked cotton in gangs under the supervision of the planter or his overseer. There was a roughly equal division of labor among the croppers, and accounts were settled on the ba-

28. Taylor, *Louisiana Reconstructed*, 364–72; J. Carlyle Sitterson, *Sugar Country: The Cane Sugar Industry in the South, 1753–1950* (Lexington, Ky., 1953), 233–34, 239–41; Hair, *Bourbonism and Agrarian Protest*, 176–86.

sis of production on the acres assigned to particular families, but working conditions were far more like those that had existed under slavery than is commonly realized.[29]

It may well be that from a purely material point of view the sharecropper was worse off than the cotton plantation slave had been. Diseases associated with malnutrition were so rare among Louisiana slaves before the Civil War that it is difficult to prove that any at all existed. But apparently the sharecropper's largely unsupervised diet did not afford as much variety and as satisfactory nutrition as the slave's. The slave had eaten pork and cornbread supplemented by beef, fish, game, vegetables, and wild and cultivated fruits. The sharecropper ate pork and cornbread as his basic diet; but the pork, was usually commercially produced rather than killed and cured on the plantation and seems to have had a much larger proportion of fat than the pre-war ration. Too few families seem to have supplemented their diet of cornbread and pork. Deadly pellegra was the most obvious result of this inadequate diet, but poor nutrition must have made many people more susceptible to other diseases.[30] Since most black families in the South were sharecroppers (and also millions of white families before sharecropping came to an end), one is forced to the conclusion that Reconstruction not only did not succeed in improving the economic condition of black people, or poor people generally, in Louisiana, but that it left many of them in a worse economic condition than had been the case under the slave regime.

Since Reconstruction in Louisiana was demonstrably such a failure, inquiry into the reasons for that failure are in order. As stated at the beginning of this essay, this writer is convinced that there was never a chance of success in the sense that the "Second Reconstruction" of the twentieth century has been a success, and he emphatically disagrees with any assertion that

29. Taylor, *Louisiana Reconstructed*, 372–80, 508.
30. Sam Bowers Hilliard, *Hog Meat and Hoecake: Food Supply in the Old South, 1840–1860* (Carbondale, Ill., 1972), 68–69; Joe Gray Taylor, *Negro Slavery in Louisiana* (Baton Rouge, 1963), 107–10, 114–21.

earlier, stronger, and more radical action by the Lincoln administration could have prevented failure.[31] But the reasons for failure were several, and they deserve some discussion.

A frequently cited reason for failure, though cited more often in earlier writings than today, is that the freedmen were not adequately prepared for participation in politics or complete citizenship. There need be no racist connotation to the assertion that neither slaves nor free people of color in Louisiana had any antebellum experience whatsoever at participating in a representative democracy. It is well known that insofar as slaves were concerned, it was a criminal act under the slave code to teach them to read or write. Most lived isolated lives on rural plantations where they had minimal contact with any part of the outside world. Some notion of what went on elsewhere did filter down to them through those slaves whose work made it possible to overhear white conversation and to meet with slaves belonging to other masters, but a conception of reality thus derived at second and third hand was inevitably a distorted conception. It is no reflection on the intelligence of the typical slave to point out that circumstances made it almost inevitable that he should be ignorant except of matters pertaining to the plantation and its immediate environs. The marches and counter-marches of the war brought some additional knowledge, it is true, but knowledge of an abnormal state of affairs. It would be difficult to point out any part of the life of the ordinary slave that would qualify him for active political participation. It is worth noting that many northern Radicals opposed black suffrage during the early years of Reconstruction, whether because of their own beliefs or because they feared the reaction of northern voters.[32]

31. Ripley, *Slaves and Freedmen.*
32. Eugene D. Genovese, *Roll, Jordan, Roll: The World the Slaves Made* (New York, 1974), 561–66; Kenneth M. Stampp, "Radical Reconstruction," in Edwin C. Rozwenc (ed.), *Reconstruction in the South* (Lexington, Mass., 1972), 62–63; Lawanda Cox and John H. Cox, *Politics, Principle, and Prejudice, 1865–66: Dilemma of Reconstruction America* (New York, 1963), 77–79, 198, 226–28; McKitrick, *Andrew Johnson and Reconstruction,* 332.

On the other hand, as pointed out earlier, there were Louisiana Negroes who were eminently qualified to serve as political leaders. Most of them were educated members of the prewar community of free people of color, but there also were some ex-slaves who had managed to acquire an education. Additionally, many men who had been slaves in New Orleans or who had practiced trades that took them out into the world, had acquired a large measure of practical experience, even though their ability to read and write might be meager or nonexistent. And even though the illiteracy and lack of political experience of the great mass of blacks cannot be denied, it would be most difficult to argue that they voted any less intelligently than the mass of whites. The fact that they voted overwhelmingly for the Radical Republicans when they were permitted to do so indicates that the freedmen were well aware of where their interests lay. The implied assumption that white voters in the nineteenth century, or the twentieth, calmly considered the issues, calculatingly weighed the qualifications of the candidates, and carefully evaluated the principles of opposing parties is, to put it mildly, balderdash. If voting behavior really is determined, as the political scientists tell us, by impulse, candidate personality, party loyalty, ethnic prejudice, and countless other irrational considerations, who can prove that black voters during Reconstruction were any less prepared for political responsibility than a host of Ph.D.s in history? Incidentally, it was in largely Anglo-Saxon West Virginia in 1960, not in half-black Louisiana in 1870, that the vote of a whole state was bought in order to launch a successful campaign for the presidency by the son of a multi-millionaire.

Louisiana blacks did definitely lack one quality needed for participation in Reconstruction politics. For reasons difficult to comprehend, groups of black men were unable to match groups of whites no more numerous and no better armed in violent confrontation. In the New Orleans Riot of 1866 the white police were armed and most of the blacks were not, but the blacks were much more numerous. Yet the blacks fled, leaving many dead and wounded behind, and the white attackers lost only one man. In New Orleans and many of the country parishes relatively small groups of whites belonging to Democratic "clubs" or openly to the Knights of the White Camellia were able to keep so many blacks from the polls in 1868 that what had been a heavily Republican state in April was apparently a strongly Democratic state in November. At Colfax well-armed and, to some extent, well-drilled blacks, holding a fortified position, were easily dispersed with heavy casualties by a "posse" of whites certainly no more numerous and probably lesser in number. The well-equipped and well-led Metropolitan Police defeated by the White League in New Orleans' Battle of Liberty Place in September 1874 were largely black.[33] Similar events took place in other southern states.[34]

One can only speculate upon the reason or reasons that blacks were unable to defend themselves. To assert that lack of fighting ability was a racial characteristic is ridiculous. The peoples of Africa have not lagged behind those of other continents in studying and practicing the art of killing one another in large numbers. The Zulus were very black, and Kipling's Fuzzy Wuzzies were at least a very dark brown. Black men had fought in all American wars, and Louisiana blacks had a particularly commendable military record.[35] Perhaps generations of subordination under slavery had made it psychologically impossible for most black men of the mid-nineteenth century to stand up to white aggression with equal force. Perhaps, even, the white assumption of white superiority had to some extent, consciously or subconsciously, been accepted by blacks. The explanation may, of course, be something not yet suggested. It cannot be maintained that lack of physical courage was responsible for the

33. Taylor, *Louisiana Reconstructed*, 103–13, 267–73, 291–96.

34. See, for example, Francis Butler Simkins and Robert Hilliard Woody, *South Carolina During Reconstruction* (Reprint; Gloucester, Mass., 1966), 499–508; William C. Harris, *Presidential Reconstruction in Mississippi* (Baton Rouge, 1967), 75–76; Jerrell H. Shofner, *Nor Is It Over Yet: Florida in the Era of Reconstruction, 1863–1877* (Gainesville, Fla., 1974), 226–37.

35. Roland C. McConnell, *Negro Troops of Antebellum Louisiana: A History of the Battalion of Free Men of Color* (Baton Rouge, 1968).

poor black showing in conflict with whites; blacks were frequently engaging in sanguinary affrays with each other that would match the equally bloody outcome of quarrels between whites.

Probably if the white mob at Colfax had been routed by the blacks, or if the Metropolitan Police in New Orleans had defeated the White League at Liberty Place, Radical government in Louisiana could have accomplished more and remained in power longer. Certainly the dependence of Republican state government on federal troops was a great weakness. On the other hand, one must ask what the reaction of the North would have been to a riot in which blacks slaughtered large numbers of whites. It is not without significance that the Yankee reaction to the Coushatta Massacre of 1874, when five white Republicans were murdered, was far stronger than the reaction to the Colfax Riot of 1873 in which at least sixty-nine blacks died.

Another reason for the failure of Radical Reconstruction in Louisiana and elsewhere was the climate of economic thought of the day, especially the emphasis on the sanctity of property rights that prevailed in the mid-nineteenth century. In the heat of war, Republicans could countenance the Emancipation Proclamation, but once the war was over, they could not bring themselves to carry out any general confiscation of private property. One of the primary reasons for extending suffrage to freedmen in the South was to enable those freedmen to protect themselves from hostile whites. Yet most politicians should have known that without some form of economic foundation, black political power was, at best, uncertain. Yet very few of the Radical Republican leaders, Thaddeus Stevens the one of most importance, were willing to violate property rights, even those of the hated Rebels, in an attempt to turn the freedmen into an independent peasantry. On the contrary, as has been demonstrated, they were allowed to become the equivalent of serfs or peons. On the Sea Islands, where land abandoned by fleeing Confederates had actually been divided among black families, the United States Army eventually assisted the prewar owners in recovering their property. It is quite possible, even probable, that the experiment of dividing up the plantations and giving freedmen "forty acres and a mule" would have failed if it had been attempted. Certainly, also, there were almost insuperable constitutional obstacles. But it is significant that men who were willing to force Negro suffrage upon the southern states were unwilling to make any effort to secure this suffrage with property rights.[36]

Another important factor in the failure of Louisiana Reconstruction was the racism of white Republicans in the state. This writer can name only three white men in Louisiana during Reconstruction, and some of them not long in the state, who seem honestly to have believed that all men were created equal. These three were Emerson Bentley, practically a boy, driven from his teaching job in St. Landry Parish; Paul Trevigne, the Belgian-born true radical who edited that excellent black-owned newspaper, the New Orleans *Tribune*; and Thomas Jefferson Durant, longtime resident of New Orleans and United States attorney under President James K. Polk, a follower of Fourier, who left the state forever after the New Orleans Riot of 1866. Probably there were a few others, but they were careful to conceal their views.

It was to be expected, of course, that such scalawags as James Madison Wells, John Ray, John Lynch, and Jasper Blackburn would be no more willing to accept black men as equals than would the most ardent members of the Knights of the White Camellia. Probably they were Republicans primarily because they were opportunists; this certainly was true of Wells who, although he had been a Unionist during the war, followed what he thought was the main chance until General Sheridan said, in removing him from his office as governor, that "his conduct has been as sinuous as the mark left in the dust by the movement of a snake."[37]

36. Lawanda Cox, "The Promise of Land for the Freedmen," *Mississippi Valley Historical Review*, XLV (December 1958), 413–40; Ripley, *Slaves and Freedmen*, 194–96.

37. P. Sheridan to Edwin M. Stanton, June 3, 1867, in *Senate Executive Documents*, 40th Cong., 1st Sess., No. 14, p. 213.

Henry Clay Warmoth, the first Republican governor of Louisiana, boasted in his old age that he had prevented the "Africanization" of his adopted state. He was overstating his role when he wrote this, attempting to please Louisiana whites, but he certainly did nothing to promote the civil rights of black people as was required by the state constitution. Indeed, he openly ridiculed blacks in some of his public speeches, even as he sought their votes. In the election of 1872, when he went over almost, if not entirely, to the Democrats, he joyfully used the not inconsiderable power of the governor over the election machinery to prevent voting by as many black citizens as possible.

Warmoth had come to power by overcoming the educated blacks of New Orleans in the Republican convention of 1868; they seem to have been aware of his racial attitudes from the beginning. Such perceptive black politicians as Oscar J. Dunn and P. B. S. Pinchback soon became aware of his views. Yet if blacks did not follow Warmoth, their only other recourse was to ally themselves with the so-called "Custom-House Ring." The racial attitudes of Stephen Packard, James F. Casey, and William Pitt Kellogg were not so obviously Negrophobic as those of Warmoth and the scalawags mentioned earlier, but these men did not crusade for black rights, only for black votes. Pinchback expressed the dilemma of Louisiana blacks in 1872 when he said: "As a race [we] are between the hawk of Republican demagogism and the buzzards of Democratic prejudices. The aspirants for position in our party threaten us with excommunication if we do not follow every jack o'lantern who raises his feeble light, and the Democrats invite us to annihilation if we turn away from these Republican jack o'lanterns." [38]

The attitude of Republican leaders in Louisiana toward black people should be no cause for wonder. It simply reflected the general attitude of the country as a whole, most definitely in-

38. Quoted in Elsie M. Lewis, "The Political Mind of the Negro, 1865–1900," *Journal of Southern History*, XXI (May 1955), 197. See also Taylor, *Louisiana Reconstructed*, 156, 212–13, 237–40; Ripley, *Slaves and Freedmen*, 160–80.

cluding the North. It is well to remember that the Republicans, even at the height of Reconstruction, were but a small majority of the voters, that so-called Radicals were only a part of the Republicans, and that only a few of the Radicals really believed in full and equal citizenship for blacks. Abraham Lincoln's undisguised belief in white superiorty was that of most Republicans; the views of Thaddeus Stevens and Charles Sumner were not shared by many in their party. "The fact was that the constituency on which the Republican congressmen relied in the North lived in a race conscious, segregated society devoted to the doctrine of white supremacy and Negro inferiority."[39] In advocating emancipation and the Reconstruction amendments Republican congressmen had to assure their constituents that there would be no migration of freedmen to the North; indeed, the safest assertion was that newly freed blacks would be deported and colonized somewhere outside the United States.[40]

In response to southern violence against freedmen, to the Black Codes, to the election of high Confederate officials to office, and to what seemed generally to be an unrepentant attitude on the part of the South, a majority of Republicans, and probably a majority of the people in the North, wished, at least for a time, to do whatever was necessary to prevent the reenslavement of black people and to protect them from bodily harm. But there was no strong commitment to civil or political rights, not even to the right to vote. The people of the North were not quite so fanatical on the question of race as the "last ditch" Democrats of Louisiana, but the difference was one of degree, not of principle. It can be suggested, though it cannot be proven, that a desire to punish the South for the tragedy of the Civil War played a larger part in bringing on Radical Reconstruction than did a concern for black people, and this as late as 1868.

If Republicans were to a great extent racist, they were none-

39. C. Vann Woodward, "Seeds of Failure in the Radical Race Policy," in Rozwenc (ed.), *Reconstruction in the South*, 245.
40. Avins (ed.), *Reconstruction Amendment Debates*, 30–36, 40–41, 220, 236.

theless moderate when compared with the strident racism of northern Democrats. Throughout the Civil War and Reconstruction, these Democrats invoked the race question at every opportunity. They charged that Lincoln and his "nigger crazed counselors" planned to encourage "hordes" of blacks to overrun the North. The Republicans would do this because they had nothing but "nigger on the brain." The Emancipation Proclamation was "that masterpiece of folly and treachery."[41] Radical Reconstruction was a malignant effort "to degrade the white inhabitants of the Southern states and place them at the mercy of an inferior race."[42] The Democrats did not emphasize their uncompromising disagreement with the racial policies of the Republicans because all Democrats were paranoid on the subject. On the contrary, they believed that if they could create a situation where the only issue between Democrats and Republicans was race, the Democrats were sure to win. They may have been right, but "the Republicans were always very adept at ignoring, confusing, and cross-pressuring so effectively as to prevent any clear referendum's ever taking place on the one issue that probably would have helped the Democrats."[43] It is certainly obvious that public opinion in the North would not indefinitely keep pressure on the government to support and maintain in Louisiana a Radical Republican state government that depended on Negro voters and federal troops to remain in existence.

Louisiana Republicans definitely did depend on federal support in order to remain in power. Black voters were either a slight majority or numerically equal to white voters, but they still were not able to maintain themselves politically. A definite reason for the failure of the Radicals in Louisiana was the relentless and unceasing resistance of white Louisianians to "Black Reconstruction." It is highly significant that there was

41. Joel H. Sibley, *A Respectable Minority: The Democratic Party in the Civil War Era, 1860–1868* (New York, 1977), 180–83.
42. Quoted in *Ibid.*, 190.
43. *Ibid.*, 232.

only one locally inspired attempt to compromise during the entire period, and this "Unification Movement" was confined almost entirely to New Orleans and was an abject failure. The Wheeler Compromise of 1875, temporarily resolving an election dispute, was in effect imposed by a congressional committee.[44] Louisiana "Conservatives" bitterly contested Radical government every step of the way; they never recognized the legitimacy of Kellogg's administration; and they did not hesitate to use any practical means of destroying their political enemies.

Their methods included vote fraud, economic and physical intimidation, and if necessary murder. Louisianians were accustomed to using violence against one another, and violence against northerners and blacks was endemic in the state from 1865 to 1868. It is difficult to say how much of this early Reconstruction violence was the result of simple race hatred and resentment because of the South's defeat and how much calculated for political purpose. In the autumn of 1868, however, violence definitely became political. In the April 1868 election under the Military Reconstruction Acts, the vote in favor of ratification of the newly drawn constitution was by 17,000 out of some 110,000 votes cast. In the gubernatorial election Radical Henry Clay Warmoth polled 65,000 votes as compared to 38,000 for his Conservative opponent. Yet in the November presidential election Horatio Seymour, the Democratic candidate, polled over 80,000 votes to Ulysses S. Grant's slightly more than 33,000.[45] This abrupt reversal in less than seven months resulted from a deliberate campaign of intimidation and terrorism by white Louisianians.

The Knights of the White Camellia, a Louisiana version of

44. Unification Movement Papers, 1873, in Department of Archives, Louisiana State University; New Orleans *Daily Picayune*, June–July 1873; T. Harry Williams, *Romance and Realism in Southern Politics* (Baton Rouge, 1966), 21–43; Taylor, *Louisiana Reconstructed*, 308–10.

45. Donald W. Davis, "Ratification of the Constitution of 1868—Record of Votes," *Louisiana History*, VI (Summer 1965), 301–305; Taylor, *Louisiana Reconstructed*, 160.

the hooded terrorism exemplified in the upper South by the Ku Klux Klan, was the main instrument of this campaign, but there were lesser organizations such as the Blair Guards, the New Orleans Crescent Club, and even an organization of Italian immigrants known as the "Innocents" who played a role. These groups did not, as legend would have it, depend on black superstitions to accomplish their ends. They depended on fear, pure and simple. Probably a few blacks were persuaded by argument to vote the Democratic ticket, but most who voted Democratic or who stayed away from the polls did so because they were afraid. They had good reason for fear; sizable numbers of blacks were killed in St. Tammany Parish, St. Bernard Parish, St. Landry Parish, and Bossier Parish, and these were simply the bloodiest parishes. In St. Mary Parish two leading white Republicans were shot and stabbed to death while the wife of one of them looked on. In New Orleans "Democratic Clubs" took over patrols after Republican policemen had been driven from the streets and thus were in good position to control access to the polls. Probably it should be surprising that as many as 33,000 brave men voted for Grant.[46]

The installation of President Grant, which increased the likelihood of federal intervention in case of major disorder, and probably the ratification of the Fifteenth Amendment, brought a reduction in openly terrorist activity from 1868 through 1872, though individual crimes against blacks in general certainly continued to take a heavy toll. Then, after the disputed state election of 1872, incidents of violence increased dramatically. The economic debacle of 1873, which hit Louisiana especially hard, probably contributed to the increase in violence. First

46. Ficklen, *History of Reconstruction in Louisiana*, 215–18; Walter Prichard (ed.), "The Origin and Activities of the 'White League' in New Orleans (Reminiscenses of a Participant in the Movement)," *Louisiana Historical Quarterly*, XXXIII (April 1940), 528–29; Grady H. McWhiney and Francis B. Simkins, "The Ghostly Legend of the Ku Klux Klan," *Negro History Bulletin*, XIV (February 1951), 109–12; New Orleans *Daily Picayune*, August–November 1868; Georges Clemenceau, *American Reconstruction, 1865–1870, and the Impeachment of President Johnson* (New York, 1928), 228–29.

came the Colfax Riot, already mentioned, and the death of perhaps 100 black men. Next was an almost bloodless conflict between the Metropolitan Police (really a Republican militia) and "Tax Resisters" near St. Martinville. When the Colfax Riot and incidents in other states made it clear that federal intervention was no longer a real danger to individuals participating in acts of terrorism, the paramilitary White League made its appearance. This organization forced dozens of Republican officeholders in rural parishes to resign, lynched five white Republicans in the Coushatta Massacre, and finally defeated the Metropolitan Police in the pitched Battle of Liberty Place in New Orleans in September 1874. Federal troops did respond to Liberty Place, tardily, but their intervention merely emphasized the fact that a Radical Republican regime could not survive in Louisiana without outside support.[47]

Organized terrorism crested again during the election campaign of 1876 which, when finally resolved, brought "redemption," the end of Radical rule in Louisiana. This last phase of Reconstruction terrorism seems somewhat more modern, because it was more or less carried out in the presence of United States troops, though the troops were few in number and widely scattered. Intimidation, that is the threat of force, was usually sufficient in 1876, but when this did not work, sterner methods were available. A participant noted later, "Occasionally there were a few necks broken and straps used among the worst."[48]

In 1876, as earlier, violence was not confined to the persons of black Republicans. By that year almost all the white Radicals remaining in Louisiana were carpetbaggers, and they were fair

47. Manie White Johnson, "The Colfax Riot of April, 1873," *Louisiana Historical Quarterly*, XIII (July 1930), 391–427; New Orleans *Daily Picayune*, April–May 1873; Taylor, *Louisiana Reconstructed*, 274–76, 279–86; Ida Waller Pope, "The Coushatta Massacre" (M.A. Thesis, McNeese State College, 1968); Stuart Omar Landry, *The Battle of Liberty Place: The Overthrow of Carpetbag Rule in New Orleans—September 14, 1874* (New Orleans, 1955), 63–178.
48. Charles M. Barrow to Mrs. Hugh M. Bone, November 23, 1927, Fanny Z. Lovell Bone, "Louisiana in the Disputed Election of 1876," *Louisiana Historical Quarterly*, XV (January 1932), 100–101.

game. One man was killed and a Republican state senator maimed at Coushatta in May; the tax collector of Ouachita Parish was shot dead from ambush in August; other white Republicans were murdered in Caddo, Natchitoches, Red River, and East Baton Rouge Parishes. Others fled to save their lives. It can be argued that intimidation was not the most decisive factor in the Democratic victory in 1876, if it was a Democratic victory, but it certainly did great harm to the Republican cause.[49]

A last factor that assured the failure of Radical Reconstruction in Louisiana was the simple fact that the North lost whatever will it had had to impose a political revolution on the South, even as it had never had the will to impose social and economic revolution. It is quite possible, as noted above, that a majority of voters in the North never favored political equality for Negroes. As the years passed, the idea of expending northern treasure to protect Republican governments in the South, governments that obviously could not survive without the assistance of the United States Army, was less and less acceptable to the people of the North. Even the more Radical northern Republicans began to grow weary of the struggle and began more and more to manifest the race prejudice which had never been far below the surface. As early as 1873 Ben Wade of Ohio, who would have become president if Andrew Johnson been convicted in the impeachment trial, could write in a letter to a friend that he was "sick of niggers."[50] Attorney General George H. Williams was speaking not only for the Grant administration but for most northerners when he refused aid to Mississippi Radicals in 1875, pointing out that the people were growing weary of "autumnal outbreaks" in the South. Republican presidential candidate Rutherford B. Hayes was a prince of hypocrites when he said that he did not mind for himself if he was not elected

49. Taylor, *Louisiana Reconstructed*, 485–89; T. B. Tunnell, Jr., "The Negro, the Republican Party, and the Election of 1876 in Louisiana," *Louisiana History*, VII (Spring 1966), 101–11.

50. Patrick W. Riddleberger, "The Radicals' Abandonment of the Negro During Reconstruction," *Journal of Negro History*, XLV (April 1960), 91.

president, but that he was full of sorrow for the poor black people of the South who would be left without the protecting hand of the Republican party. When he became president, he made an effort, though not a successful one, to create a white Republican party in the South, leaving black voters in political limbo.[51]

Thus Radical Reconstruction in Louisiana went down to ignominious defeat. Except for the vote, which was meaningless after 1876, black Louisianians in 1880 were back almost to where they had been in 1860, and by 1900 the vote was gone. The white South, including white Louisianians, had lost the conventional war that followed secession, but with northern allies it had won the political and guerrilla war of Reconstruction. White Louisianians emerged victorious from the decade-long postwar struggle because the economic views of the day would not sanction the confiscation of private property on any significant scale; because white Radical Republicans in Louisiana believed about as much in white supremacy as their Conservative opponents; because a substantial majority of the people of the North shared the racial attitudes of white Louisianians; because black Louisianians proved unable to physically defend themselves against white aggression; because white Louisianians, like other southerners, resisted any attempt at racial equality of any sort as fiercely and as brutally as was necessary to accomplish their ends; and because the intransigence of the white South, and especially Louisiana, wore down the will of the North to impose Reconstruction upon the conquered region.

51. Vincent P. DeSantis, "President Hayes' Southern Policy," *Journal of Southern History*, XXI (November 1955), 476–94; C. Vann Woodward, *Reunion and Reaction: The Compromise of 1877 and the End of Reconstruction* (Garden City, N. Y., 1956), 25.

Bibliographical Essay

THE SOURCES AVAILABLE FOR THE STUDY OF RECON-
struction in Louisiana are so many that only the most important can be mentioned in a brief essay, and those only briefly.
The Centenary College Library at Shreveport, Louisiana, and
the Presbyterian Historical Foundation at Montreat, North Carolina provide much manuscript material dealing with religious
developments. The two most extensive and most important collections of manuscript materials are located in the Department
of Archives of Louisiana State University at Baton Rouge and in
the Southern Historical Collection of the University of North
Carolina at Chapel Hill. Dozens of collections in these deposi-
tories are useful, especially in the study of social and economic
developments, and the Henry Clay Warmoth Papers of the
Southern Historical Collection are absolutely essential.

Important state documents and publications include the various parish tax assessment rolls, the *Acts of Louisiana* for the
years 1864 through 1877, the published debates of the Reconstruction legislatures, and the debates of the constitutional conventions of 1864 and 1868. Federal documents essential to
research in the period include *United States House of Representatives Miscellaneous Documents, Executive Documents,*
and *Reports,* and *United States Senate Executive Documents*
and *Reports* for the years 1866 through 1878 when these per-
tain to Louisiana. Finally, the Freedmen's Bureau Papers for
Louisiana, located in the National Archives, will soon be available on microfilm.

Among travel accounts the most useful are Edward King,

The Great South: A Record of Journeys in Louisiana . . . and Maryland (Hartford, Conn.: American Publishing Company, 1875), Charles Nordhoff, *The Cotton States in the Spring and Summer of 1865* (New York: D. Appleton and Company, 1876), and Whitelaw Reid, *After the War: A Southern Tour* (Cincinnati: Moore, Wilstach, and Baldwin, 1866). Necessary memoirs include John Eaton, *Grant, Lincoln, and the Freedmen: Reminiscenses of the Civil War with Special Reference to the Work for the Contrabands and Freedmen of the Mississippi Valley* (New York: Longman, Green, and Company, 1907), and Henry Clay Warmoth, *War, Politics and Reconstruction: Stormy Days in Louisiana* (New York: Macmillan, 1930). The latter must be used with caution, because the aged Warmoth was setting himself forth as he hoped to be remembered by posterity, but his memory and his wit were still excellent. George Washington Cable's *The Negro Question: A Selection of Writings on Civil Rights in the South*, ed. Arlin Turner (Garden City, N.Y.: Doubleday, 1958) and his *The Silent South: Together with the Freedman's Case in Equity and the Convict Lease System* (New York: C. Scribner's Sons, 1885) tell among other things what an enlightened southerner saw in New Orleans during Reconstruction. George Clemenceau's *American Reconstruction, 1865–1870, and the Impeachment of President Johnson* (New York: Dial Press, 1928) contains many shrewd comments on events of the day. *They Came to Louisiana: Letters of a Catholic Mission, 1854–1882*, ed. and trans. Sister Dorothea Olga McCants (Baton Rouge: Louisiana State University Press, 1970), is a valuable and delightful source. Many other letters, diaries, and memoirs have been published in the *Louisiana Historical Quarterly, Louisiana History, The Journal of Southern History*, and the *Mississippi Valley Historical Review* (now the *Journal of American History*), but there are far too many of these for even the best ones to be listed here.

Dozens of newspapers, good and bad, were published in Louisiana during Reconstruction. The New Orleans *Daily Picayune*, which came out regularly throughout the era, has consistent though biased coverage of political events. The New

Orleans *Republican*, first Warmoth's organ and then spokesman
for the administration of William Pitt Kellogg, was even more
biased, though in the opposite direction, and much less complete in its coverage. Probably the best paper published in the
state during Reconstruction was the bilingual New Orleans
Tribune, but it ceased publication when carpetbaggers took over
the Republican party and threw state printing to the *Republican*. The Baton Rouge *Weekly Advocate*, available issues of the
Shreveport *Times*, and numerous other short runs of "country"
papers throw light on developments outside of New Orleans.

The most pertinent older secondary sources are John Rose
Ficklen, *History of Reconstruction in Louisiana (Through 1868)*
(Baltimore: Johns Hopkins Press, 1910), Willie M. Caskey,
Secession and Restoration of Louisiana (Baton Rouge: Louisiana State University Press, 1938), and Ella Lonn, *Reconstruction in Louisiana after 1868* (New York: G. P. Putnam's
Sons, 1918). These volumes were the result of thorough research, but each one reflects the biases and racial prejudices of
the early twentieth century. Joe Gray Taylor's *Louisiana Reconstructed, 1863–1877* (Baton Rouge: Louisiana State University
Press, 1975) is a one-volume revisionist study that attempts to
treat economic, social, and cultural developments as well as political ones. Other useful monographs dealing directly with Reconstruction in Louisiana are John W. Blassingame, *Black New
Orleans, 1860–1880* (Chicago: University of Chicago Press,
1973), Gerald M. Capers, *Occupied City: New Orleans under
the Federals, 1862–1865* (Lexington: University of Kentucky
Press, 1965), Garnie W. McGinty, *Louisiana Redeemed: The
Overthrow of Carpetbag Rule, 1876–1880* (New Orleans: Pel-
ican Publishing Company, 1941), Howard Ashley White, *The
Freedmen's Bureau in Louisiana* (Baton Rouge: Louisiana State
University Press, 1970), Charles Vincent, *Black Legislators in
Louisiana During Reconstruction* (Baton Rouge: Louisiana State
University Press, 1976), and T. Harry Williams, *Romance and
Realism in Southern Politics* (Baton Rouge: Louisiana State
University Press, 1966).

More general but nonetheless useful books for the study of

Louisiana Reconstruction include W. R. Brock, *An American Crisis: Congress and Reconstruction, 1865–1867* (London: Macmillan, 1963), Lawanda Cox and John H. Cox, *Politics, Principles and Prejudice, 1865–1866* (New York: Free Press of Glencoe, 1963), Richard Nelson Current, *Three Carpetbag Governors* (Baton Rouge: Louisiana State University Press, 1967), Otis A. Singletary, *Negro Militia and Reconstruction* (Austin: University of Texas Press, 1957), James E. Sefton, *The United States Army and Reconstruction, 1865–1877* (Baton Rouge: Louisiana State University Press, 1967), Harold D. Woodman, *King Cotton and His Retainers: Financing and Marketing the Cotton Crop of the South, 1800–1925* (Lexington: University of Kentucky Press, 1968), and C. Vann Woodward, *Reunion and Reaction: The Compromise of 1877 and the End of Reconstruction* (Rev. ed., Garden City, N.Y.: Doubleday, 1956).

Articles in historical journals are at least as important as books to the student of Louisiana Reconstruction. Scores of good articles have been published, but Agnes Smith Grosz, "The Political Career of Pinckney Benton Steward Pinchback," *Louisiana Historical Quarterly*, XXVII (1944), 1119–1225 and Walter M. Lowrey, "The Political Career of James Madison Wells," *Louisiana Historical Quarterly*, XXXI (1948), 995–1123 are still the best sources available on these two important figures. Also worthy of special mention here are Thomas J. May, "The Freedmen's Bureau at the Local Level: A Study of a Louisiana Agent," *Louisiana History*, IX (1968), 5–19; T. B. Tunnell, Jr., "The Negro, the Republican Party, and the Election of 1876 in Louisiana," *Louisiana History*, VII (1966), 101–16; and Charles Vincent, "Negro Leadership in the Louisiana Constitutional Convention of 1868," *Louisiana History*, X (1969), 339–51. It must be emphasized that these are but a few of scores of useful articles on the subject.

The economic history of Reconstruction in Louisiana has not yet been thoroughly investigated, though it probably should not be separated from the general economic history of the state from the Civil War to some time in the early twentieth century. More important, no study has yet been made of Louisiana's carpetbaggers and scalawags. Also needed is a detailed investigation of the rise and development of the general merchant and of the relationship between the general merchant and the planter.

Notes on Contributors

JERRELL H. SHOFNER is chairman of the Department of History at the University of Central Florida. His publications include *Nor Is It Over Yet: Florida in the Era of Reconstruction, 1865–1877* (1974); *History of Jefferson County, Florida* (1976); and *Daniel Ladd: Merchant Prince of Frontier Florida* (1978). He is presently preparing a study of black laborers and race relations in post–Civil War Florida.

SARAH WOOLFOLK WIGGINS is editor of the *Alabama Review* and a professor of history at the University of Alabama. Her publications include *The Scalawag in Alabama Politics, 1865–1881* (1977).

WILLIAM C. HARRIS is a professor of history at North Carolina State University at Raleigh. His publications include *Leroy Pope Walker: Confederate Secretary of War* (1962); *Presidential Reconstruction in Mississippi* (1967); and *The Day of the Carpetbagger: Republican Reconstruction in Mississippi* (1979). He is presently working on a biography of William Woods Holden of North Carolina.

JACK P. MADDEX, JR., is professor of history at the University of Oregon. His publications include, among others, *The Virginia Conservatives, 1867-1879: A Study in Reconstruction Politics* (1970); and *The Reconstruction of Edward A. Pollard: A Rebel's Conversion to Postbellum Unionism* (1974). He is presently completing a history of southern Presbyterianism in the Civil War era.

OTTO H. OLSEN is a professor of history at Northern Illinois University. His publications include *Carpetbagger's Crusade: The Life of Albion Winegar Tourgée* (1965), and *The Negro Question: From Slavery to Caste, 1863–1910* (1971). He is presently completing a study of Reconstruction in North Carolina.

JOE GRAY TAYLOR is head of the Department of History at McNeese State University. His publications include *Negro Slavery in Louisiana* (1963); *Louisiana Reconstructed, 1863–1877* (1974); and *Louisiana: A Bicentennial History* (1976). At present he is completing a study of "Food, Drink, and Hospitality in the South, 1607–1977."

Index